Biblical, Traditional, and Theological Framework for Understanding Christian Prophetism in Ghana Today

Biblical, Traditional, and Theological Framework for Understanding Christian Prophetism in Ghana Today

DANIEL NII ABOAGYE ARYEH

RESOURCE *Publications* • Eugene, Oregon

BIBLICAL, TRADITIONAL, AND THEOLOGICAL FRAMEWORK FOR UNDERSTANDING CHRISTIAN PROPHETISM IN GHANA TODAY

Copyright © 2019 Daniel Nii Aboagye Aryeh. All rights reserved. Except for brief quotations in critical publications or reviews, no part of this book may be reproduced in any manner without prior written permission from the publisher. Write: Permissions, Wipf and Stock Publishers, 199 W. 8th Ave., Suite 3, Eugene, OR 97401.

Resource Publications
An Imprint of Wipf and Stock Publishers
199 W. 8th Ave., Suite 3
Eugene, OR 97401

www.wipfandstock.com

PAPERBACK ISBN: 978-1-5326-1863-5
HARDCOVER ISBN: 978-1-4982-4437-4
EBOOK ISBN: 978-1-4982-4436-7

Manufactured in the U.S.A.   JANUARY 11, 2019

I dedicate this work to my wife Tina Aboagye Aryeh; children: Michelle Naa Aboagyewaa Aryeh, Samuel Nii Aboagye Aryeh (Jr), and Beulah Naa Aryeki Aryeh. To Manfred Otchere, and Mawulawe Keleglo. I also dedicate this work to all genuine Christian prophets.

Contents

Preface | ix
Acknowledgments | xi
General Introduction | xiii

Chapter One: Prophetism in *Akan* Traditional Religion | 1

Chapter Two: Prophetism in *Gã* Traditional Religion | 12

Chapter Three: Early Christian Prophetism in Ghana | 24

Chapter Four: Phases of Neo-Prophetism in Ghana's Christianity | 35

Chapter Five: Contemporary Prophetic Ministry in Ghana | 44

Chapter Six: Contemporary Prophetic Ministry: A Case of Gã South Municipal Area | 72

Chapter Seven: Prophetism in the Old Testament | 82

Chapter Eight: Prophetism in the Gospels | 97

Chapter Nine: Prophetism in Early Christianity | 105

Chapter Ten: Prophetism in *Corpus Paulinum* | 115

Chapter Eleven: Conclusions, Implications, and Recommendations | 138

Appendix | 145
References | 157
Index of Authors | 171
Index of Subjects | 175
Index of Scripture | 197

Abbreviations

ACI | Alive Chapel International
AICs | African Initiated/Instituted/Indigenous Churches
AIDS | Acquired Immune Deficiency Syndrome
ANE | Ancient Near East
BCE | Before Common Era
CAFM | Christian Action Faith Ministry
CE | Common Era
CMs | Charismatic Ministries
CoP | Church of Pentecost
EP | Evangelical Presbyterian Church
EVD | Ebola Virus Disease
FCIC | Fruit of Christ International Church
FIC | Faithway International Church
HGMI | Hope Generation Ministry International
HIPC | Heavily Indebted and Poor Country
HIV | Human Immunodeficient Virus
NDC | National Democratic Congress
NPP | New Patriotic Party
NT | New Testament
PSIC | Prophetic Seminar & Impartation Conference

OT | Old Testament
SU | Scripture Union

Preface

THIS STUDY WAS ORIGINALLY my Master of Theology (MTh) thesis submitted to Trinity Theological Seminary (TTS) Legon, Ghana, which has been updated, expanded, and revised for publication. This book is intended to provide a succinct account of prophetism in Ghanaian traditional religions, prophetism in the Old Testament, prophetism in the New Testament, and prophetism in contemporary Christianity in Ghana so as to determine the affiliation of contemporary prophetic ministry in Ghana. As a lecturer of biblical hermeneutics and New Testament studies, it has been my desire to interpret 1 Corinthians 12-14 in the context of Ghanaian Christianity. This is due to Paul's instructions concerning pneumatic activities in the Church at Corinth, particularly prophetism; and the re-emergence of prophetism in varied shades and expressions in Ghana since the 1920s. The enterprise is to evaluate biblical prophetism and contemporary prophetism in Ghana. The book is a first step into realizing my overarching vision.

There have been many publications concerning the alignment or relationship between the fore-runners of prophetism in Ghana and the Bible. Many of the publications show that the fore-runners of prophetism in Ghana largely draw on the Old Testament and traditional religions for their practices. As a practicing Pentecostal/Charismatic Christian, it has been my desire to examine some practices by contemporary prophet ministry using the gospels, and Pauline stipulations as a canon. This desire was driven by accusations and counter-accusations by Ghanaians and prophets that the practices of contemporary prophets is based on the gospels and Pauline expose.

Daniel Nii Aboagye Aryeh

September 2018

Accra Ghana

Acknowledgements

I AM EXTREMELY GRATEFUL to the Almighty God for granting me His grace, insight, and good health throughout the period of writing the thesis and converting it into a book. I acknowledge the tremendous encouragement, friendship, and supervision of Very Rev. Prof. John David Kwamena Ekem. In addition, I thank Prof. Ekem for recommending this book to Wipf and Stock for publication. I acknowledge the encouragement I received from the Very Rev. Prof. J. Kwabena Asamoah-Gyadu to be focused and publish. I thank Rev. Frederick Mawusi Amevenku who discovered me during my Bachelor's study at Trinity Theological Seminary, Legon Ghana. Since then, he has been my academic counsellor. He introduced me to Pentecost University College (PUC), School of Mission and Theology, in 2015 to teach biblical hermeneutics. I sincerely appreciate Rev. Prof. Prince S. Conteh of the University of Sierra Leone for the opportunity he gave me to publish my first journal article is 2014.

My gratitude to Bib Hughes for reading the work and suggesting very insightful and critical inputs. My appreciation goes to my students who always pursue me with questions concerning the biblical allegiance and support for contemporary prophetic ministry. I thank my wife, Tina Aboagye Aryeh for her immeasurable support and unflinching attention given to our children so I can find time to research. I express my gratitude to my children: Michelle Naa Aboagyewaa Aryeh, Samuel Nii Aboagye Aryeh (Jr.), and Beulah Naa Aryeki Aryeh for the jokes they share with me to help me relax during tensed moments. Finally to Manfred Otchere, and Mawulawe Keleglo for their support and love.

General Introduction

THE RECEPTION OF AN oracular message from a deity to its subjects is a hall mark of the potency of the deity and its intermediaries. In many societies in Africa, the services of religious intermediaries who frequently diagnose and prescribe solutions and, in addition, predict future events through spiritual means are patronized. In that regard, many shrines are oracular in nature, which may be precipitated by the African quest and belief of spiritual causality of any physical happenings/situations that defies economic, social, scientific etc. prescription. It may also be due to poverty levels in Africa, which impedes on education and innovation in science and technology. According to A. E. Southon:

> Prophetism in religion goes far back into human history and is found among all races. It is not easy to explain, and in many of its manifestations baffles human understanding. At times it may prove to be of infinite blessing, smashing through the barriers of ignorance or formalism, and setting free the souls of multitudes. It has its perils, too; for being mainly an appeal to the emotions it opens the way to grave moral evils.[1]

Since every theology is contextual, in other words, it is influenced by the socio-cultural issues prevailing at the time, the phenomena has found its way into the church in Africa, particularly Ghana. Members of the church mainly recognized God as one who speaks to provide solutions for their needs. Therefore Ministers must be able to hear the voice of God that diagnoses the cause of problems, prescribe solutions, and predict/prophesy future events accurately.

This agrees with the ministry of some non-literary prophets in the Old Testament; prophets such as Moses, Samuel, Elijah, Elisha, etc. who

---

1. Cited in F. L. Bartels, *The Roots of Ghana Methodism* (Cambridge: The Cambridge University Press in Association with Methodist Book Depot Ltd Ghana, 1965), 174-175.

ministered oracularly to the specific needs of individuals. However, it was not their core function, but a sublet of the function as covenant enforcers, and social reformers between Adonai and Israel. It raises the question of the use of the Old Testament by Christians today. J. K. Asamoah-Gyadu asserts that, although contemporary prophetic ministry in Ghana is aimed at replicating and perpetuating prophetism as expressed in the book of Acts and the Early Church, they also "strike a response cord with the primal religious idiom of African societies like that of Ghana."[2]

Analyzing the charisma of prophets as captured in the translation of the Bible in some African languages and how it resonates with African religio-cultural and political world views, L. Sanneh states that "for the Gbeapo people of Liberia the word for a prophet of the Bible is 'God's town-crier,' who is the official mouthpiece of the chief. As such he [or she] is more readily acceptable as God's spokesperson".[3]

The Spirit of prophecy, which was believed to have ceased in Judaism and during the intertestamental period, has now been restored at the inauguration of Christianity. David E. Aune holds that 1 Thessalonians is the earliest epistle of Paul that advocated that Christians must not despise prophecy (1 Thes. 5:19-22), and the book of Acts portrays the Holy Spirit as the Spirit of prophecy who speaks through prophets.[4] Paul gave stipulations for prophets and prophecy in the church in 1 Corinthians 14. This confirms that prophets and prophecy was a common phenomenon in the Early Church and Pauline communities.[5] Contemporary prophetic ministry claim to have conformed to Pauline stipulations concerning prophets and prophecy in the church: but what is their level of conformity?

C. N. Omenyo and W. A. Arthur argue that contemporary prophetic ministry is becoming popular due to their appeal and compatibility with religious world views and its pragmatic outlook that resonates with the Ghanaian phenomenon of religion.[6] They further postulate that, as an ad-

---

2. J. Kwabena Asamoah-Gyadu, "Pentecostalism and the Missiological Significance of Religious Experience in Africa Today: The Case of Ghana 'Church of Pentecost,'" in *Trinity Journal of Church and Theology* XII, no. 1&2 (July/December 2002), 34. , 30-57.

3. Lamin Sanneh, *Translating the Message: The Missionary Impact on Culture* (Maryknoll, New York: Orbis Books, 2009), 235.

4. David E. Aune, *Prophecy in Early Christianity and the Ancient Mediterranean World* (Grand Rapids, Michigan: William B. Eerdmans Publishing Company, 1983), 191.

5. David Hill, *New Testament Prophecy* (London: Marshall, Morgan & Scott, 1979), 120.

6. Cephas N. Omenyo and Wonderful Adjei Arthur, "The Bible Says! Neo-Prophetic

General Introduction

herent of *Akan* Traditional Religion would go to a religious intermediary for *ebisa* (literally, to inquire or ask) into present or future happenings, contemporary prophets have positioned themselves to be agents of *ebisa* in Ghanaian Christianity.[7] Their ability to reveal secrets have won them the sobriquet "ditto-ditto" (detail, detail). J. Quayesi-Amakye states that "these prophets [and prophetesses] who present themselves as offerers of spiritual panacea to the Ghanaian lack, and exploit the traditional desire to probe into the unknown cannot be ignored".[8] To the extent that some Christians flock to their services and testify to the efficacy of their prophetic power, these prophets have succeeded in presenting themselves as the "'last stop' for life challenges".[9] To what extent do contemporary prophetic ministry appeal to traditional prophetism or religiosity?

Although there were elements of prophetism in the church in Ghana, it was first and foremost experienced during the period of the African Initiated/Instituted/Indigenous Church (AICs). Their founders and leaders were prophets/prophetesses who claimed to have the power to discern the presence of angels to receive messages for members of the Church. By implication, they redefined the qualification of being a leader in the church. Theological education was not a prerequisite for Ministers but the possession and demonstration of charisma.

Neo-prophetism began to attract the attention of many scholars with the decline of the AICs in the 1950s. By neo-prophetism, we refer to prophetic ministries that emerged in Ghana after the AICs. The words "Prophet" and "prophecy" have become household terms both in Ghanaian Christianity and non-Christian institutions. The title "Prophet" has become an important ecclesiological designation that attracts people to church services of Pentecostal and Charismatic Churches who believe and manifest some level of prophetic ministries. In the newer Charismatic Ministries in Ghana, the term has become a marketing tool, side attraction, and indispensable ecclesio-charismatic element in church life. In this study, the expressions contemporary prophetic ministry or contemporary prophets

---

Hermeneutics in Africa" *Studies in World Christianity* 19, No.1 (2013): 51, 50–70.

7. Omenyo and Arthur. "The Bible Says!" 57.

8. Joseph Quayesi-Amakye, *Prophetism in Ghana Today: A Study of Trends in Ghanaian Pentecostal Prophetism* (n.c.: n.p., 2013), 122.

9. Daniel Nii Aboagye Aryeh, "A Study of Prophetism in the Gospels and Ga South Municipal Area: A Way Forward for Prophetic Ministry in Ghana's Christianity," *All Nations University Journal of Applied Thought* Vol. 4, No. 1 (2015), 196, 196-221.

General Introduction

refers to prophetic ministries or prophets who emerged in Ghana from early 2000s to 2017.

Amazingly, many contemporary Ghanaian prophets are making the prophetic gift become an office in the Church.[10] By office, they refer to a statutory position that has to be always occupied; therefore the church would have to ordain someone to occupy the position despite the bestowal of charisma largely being dependent on the Holy Spirit. They also put forth the argument that all church denominations must have a prophetic positions because the prophet is the mouth piece of God.[11] These claims could be likened to the claims of Montanism[12] that they are the mouthpiece of the Holy Spirit and that their utterances are equal to scripture and should be added to it.[13] In view of the large numbers of Pentecostal and Charismatic Christians in Africa,[14] misinterpretation of the prophetic gift would have a wider effect. This necessitated the study.

Although prophetism largely points to the Old Testament as the primary cradle of authority, contemporary prophets have begun to claim the principal source of authority from the New Testament, particularly from the epistles of Paul. J. K. Asamoah-Gyadu states that "it is noteworthy that Pentecostals point to Scripture, particularly Pauline thought, as the primary source of authority in matters of faith".[15] It is evident in the writings of some contemporary Ghanaian Prophets that, although they may occasionally refer to the Old Testament, Paul's teachings regarding prophetism in the church is their foundation for prophetic ministry. Prophet Richard Oswald Commey postulates that Paul's teachings in 1 Corinthians 12-14 are the

---

10. Isaac Anto, *The Office of the Prophet* (rev.edi) (Accra: Nobles Multimedia, 2011), 85-94.

11. Richard Oswald Commey, *Ministry Gifts: Apostles, Prophets, Evangelists, Pastors and Teachers* (Summerville, SC: Holy Fire Publishing, 2008), 78, 147-153.

12. Montanism was a second century prophetic group led by its founder Montanus from Phrygia.

13. Williston Walker, *History of the Christian Church* (New York: Charles Scribner's Sons, 1922), 57-59.

14. David Maxwell, *African Gifts of the Spirit: Pentecostalism & the Rise of a Zimbabwean Transnational Religious Movement* (Oxford, Ohio and Harare: James Currey, Ohio University Press and Weaver Press, 2006), 5-13.

15. J. Kwabena Asamoah-Gyadu, "'The Promise is for you and your Children': Pentecostal Spirituality, Mission and Discipleship in Africa" in Wonsuk Ma and Kenneth R. Ross (Eds.) *Mission Spirituality and Authentic Discipleship* (Oxford: Regnum Books International, 2013), 11.

bedrock for prophetic presbytery in the church.[16] Prophet Isaac Anto adds that the office of a Christian prophet is established in Ephesians 4:11-12.[17] By this, they differ from the AIC prophets who take authority mainly from the Old Testament. Hence, there is the need to investigate what Paul meant by the designation "προφητης" and whether it was supposed to be an office or a function.

Prophetic office in this study refers to public proclamation and acceptance by the leadership of the Church that a person has a prophetic gift and is authorized by the Church "to minister that gift in what might be termed an official capacity" of the Church,[18] similar to institutionalized prophets in the Church of Pentecost (CoP).[19] Prophetic gift, as a function, refers to any individual Christian through whom the Holy Spirit decides to speak at any time to the Church or an individual who occasionally prophesies without ecclesiological recognition as a prophet. He/She could belong to the Lay or Clergy. Prophetism refers to a system or means of receiving oracular information from God/god by a Christian prophet/religious functionary.

There are various assertions with respect to the source of Paul's teaching concerning "προφήτης". We have not found any evidence to show that Paul was involved in Hellenistic religious practices in Tarsus, during his early education in the city. However, Paul's admonition for the Corinthian prophets in the Church to acknowledge his writings as what he had received from God (1 Cor. 14:37-38), indicates that Paul had knowledge of Hellenistic "προφήτης", which was dominated by frenzied experience.

As a Jew who studied at the feet of Gamaliel I, a renowned rabbi during the time of Paul, Paul might have had good knowledge concerning prophetism in the Old Testament and Judaism. D. Hill[20] postulates that Paul held Old Testament prophets in high esteem (Acts 13:27; Rom. 1:2). He concludes that Paul was a Christian prophet who never used the title "προφήτης". Hill rationalized his observations by positing that Paul's

---

16. Richard Oswald Commey, *Prophecy and Prophets* (Summerville, London: Holy Fire Publishing, 2007), 49-50.

17. Isaac Anto, *Deeper Insight into the Prophetic* (Accra: Nobles Multimedia, 2014), 17.

18. Jimmy D. Bayes, "Five-Fold Ministry: A Social and Cultural Texture Analysis Of Ephesians 4:11-16" in *Journal of Biblical Perspectives in Leadership* 3, no. 1 (Winter 2010), 113-122.

19. Joseph Quayesi-Amakye, *Prophetism in Ghana Today: A Study on Trends in Ghanaian Pentecostal Prophetism* (n.c.: n. p., 2013), 78.

20. David Hill, *New Testament Prophecy* (London: Marshall, Morgan & Scott, 1979), 111-117.

call event, which took place on the road to Damascus can be favorably compared to the call event of Prophet Jeremiah (Jer. 1:4-5). And the call narrative of Paul could be parallel to the call event of an unnamed servant of YHWH (Isa. 49:1). Hill added that Paul's statement "I received from the Lord what I also handed on to you, that the Lord Jesus on the night when he was betrayed took a loaf of bread" (1 Cor. 11:23) points to the notion that he was a prophet in continuity of the prophets of the Old Testament.

Hill's view suggests that Paul is deeply indebted to Old Testament prophetism and that his teaching concerning prophetism in the Church might be informed by the Old Testament. If this is correct, it suggests that the inspiration of prophets in the Church and that of the Old Testament is on the same level. However, this could lead to the claims of the Montanists, that their revelation is equal to scripture and that it should be added to it. Undeniably, Paul was an apostle whose functions included prophetic ministry. D. E. Aune separated the prophetic experience of Paul and that of the Corinthians when he states that "Paul's conception of the prophetic role was primarily informed by the OT models, though the same assumption cannot be made of the Corinthian Christians themselves."[21] It is obvious that Paul was aware of prophetism in the Hellenistic societies, the Old Testament, and Judaism. However, his teaching on prophetism is unique.

Some scholars have used various exegetical methods to interpret 1 Corinthians 14:26-40 and this has led to varying understandings of what Paul meant by the designation "προφήτης" in the church. Others commented on the pericope without interest in examining what Paul meant by "προφήτης". A. J. Rowe used structural exegesis on 1 Corinthians 12-14 to show that Paul did not give licence to anyone who claimed some spiritual endowment in the church to be given an opportunity to be heard in every meeting of the Church. He did not examine what Paul meant by "προφητης" in the Church.[22]

Discussing cessation of prophecy, F. D. Farnell used 1 Cor. 14:29-31 to state the function of a prophet as the announcer of God's message. However, He did not examine "προφήτης" in the Corinthian context and what Paul meant by "προφήτης" in the text. His comment seems to have been

---

21. David E. Aune, *Prophecy in Early Christianity and the Ancient Mediterranean World* (Grand Rapids, Michigan: William B. Eerdmans Publishing Company, 1983), 196-197.

22. Arthur J. Rowe, "1 Corinthians 12 - 14: the Use of a Text for Christian Worship" in *Evangelical Quarterly* 77.2 (2005), 119-128.

General Introduction

informed by the Old Testament designation of "*Nabi*".[23] Interpreting 1 Cor. 14:26-40, S. Kissi emphasized Paul's admonition for orderliness in Christian worship stating that the Spirit that possessed the prophet is the Spirit of orderliness in the Church. He did not examined "προφήτης" in the context of the pericope and Corinth.[24] This is not to suggest that the above scholars did not do a good research work, it is a matter of method and focus.

J. L. Boyer[25] asserts that the function of a prophet in the New Testament is in direct continuity of prophets in the Old Testament. This is due to the opening of the gospels with the proclamation of John the Baptist who was a prophet and the New Testament reference to Old Testament prophets such as Samuel, Elijah, Jeremiah, Daniel just to mention a few. In view of the proliferation of the use of the title "prophet" by prophetic Church leaders in Ghana, and the view of Boyer being considered as a sweeping generalization; this study undertook an in-depth grammatico-historical and religio-cultural exegesis of 1 Corinthians 14:26-40 for an understanding of "προφήτης" in Pauline thought and its implications for contemporary prophetic ministry in Ghana.

Assessing Christian prophetism in Ghana in the light of 1 Corinthians. 14:26-40 will help appreciate the similarities and differences between the two. Although there are some publications on prophetism in the CMs and AICs,[26] no studies have been developed to assess prophetism in Pauline literature especially 1 Corinthians 14:26-40 and prophetism in Ghana were found during the period of writing this book.

---

23. F. David Farnell, "When Will the Gift of Prophecy Cease? In *Bibliotheca Sacra* 150 (April-June, 1993), 171-202.

24. Seth Kissi, *The Gifts and Spirituality: Understanding the Subject in the Context of First Corinthians, Addressing Some Popular Misconceptions* (Accra, Ghana: African Christian Press, 2014), 80-81.

25. James L. Boyer, "The Office of the Prophet in the New Testament" in *Grace Journal* on http/www.biblicalstudies.org.uk/pdf/grace-journal/01-1_13.pdf. Accessed 18/72014.

26. See Christian G. Baëta, *Prophetism in Ghana: A Study of Some 'Spiritual' Churches* (Achimota, Ghana: Africa Christian Press, 2004); J. Kwabena Asamoah-Gyadu, *African Charismatics: Current Development Within Independent Indigenous Pentecostalism in Ghana* (Leiden: Koninklijke Brill NV, 2005); Kofi Asare Poku, "A Brief History of Independent Church Movement in Ghana Since 1862" in *The Rise of Independent Churches in Ghana* (Accra: Asempa Publication, 1990); Cephas O. Omenyo, *Pentecost Outside Pentecostalism: A Study of the Development of Charismatic Renewal in the Mainline Churches in Ghana* (Boekencentrum The Netherlands: Publishing House, 2002); James Annorbah-Sarpei, "The Rise of Prophetism: A Socio-Political Explanation" in *The Rise of Independent Churches in Ghana* (Accra: Asempa Publication, 1990).

General Introduction

The significance of contemporary prophetic ministry in Ghana taking its nature and structure in the New Testament, especially Pauline literature, cannot be understated. In comparison with the Old Testament, one wonders why the New Testament has little to offer concerning prophetic ministry. However, 1 Corinthians 12-14 can be largely considered as a block of literature where Paul dealt extensively with manifestations of pneumatological phenomena in the Church as against those of non-Christian groupings in the Corinthian context.[27] 1 Corinthians 12-14 has become the main reference material when guidelines for the perennial issue of prophetism in the church cropped-up. In 1 Cor. 14:26-40, Paul seemed to have drawn a conclusion on issues pertaining to spiritual gifts and manifestations that he began to discuss in chapter 12.

P. Gifford argues that, by the year 2000, in Ghana, almost every Christian activity was labelled prophetic and is attracting many to Churches that market themselves as prophetic.[28] However, one can hardly find a biblical and theological understanding of "προφήτης" in the New Testament, particularly Pauline literature. In view of the proliferation of prophets and prophecies in contemporary Christianity in Ghana, and the scared scholarly work using grammatico-historical and religio-cultural exegetical method, it is imperative that reference be made to Pauline stipulations concerning prophets and prophecies in the church. Although some contemporary prophets claimed Pauline support for their ministry, unfortunately, it is partial and in some cases tantamount to total neglect of Pauline teachings governing prophets and prophecies in the church.

The study will primarily be concerned with what Paul meant by "προφήτης" in the context of 1 Corinthians 14:26-40 and its relevance for an understanding of the meaning of "prophet" in the Ghanaian context. It is also limited to the ministry of Prophet Dr. Eric Nana Kwesi Amponsah due to his availability for research work and belief in Pauline teaching in 1 Cor. 14:26-40 as part of guidelines for prophetism in the church. Prophet Dr. Amponsah was used as a microcosm for contemporary prophetic ministry and contemporary prophets in Ghana.

The noun 'prophet' is derived from the Greek compound "προφήτης"; the prefix προ-before, φή-'to say' or 'to speak', and της- the gender. J. R.

---

27. John Ruff, *Paul's First Letter to Corinth* (London: SCM Press Ltd, 1977), 124-125.
28. Paul Gifford, *Ghana's New Christianity: Pentecostalism in a Globalizing African Economy* (Bloomington, Indiana: Indiana University Press, 2004), 38, 90.

General Introduction

C. Cousland aptly puts it as προ-on behalf of, and φήτ-to speak.[29] Hence, "προφήτης" means speaking on behalf of/for God or gods. Therefore a prophet in the New Testament is someone who speaks or proclaims a message from a deity to its subjects, the message may be relating to present happenings or about the future. The term "προφήτης" is not limited to early Christian usage. It is closely associated with the Greek famous oracle at Delphi presided over by Apollo.[30]

Prophecy is made up of forth-telling and fore-telling. The prefix "προ" is originally concerned with forth-telling more than fore-telling. This is due to the temporary nature and expiration nature of prediction, after it has been fulfilled. Therefore, as suggested by David Hill, the working definition of "προφήτης" must be related to the way in which the word and the word-group of which it is related is used in the context where it appears.

Forth-telling is basically preaching the gospel. Fore-telling is declaring the message of God as revealed to the prophet.[31] The message of the prophets, in many situations, do not come from tradition (even though the style of delivery can be comparative) or does not follow laid down protocols (Jer.1:7-8). This aspect of the prophetic ministry deals with current issues, which need God's immediate guidance and direction. It is this that distinguishes the prophets from other preachers. Hill defines a Christian prophet as:

> ... a Christian who functions within the Church, occasionally or regularly, as a divinely called and divinely inspired speaker who receives intelligible and authoritative revelations or messages which he is impelled to deliver publicly, in oral or written form, to Christian individuals and/or the Christian community.[32]

Admittedly, no definition will be universally accepted as sacrosanct, yet it is very necessary to have some kind of reference, a basic understanding of what we are embarking on. Hill's definition lacks certain elements that, can be added to widen the scope of the definition. In this regard, I adopt a definition I stated elsewhere

---

29. J. R. C. Cousland, 'Prophets and Prophecy' in Craig A. Evans & Stanley E. Porter Eds, *Dictionary of New Testament Background* (Illinois: Inter Varsity Press, 2000), 830-835.

30. Verlyn D. Verbrugge, *New International Dictionary of New Testament Theology*, Abridged Edition (Grand Rapids: Michigan, Zondervan, 2000), 499.

31. Hill, *New Testament Prophecy*, 2-4.

32. Hill, *New Testament Prophecy* 7.

General Introduction

A Christian prophet is a trained Christian, who has been called by God to function both within and outside the Church as a charismatic or ecclesiastical leader. Occasionally or regularly receiving intelligible and authoritative solicited or unsolicited revelations and messages, which do not contradict the written word of God as recorded in the Bible. And he/she is impelled to deliver the message either publicly or privately, in oral or written form to the individual Christian or non-Christian or to the community without any charges.[33]

A Christian prophet must combine both forth-telling and fore-telling. Over reliance and giving priority to fore-telling at the detriment of forth-telling has the potential of producing soothsayers/diviners or make Christian prophets appear as soothsayers/diviners. The phrase "Christian prophet" is used to distinguish it from Old Testament prophets, Traditional prophets or soothsayers.

ORGANIZATION OF THE STUDY

The study is organized into eleven (11) chapters. Chapter one discusses prophetism in *Akan* Traditional Religion. *Akan* tradition is one of the most popular traditional thoughts in Ghana. Its religious thoughts and tenets are wide spread in Ghana and beyond. A study of its prophetism with a case of the exploits of Ɔkomfo Anokye will be key in determining the influence of *Akan* understanding of prophets on contemporary Christian understanding of prophets. Chapter two (2) focuses on prophetism in *Gã* Traditional Religion with a case of Gbawe traditional area. The *Gã* people have a large population in Ghana, the celebration of *hɔmɔwɔ* festival has attracted academic studies and assumed international dimension. The goal is to study prophetism among the *Gã* people and their religious intermediaries. It will give a clue to the understanding of prophet in contemporary prophetic ministry in Ghana today.

Chapter three (3) studies the emergence of prophetism in Ghana's Christianity. It seeks to discuss issues that led to the emergence of the phenomenon, the response of the members of the Church, and the main actors/founders involved. Chapter four (4) focuses on phases of prophetism

---

33. Daniel Nii Aboagye Aryeh, "A Study of 'Prophetism' in the Gospels and Ga South Municipal Area: A Way forward for Prophetic Ministry in Ghana's Christianity" in *Journal of Applied Thought*, Vol. 4; No 1 (Jan. 2015), 196-221 at 199.

General Introduction

in Ghana's Christianity. It seeks to appreciate various phases and shades of prophetisms that Ghanaian Christianity has taken over the period under study. The goal is to emphasize issues that necessitate the phenomenon and the various understandings attached to them.

Chapter five (5) discusses the issues of contemporary prophetic ministry, a case of the ministry of Prophet Dr. Eric Nana Kwesi Amponsah of Hope Generation Ministry Int. It seeks to discuss issues that motivated the rise of contemporary prophetism, and how contemporary prophets understand and appropriate the term "prophet". Chapter six (6) focuses on contemporary prophetic ministry, a case of Gã Municipal Area. The goal is to access the views of various Christians in the municipality concerning claims by contemporary prophets. A sample size of 297 respondents were engaged to answer questionnaires to obtain the result. The findings are then analyzed and interpreted.

Chapter seven (7) discusses prophetism in the Old Testament. It seeks to analyze the categories of prophets in the Old Testament. It provides a background for the understanding of "prophet" in contemporary prophetic ministry. A qualitative analytical approach is used to the discussion of issues. It involves archival and library research, as well as interpretation and analysis of findings. Chapter eight (8) discusses prophetism in the gospels. It seeks to analyze statements that have prophetic undertones and individual prophets or perceived prophets as recorded in the gospels.

Chapter nine (9) analyzes prophetism in early Christianity. It seeks to discuss prophets and prophetic instances in the Acts of the Apostles and the early Pauline epistles. The goal is to identify and analyze early Christian prophetism and how it can be appropriated in contemporary Christianity in Ghana. Chapter ten (10) interprets 1 Corinthians. 14:26-40 to ascertain the meaning and ministry of prophets in Pauline corpus. Grammatico-historical and religio-cultural exegesis is used for the study. Chapter eleven (11) draws conclusions, and implications for the study. The method for the study is eclectic. Generally, a qualitative historical analytical approach to the discussion of issues is used. It involves archival and library research, as well as interpretation and analysis of findings. Where texts are involved, historical critical method is used.

Chapter One

Prophetism in *Akan* Traditional Religion

INTRODUCTION

PROPHETISM EXISTS IN MANY traditional religions in Ghana. The *Akan* people of Ghana are not exempted. They have experienced and benefited from the ministry of traditional prophets during difficult and challenging moments. Some have also suffered as a result of instructions by traditional prophets. The goal of this chapter is to explore prophetism in traditional religion as a preamble for later determination of the influence of *Akan* traditional prophetism, and its impact on the understanding and expression of Christian prophetism in contemporary Pentecostal and Charismatic Churches in Ghana. The chapter undertakes a study of the exploits of the famous Ɔkomfo Anokye, a traditional priest/prophet who assisted in the establishment of the Ashanti Kingdom in Ghana.

The prophetic phenomenon is not the preserve of Israelite religion. Many religions of the world have recorded the activities of prophets and prophecy at various levels of their existence.[1] The distinction is that these prophets speak for different deities or God/gods. For example, the *Akans* have experienced the activities of 'Priests/Priestesses, diviners and seers' who functioned as prophets and prophetesses and were consulted on many

---

1. Emmanuel K. Asante, *The Prophetic and Apocalyptic Phenomena in Israel: A Theological Introduction* (Accra: Son Life Press, 2011), xix.

Biblical, Traditional, and Theological Framework

occasions.² The services of traditional prophets were frequently patronized. This was due to the communal nature of the visible and invisible worlds in African/Ghanaian cosmology, and the belief in the complementary role of spirit beings to the welfare of humans.

The *Akan* language is one of the few local languages that has been developed to the literary level starting from the Basel missionary days in 1828; and is being taught in many basic schools, secondary schools, and some theological seminaries. Gradually, it is being used in academic writings. The *Akan* language belongs to the Kwa group of languages. According to Kwesi Yankah, it is spoken by 42% of Ghanaians as their first language and a good number of Ghanaians as second language.³ *Akan* is a major language in Ghana with many dialects spoken largely in the Ashanti, Brong Ahafo, Eastern, Central, and Western Regions. The term *Akan* applies to "the largest ethnic group in Ghana". They constitute about two thirds of Ghana's land space and population.⁴ The principal language of the *Akans* is *Twi*. There is the Asante *Twi* and Akwapim *Twi*.

At the heart of prophetism in *Akan* Traditional Religion is the ɔkomfo, a traditional priest/priestess. The term is used to refer to both male and female. Ɔkomfo is singular and *akomfo* plural. The prefix ɔkom means prophesying "authentically about present and future events under the inspiration of deities" and *fo* is the person.⁵ Hence, ɔkomfo is one who is ascetically "disciplined for physical and spiritual alertness, possession/cultic dancing, and above all, prophecy (*Akan*: nkɔnhyɛ), help to define and describe the nature of priesthood in *Akan* Traditional Religion".⁶

---

2. John D. K. Ekem, *Priesthood in Context: A Study of Priesthood in Some Christian and Primal Communities of Ghana and its Relevance for Mother-Tongue Biblical Interpretation* (Accra: Son Life Press, 2008), 41–42.

3. Kwesi Yankah, *Education, Literary and Governance: A Linguistic Inquiry into Ghana's Burgeoning Democracy* (Accra: Ghana Academy of Arts and Sciences, 2006), 13.

4. K. Nkansa Kyeremanteng, *The Akans of Ghana: Their Customs, History and Institutions* (Kumasi: Sebewie De Ventures, 2010), 26–27.

5. Ekem, *Priesthood in Context*, 44–45.

6. Ekem, *Priesthood in Context*, 45.

Prophetism in Akan *Traditional Religion*

A BRIEF HISTORY OF THE ASANTE (*AKAN*) PEOPLE OF GHANA

The Asante people are part of the *Akans* with strong socio-political and cultural affiliations and influence. Traditionally, it is believed that they emerged from the earth or the sky. However, research has argued that they hailed from ancient Israel or Mesopotamia. They were part of the Ancient Ghana Empire. From Israel or Mesopotamia, they first settled in the present day Northern Region, specifically Gonjaland in the 13th century when it was a forest zone. [7] By the exploits of the hunters among them, they gradually moved and settled in the present location (in the Asante Region) and lived according to clans: Oyoko, Adako, Biretuo, Agona, Asona, Aduana, Asenie, Ekuona, and Asakyiri.

There are two opinions concerning the origin and meaning of the term Asante. The Asantes used to be vassal to the Denkyira Kingdom (which is also *Akan*). The responsibilities of the Asantes include sending plantain fiber to the Denkyira Kingdom. In addition, they sent red clay, which was a special commodity at the time. The *Akans* call red clay "*Asan*", hence they were being referred to as *Asantefoɔ*, meaning people who dig clay.[8] The other view is that, due to the dehumanizing demands and economic exploitation of the Denkyira Kingdom over the Asantes, in 1695, during the rule of King Osei Tutu I, the various clans/states of the Asantes decided to unite and fight to liberate themselves from the rule of the Denkyira Kingdom. Hence the name ɛsa-nti-foɔ meaning united to overcome our overlord. The name was later revised/corrupted to read *Asantefoɔ*.[9]

From the above discussion concerning the origin and meaning of the name Asante, it is obvious that there are varied opinions. However, in recent times, ɛsa-nti-foɔ is often used as the origin and meaning of Asante due to the bravery of the people. The use of ɛsa-nti-foɔ has both political and economic values, while the use of "*Asan*" as the origin and meaning of Asante limits them to a perpetual vassal state and economically handicapped. The unity and victory of the Asantes over their overlord—Denkyira Kingdom - was precipitated by the traditional prophetic exploits of *Ɔkomfo Anokye*. I

---

7. Osei Kwadwo, *An Outline of the Asante History* 3rd Edi (Kumasi: O. Kwadwo Enterprise, 2004), 1.

8. Osei Kwadwo, *An Outline of Asante History* Vol. 1 (Kumasi: O. Kwadwo Enterprise, 2014), 1.

9. Osei Kwadwo, *A Handbook on Asante Culture* (Kumasi: O. Kwadwo Enterprise, 2002), 87.

Biblical, Traditional, and Theological Framework

now discuss the history of Ɔkomfo Anokye and then continue to analyze his prophesies that led to the establishment of the Asante Kingdom.

Early Life of Ɔkomfo Anokye

There is no consensus concerning where Ɔkomfo Anokye hails from. It is popularly accepted that he was born to Agya Ano and his wife Kobe on a Saturday in Awukugua, Akwapim in the Eastern Region of Ghana, in 1645 CE.[10] He was the only child of the parents after many years of barrenness. It seem to run parallel to the birth narratives of Samson (Judg. 13), and Samuel (1 Sam.1) who later in life undertook landmark events which greatly benefitted posterity. Some believe that Ɔkomfo Anokye was raised at Awukugua, Akwapim but he did not hail from there. He hailed from Agona-Mampong, in the Asante Region. The name of his parent were given as Kyei Patua (father) from Adansi Akrokyere and Dweriyikwaa (mother) from Agona in the Ashanti Region.[11] At birth, Ɔkomfo Anokye had some teeth already grown in his month, a short beard, and his right hand was rolled into fist. When it was forced opened, a little magic wound and *dufa* (traditional substance for protection) was found in his hand. These are critical elements in Traditional Religion in Africa. In traditional prophetism, it suggests that Ɔkomfo Anokye was gifted from birth by the deities/spirits to be a priest/prophet a kind of Jeremiah's calling to the prophetic ministry (Jer. 1:4–19).

According to *Akan* tradition of naming, he was named Kwame Agyei Frimpong by the parents, and was named after his grandfather Agyei Frimpong. After one week of his birth, news about him spread all over Awukugua, and many came to see the little boy. As a little boy, Ɔkomfo Anokye sometimes disappears during the night and reappears the next day. The mother would often call the father in the native Guan language "Ano, Kye" meaning Anor see the wonders of your son, which later became his name. Nonetheless, as was the norm in those days to inquire from medicine men concerning strange happenings, the father inquired about the destiny of the baby and was told that he would become a great person; and that all the

---

10. Kwame Dwoben Poku Afriyie, *The Legendary Komfo Anokye of the Asante Kingdom* (Accra: Oriental Bookshop Agency, 2005), 4.

11. Author interview with Gordon Frimpong, general purpose officer at Manhyia in charge of Ɔkomfo Anokye sword site and Grandson of Osei Kwadwo, former Curator of Manhyia Palace. Interviewed at the sword site on Dec.22, 2017.

Traditional Religious priestly elements that were found in his right hand at birth should be kept.[12]

Ɔkomfo Anokye did not receive formal education. In other words, he never went to school. At age twelve (12), he went for the magical elements that were found in his hands at birth and began performing wonders. According to the family historian at Awukugua, the first of the wonders Ɔkomfo Anokye performed was to charm *fufu* (boiled pounded cassava eaten with soup) for his hungry friends after playing for a while. This wonders seem to present Ɔkomfo Anokye as the biblical Moses who prayed to God for the supply of Manna and quail for the Israelites on their journey to "The Promised Land," Canaan (Ex. 16). It can also be liken to the feeding of the five thousand persons by Jesus (Mt. 14:13–22; Mk. 6: 30–44; Lk. 9:10–17).

Nonetheless, the means that Ɔkomfo Anokye used is shrouded in traditional religio-cultural rituals, whiles that of Moses and Jesus was by prayer. This may be so because in ATR, prayer and ritual can hardly be dichotomized. Afriyie[13] chronicled twenty one (21) wonders that Ɔkomfo Anokye performed in Awukugua. These include planting cooked yam and commanding it to grow to maturity and harvest on the same day; transforming himself into a crab in order to spy on his enemies; and walking on 150 meters of long black sewing thread suspended in mid-air.

The Works of Ɔkomfo Anokye

After sometime, there arose a misunderstanding between the elders of Awukugua and Ɔkomfo Anokye concerning hunted animal parts. By tradition, hunters were expected to give animal shoulders and livers to the chiefs and elders of the community. However, Ɔkomfo Anokye began to receive the animal parts instead of the chiefs and elders: although he used to be consulted on some spiritual issues bothering the community, it was interpreted as taking the due of the chiefs and elders from the hunters. However, it is claimed that when the chiefs and elders stopped the giving of animal parts to Ɔkomfo Anokye, the hunters did not have as good a catch as they had beforehand; some of them died in the forest; and others were attacked by strange animals. The misfortune of the hunters was attributed to Ɔkomfo Anokye's spiritual powers. It created enmity between some elders

---

12. Author interview with Nana Larbi, historian of Anokye Family and Asokwa hene of Awukugua. At Awukugua Dec.16, 2015.

13. Afriyie, *The Legendary Komfo Anokye*, 10–21.

Biblical, Traditional, and Theological Framework

of the community and Ɔkomfo Anokye; the situation forced him to leave Awukugua.[14] It is significant to mention that the giving of animal parts to leaders is not unique to Awukugua. In the Ancient Near East (ANE), animal parts including liver were used by magicians and diviners to inquire about future events and diagnoses of current happenings. In effect, the fight for the animal parts between the elders and Ɔkomfo Anokye is not limited to economic survival but elements for spiritual empowerment. It can be cogently argued that the supply of the animal parts to either party would have assisted in their spiritual growth.

Ɔkomfo Anokye went to Adoagyiri near Nsawam and Nyanawase, in the Eastern Region, where he prophesied that, in a war between the Akwamus and the Gãs in about 1677, the Akwamus would be defeated, which did not come to pass. As he had issued a false prophesy he had to be imprisoned or sold into slavery as punishment.[15] He was imprisoned by King Ansah Sasraku of Nyanawase. During the time, Osei Kofi Tutu was a sword bearer for King Boa Amponsem of Denkyira Kingdom and had impregnated his niece. Osei Kofi Tutu then run to King Ansah Sasraku of Nyanawase to avoid imprisonment. When Ɔkomfo Anokye saw Osei Kofi Tutu, he prophesied unto him that he would become a great King.[16] Osei Kofi Tutu pleaded to King Ansah Sasraku and Ɔkomfo Anokye was later released.

The failed prophecy of Ɔkomfo Anokye that there would be a war between the Akwamus and the Gãs was later fulfilled when, in a war between the "combined forces of Akwapim, Gãs, Abuakwas and Kotokus and were badly defeated in 1730. The Akwamus were forced to flee Nyanawase to settle beyond River Volta, where they named their new capital Akwamu Fie".[17] Although legends may argue that it was the fulfillment of the prophecy of Ɔkomfo Anokye in 1677, the prophecy was, however, specific. This can be likened to Jewish means of postponed fulfillment of prophecy; where unfulfilled prophesies of renowned prophets were expected to be fulfilled later. Ɔkomfo Anokye was later engaged as a priest for King Ansah Sasraku, however, he mistakenly shoot a royal to death during hunting and was imprisoned the second time. From Brekusu and Tutu in the Eastern Region, Osei Kofi Tutu visited King Ansah Sasraku and pleaded for the release of

---

14. Afriyie, *The Legendary Komfo Anokye*, 6–7.
15. Afriyie, *The Legendary Komfo Anokye*, 6–7.
16. Author interview with Gordon Frimpong, Dec. 22, 2015 at Kumasi.
17. Afriyie, *The Legendary Komfo Anokye*, 8–9.

Ɔkomfo Anokye and took him to Asante.[18] At this point, Ɔkomfo Anokye claimed to have been commanded by God to unite the Asantes into a great kingdom. Although Ɔkomfo Anokye was received in Asante, the chiefs and elders were skeptical about his claim to unite the clans and make them into a great kingdom. They decided to test him:

> At a secret place in Kwaman [now Kumasi], two cows were put at two locations in two separate rooms. Into the first room they put a brown cow, and in the second a black one, then on the appointed day the chiefs gathered and asked Nana Akrasi [chief of Dwaben, now Juaben] to bring . . . Ɔkomfo Anokye in to tell what were in the two rooms. Ɔkomfo Anokye stood in their presence, pointed at the first room and declared that it was a cow and its color was grey. Upon opening the door, the cow was grey. He was taken to the second location. He pointed to the door and told them that there was a cow in that too, and it was white. They opened it and truly, there was a white cow. This meant that by spiritual powers he was able to change the black cow to a white one. This proved that he was a psychic who could communicate with God and understand divine messages.[19]

The narrative can be likened to the ministry of non-literary prophets in the Old Testament. Elisha was able to tell the secret plans of the King of the Arameans to the King of Israel (2 Kgs. 6:8–23). Ɔkomfo Anokye did not mention the color of the cows as initially put in the rooms, but changed them to his preferred colors. This suggested that he would be able to enhance the fortunes of the Asantes as he claimed. The doubts of the people of Asante would be changed to belief. During the period, Osei Kofi Tutu succeeded Obiri Yeboah as Chief of Kumasi. At a set date, Ɔkomfo Anokye gathered all the chiefs and leaders of the Asante people and declared that whoever the charmed golden stool settled upon would be the leader of the united Asante Kingdom. Then Ɔkomfo Anokye charmed a golden stool from the skies, and it settled on his good friend Osei Kofi Tutu I. Hence he became the first king of the Asante Kingdom, who ruled from 1695 to 1719.[20]

18. Afriyie, *The Legendary Komfo Anokye*, 24; Author interview with Gordon Frimpong, Dec. 22, 2015 at Kumasi; Author interview with Nana Larbi, historian of Anokye Family and Asokwa hene of Awukugua. At Awukugua Dec.16, 2015.

19. Afriyie, *The Legendary Komfo Anokye*, 26.

20. Kwadwo, *A Handbook*, 156. Author interview with Gordon Frimpong, Dec. 22, 2015 at Kumasi; Author interview with Nana Larbi, historian of Anokye Family and Asokwa hene of Awukugua. At Awukugua Dec.16, 2015.

Biblical, Traditional, and Theological Framework

However, King Ntim Gyakari of the Denkyira Kingdom, the overlord of the Asantes raised issues that the Asantes did not consult them prior to the united talks and the unity itself; therefore the golden stool should be sent to him; the unity should be dissolved; each chief should send his beloved and most favored wife to the palace at Denkyira and add some gold dust.[21] Having faith in the prowess of Ɔkomfo Anokye to help them overcome the Denkyira people, the Asantes killed the messengers from Denkyira and sent stones instead of gold dust. This generated war between the Asantes and the Denkyira people.

Ɔkomfo Anokye demanded that three persons be sacrificed in order for the Asantes to win the war. After the sacrifice and elaborate rituals, Ɔkomfo Anokye gave spiritual guidance and led the Asantes in the war where they were victorious.[22] As God (Adonai) used Moses to deliver the Israelite from slavery in Egypt, the spirits used Ɔkomfo Anokye to deliver the Asantes from the hands of the Denkyira people. This is not to raise Ɔkomfo Anokye to the status of Moses but to point out how the narrative rhymes with some biblical narratives. According to Afriyie,[23] Ɔkomfo Anokye performed thirty (30) wonders in Asante. These include the pushing of the end of a copper sword, into the ground at Kumasi in 1697. Walter and Slater, a construction company that built the Ɔkomfo Anokye hospital in 1954 could not pulled the sword out despite many attempts; the sword is still in the ground till date (refer to appendix ten). Ɔkomfo Anokye was said to have smite River Suben in Asante with his magic-switch causing the river to part into two (2) and he dredged the river with his bare hands. He created a river at Feyiase in Asante with his spittle and a tusk of an elephant so that the Asante warriors could drink water when they were thirsty. During the war between the Asantes and the Denkyira people, he used his magic-switch to ward off bullets directed towards the Asante warriors.

The Closing Days of Ɔkomfo Anokye

According to Afriyie[24] and Gordon Frimpong,[25] at an old age, Ɔkomfo Anokye visited his former wife Bukyia Mansa, in Kumasi. He was given

---

21. Kwadwo, *A Handbook*, 8–9.
22. Kwadwo, *A Handbook*, 10–13.
23. Afriyie, *The Legendary Komfo Anokye*, 34.
24. Afriyie, *The Legendary Komfo Anokye*, 62–64.
25. Author interview with Gordon Frimpong, Dec. 22, 2015 at Kumasi.

a resounding reception and a sumptuous meal was prepared for him with *apatere* (tilapia). In African Traditional priesthood and prophetism, intermediaries usually have taboos. They were forbidden from eating certain foods and taking certain concoctions believed to have the potential of weakening their spiritual power, and separate them from the deities. For example, trainee priests at Akonnedi shrine in Larteh, in the Eastern Region, were forbidden from eating sweet things (ripe plantain, honey, candies, and sugar); forbidden from eating kenkey on Tuesdays and Fridays; and forbidden from eating pork, and cola nuts.[26] These restrictions continue after graduation and become a norm for the practicing traditional priest/prophet.

In the case of *Ɔkomfo Anokye*, he was not supposed to eat tilapia. During the course of eating the meal prepared for him by the former wife, a tilapia bone became lodged in his throat causing it to swell. Sensing the treat of death, he informed his family members (including Kwame Siaw Anim, his nephew, who would succeed him as chief of Agona) that he was travelling to a far country in another world to look for anti-death medicine. The journey would take seven days, during which time there should not be gun shorts, and merry making in the town. He then retreated to his hut in order to undertake the spiritual journey. After seven days, the nephew opened the door of the hut to see if the uncle was still there; to his amazement, *Ɔkomfo Anokye* was not found. The nephew then ordered for gun shorts and mourning claiming that the uncle was dead. During the period of mourning, someone met *Ɔkomfo Anokye* in the forest. *Ɔkomfo Anokye* asked what the cause of mourning he could hear was. The person, without knowing that the man was *Ɔkomfo Anokye*, said the people were mourning the death of *Ɔkomfo Anokye*. *Ɔkomfo Anokye* made himself known to the man and said he is not dead; he then disappeared into the air and was not seen anywhere after this incident, which allegedly took place, in about 1740 when he was between 90 and 100 years. It was believed that *Ɔkomfo Anokye* was returning with anti-death medicine but the disobedience of the nephew prevented him from bringing it to humans.

Although the nephew might have been accused of disobedience, it is significant to state that the seven days given by *Ɔkomfo Anokye* had clearly expired. The fault of the nephew was that *Ɔkomfo Anokye* said he would return, but he did not wait beyond the seven days. The action of the nephew

---

26. Kofi Asare Opoku, *West African Traditional Religion* (Accra: FEP International Private Limited, 1978), 77.

could also be interpreted as organizing a befitting funeral mourning for the uncle. The narrative resonates with the story of some biblical prophetic figures like Moses or Elijah who did not have graves: a kind of emphasizing of the role of the divine above their humanity.

The Impact of the Work of Ɔkomfo Anokye on Akan Traditional Prophetism

The prophecies, and pronouncements of the legendary Ɔkomfo Anokye has greatly impacted *Akan* traditional prophetism. In this section, I will discuss some of the prophesies and pronouncements[27] and explore how it impacts traditional prophetism. Ɔkomfo Anokye prophesied that Osei Kofi Tutu would become a great king. This came to pass in 1695, when he became the first king of the united Asante Kingdom. He prophesied that a renowned hospital would be constructed in Kumasi. This came to pass in 1954 by the construction of Ɔkomfo Anokye teaching hospital. He again prophesied that Kyenekye, the chief priest of the Denkyira Kingdom, would die at Adansi. It came to pass during the war between the Asantes and the Denkyira Kingdom. These prophecies and their fulfillment indicates that, in traditional *Akan* prophetism, fulfilment is a critical element for authentication of the ministry of the intermediary. It is probable that, because the punishment of a failed prophecy was death or imprisonment, Ɔkomfo Anokye had to be very sure of what he heard or saw from the spirits or deities before making prophesies. The fulfillment of his prophesies leading to the establishment of the Asante Kingdom clearly emphasized dependence and harnessing the services of traditional prophets to complement human efforts for success. It also made way for religious solutions to declare future events before they happen.

Conclusion

In this chapter, I briefly discussed the history of the Asante people of Ghana, key terms relating to their traditional prophetism, and the exploits of Ɔkomfo Anokye in establishing the Asante Kingdom. The narrative concerning the objects that accompanied the birth of Ɔkomfo Anokye suggests that he was gifted by the deities/spirits from birth. His prophetic prowess,

---

27. Refer to Afriyie, *The Legendary Komfo Anokye*, 54–61 for a complete list.

which he used to free the Asantes from the Denkyira Kingdom, and the establishment of the Asante Kingdom strikes a similar cord with the use of prophets by Adonai to deliver Israel from slavery in Egypt and establish them in Canaan. The works of Ɔkomfo Anokye demonstrate that the role of traditional prophets is indispensable in the socio-political life of some Ghanaians. He projected himself above all except the King, not neglecting the fact that landmark decisions by the King cannot be taken without his input. This has placed traditional prophets on the tangent of being the spiritual heads of the community in which they live. However, the last days of Ɔkomfo Anokye show that the traditional prophets are fallible, just as any human being, and the aura accorded them must be carefully measured.

Chapter Two

Prophetism in *Gã* Traditional Religion

A Case of *Gbawe* Traditional Area

INTRODUCTION

PROPHETISM EXISTS IN MANY Traditional Religions. It is what attracts patronage to a deity and a religious intermediary. This chapter examines prophetism in Gã Traditional Religion with particular attention to Gbawe traditional area in Accra. It sought to focus on the means of receiving oracular messages by the religious intermediary to its adherents. The goal is to draw religio-cultural and social conditions that exists in Gã Traditional Religion that may influence contemporary Pentecostal and Charismatic understanding of Christian prophetism. It also intended to discuss prophetism in Gbawe traditional area as a background that may have informed some contemporary prophets' understanding of the designation "prophet".

A CONCISE HISTORY OF THE GÃ PEOPLE OF GHANA

According to M. E. Kropp Dakubu,[1] the word Gã has both ethnic and contract meanings: firstly, it represents a group of ethnic people who speak the

1. M. E. Kropp Dakubu (Ed.), Gã—English Dictionary with English—Gã Index 2nd

Prophetism in Gã Traditional Religion

Gã language as their native language. Secondly, it means "ring" as symbol of unity and mutual commitment. M. Watson-Quartey postulates that the term Gã was derived from *Gana* (dangerous black big soldier ants).[2] The term Gã was used for them due to their bravery to go to war and take other people's land. The territory of the Gã people is bordered to the north by the Akwapim Hills, to the South by the gulf of Guinea, to the West by the Awutu and to the East by *Adangbe*. The Gã language is classified among the Kwa language group, which includes Ewe, Fon, Akan, Yoruba, Nupe, Edo etc. spoken among some Sub-Saharan African people.[3] Some scholars refer to them as Gã people and others, Gã speaking people or the *Gãs*. The phrase "Gã people" can be ambiguous since it may refer to non- Gã natives who speak the *Gã* language. In this work, we used Gã people and Gãs interchangeably.

There are many versions concerning the origin of the Gã people. According to E. A. Ammah, as captured in the work of I. K. Odotei, the Gã people were of either Semitic origin (specifically Mesopotamia) from the family of Ham (son of Noah) or from Egypt.[4] H. N. Abbey intimates that the Gã people migrated from Israel and settled at an area called Ayawaso in Accra and that the Gã State was established by Nii Ayi Kushi in 1250 BCE after which some of them travelled to settle in Accra, La, Osu, Nungua, Teshie, Prampram, Aneho in Togo[5] among others. However, M. J. Field,[6] a social anthropology to the Gold Coast Government argued that the Gã people of Ghana can be categorized into six independent divisions: Tema, Nungua, Osu, Labadi, Teshie and Accra. Some of the Gã people were aborigines while others were immigrants from Nigeria, Togo, Benin and other places. He further elaborated that all the above mentioned Gã people have their own paramountcy, and were not subject to one paramountcy as

---

Ed. (Accra, Ghana: Black Mask Ltd, 2009), 74.

2. Mustapha Watson-Quartey, "Origin of the Gã Speaking People of Accra" on http://www.kpakpatseweroyalfamily. Wordpress.com/2011/06/18/origin-of-the- Gã-people-in-Ghana. Accessed 3/7/2015.

3. Irene K. Odotei, "The History of Gã people: Introduction" on http://www.justice-ghana.com/index.php/en/2012-01-24-13-47-17/6642-the-history-of-ga-people-introduction. Accessed 3/7/2015.

4. Odotei, "The History", 1, 5.

5. H. Nii Abbey, *Homoho in Ghana* (Accra, Ghana: Studio Brian Communications, 2010), 5.

6. Margaret J. Field, *Social Organization of the Gã people* (London: The Crown Agents for the Colonies, 1940), 71–81.

could be noticed in some ethnic jurisdictions; and that since Accra is called Gã (name of a city and also refers to Gã people generally) some people misunderstood it to mean that the chief of Accra (Gã) is the paramount chief of all Gãs.

Tema

The term Tema is the corrupt derivation of *Torman*, which means a city or town of gourds and calabash. The ancestors of Tema were gourd farmers. Gourd in Gã language is *tor* and *man* is city or town or nation.[7] The Gã people of Tema were aborigines who spoke the *Kpeshi* dialect, which is now extinct. This dialect was said to have some resemblance to *Twi* language and commonly called *Obutu* by the Gã people.[8] *Obutu* refers to huts made out of palm branches used as storage for newly harvested yams, which suggest that, economically, the *Kpeshi* dialect Gã speaking people of Tema were also yam farmers. Religiously, they revered "*Bleku* (the rain, the spirits of lagoons, hills, streams, pools, groves, and other works of nature, *Na Afiyei* (a grandmother deity), and *Gua* (a blacksmith god associated with thunderstorm and agricultural implements".[9] It means that they had no idol images in individual family houses. They had sacred places that were set apart in spatial areas of varied sizes earmarked for religious activities. It is usually a forest, mountain, hill, rock, cave etc. J. S. Mbiti asserted that sacred places " . . . are symbolically the meeting-point between the heaven or sky and the earth, and therefore of the visible and invisible worlds . . . .people regard them as sacred and therefore as places where they feel the symbolic presence of God".[10]

Kpeshi dialect Gã speaking people of Tema celebrate the *Kpledzo* festival in these sacred places. Two generations before the Katamanso war in 1826, it was said that some immigrant Gã people settled among the *Kpeshi* Gã people of Tema to expand and form Tema.[11] One could not ascertain the origin of the migrated Gãs who settled with the *Kpeshi* Gã people of Tema. It is significant to state that *Ashaiman* (Ashale's town) is part of Tema

---

7. The Spectator , "The Story of Tema" on http://www.ghanaculture.gov.gh/index1.php?linkid=65&archiveid=2230&page=1&adate=14/12/2013. Accessed 3/7/2014.

8. Field, *Social Organization*, 82.

9. Field, *Social Organization*, 82.

10. Mbiti, *Introduction*, 149.

11. Field, *Social Organization*, 82.

settlement. At the time when chiefs and *mankralo* (deputy chief) were not installed in Tema, the words of the *wulɔmɛi* (high priests, plural of *wulɔmɔ*) were considered as powerful laws.

Labadi

The Gã people of La or Labadi were immigrants from Bonni in the Niger Delta in Nigeria, therefore they were referred to as Gã Bɔni.[12] They were led by Oko, the *wulɔmɔ* of the deity *La-kpa* to fight against some Nungua people in the area and took over their land. However, they could not take over the worship of the *Kpeshie* lagoon deity from the aboriginals and the winning of salt from it. They were later joined by some Ewe speaking people from Aneho in Togo.[13]

Nungua

The term Nungua means little Ningo.[14] *Kpeshi* Gã people of Tema, who were aborigines, had Nungua as part of their territory. Since they were few in number, some Gã immigrants from Nigeria settled and lived among them. Before the arrival of the Nigerian immigrants, there were other immigrants believed to have come from *Akwamu* in the Eastern Region of Ghana due to "the defeat and breakup of the *Akwamu* kingdom".[15] These were hunters and therefore took large portions of the Nungua land. This resulted in the *Kpeshi* Gã people of Tema becoming a minority, allowing the *Akwamu* to take control over the land and install chiefs. *Bɔkɛte Lawei*, who was a medicine man and a *wulɔmɔ*, was the first chief of the area.

Religiously, two women were elected as *Dzranowɔyei* (market priestesses). Technically, they are traditional priestesses who were not possessed by a deity and were not succeeded by their biological daughters. These women, together with other religious officials, organized corn for use during the *Kpledzo* festival. The *Kpledzo* festival cannot be celebrated without the active involvement of *Dzranowɔyei*.[16] One other significant religious

---

12. Field, *Social Organization*, 200.
13. Field, *Social Organization*, 201.
14. Watson-Quartey, "Origin of the Gã".
15. Field, *Social Organization*, 122.
16. Field, *Social Organization*, 127.

Biblical, Traditional, and Theological Framework

functionary in Nungua was the *agba*. The term *agba*, referred to a shed, market stall, platform or bridge. Field succinctly differentiated the work of the *agba* from that of the *wulɔmɛi* thus: "The work of the *agba* on behalf of the town may be summarized by saying that, whereas the *wulɔmɛi* are concerned with the procurement of positive blessings, increase, and prosperity, the *agba* are a kind of supernatural sanitary department concerned with the cleaning away of harmful influences".[17]

Osu

The Gã term "Osu" might have originated from the Dangme word "*wasu*", which means "you have arrived".[18] By the leadership of *Nɔte Doku*, *wulɔmɔ* of the deity *Nadu*, the Osu Gã people migrated from Dangme (specifically Osudoku) in Krobo District and were given permission to settle at Osu by the chief of Labadi. They were skilful in making pots. After their settlement in the area, the few *Kpeshi* Gã people who had *klɔte* lagoon as their god, left the area and the worship of the lagoon to the newcomers.[19]

Teshie

According to E. Ago, E. A. Anang and A. Bekoe,[20] there are two different narratives concerning the origin of Gã people of Teshie. Before Teshie was established by Nuumo Okang Nmashi, there were some Fanti fishermen from Akobli (near Secondi) who had settled along the sea and Kpeshie lagoon for fishing purposes. Nmashi had fled from La due to war. He pleaded with Nii Trebi, chief of Nungua, who later agreed that he and his troop could live with him in Teshie. The other version is that the land between Teshie and Accra excluding the La land and the Kpeshie lagoon was said to belong to the chief of Nungua, Nii Afotey Okley, and that Nmashi bought it from him. Nmashi and his people lived together with the minority *Kpeshi*

---

17. Field, *Social Organization*, 129.

18. H. Nii Adziri Wellington, *Stones Tell Stories at Osu: Memories of a Host Community of the Danish Trans-Atlantic Slave Trade* (Accra, Ghana: Sub-Saharan Publishers, 2011), 9.

19. Field, *Social Organization*, 196.

20. E. Ago, E. Adzei Anang and Adjei Bekoe, *Teshi Administrative and Cultural Practices* (Tema, Ghana: Ronna Publishers, 2004), 5–6.

aborigines. Field asserts that the Teshie stool is the only stool that was occupied by a *Kpeshi* aboriginal.[21]

Accra

According to C. C. Reindorf,[22] the Gã people of Accra called themselves *Loeiabii* (progenies of *Loei*). *Loei* are dangerous evading brown ants. The Akans of Ghana refer to these ants as *nkrang*. Due to the adventure and the prowess of the Gã people of Accra in defeating the *Guan* aborigines of Accra, they were referred to as *nkrang* by the Akans: this was corrupted by the Portuguese to *Akra*. Field[23] asserts that it was towards the end of the sixteenth century that the ancestors of the Gã people of Accra began to settle among the *Kpeshi* aborigines as immigrants from Benin and other places. There were four major parties: the Gã Bɔni, Gã Wɔ, Gã Mashie and Gã Obutu.

The Gã Mashie party later split into two groups, one half was led by Ni Tɛte and Ni Moi the *wulɔmɛi* of the sea deities *Nai* (believed to be the corrupted version of the Nile—River in Egypt) and *Oyeni* respectively. This group became known as the Sempe people. The other half of Gã Mashie led by Ayi Kushi, went to settle at *Ayiwasu* (Ayi has arrived), a town on a hill. The Gã Obutu later arrived and settled together with Ayi Kushi and his people in *Ayiwasu*. Ayi Kushi later handed over leadership to his son Ayite. Ayite's grandson was Okai Kwei the founder of the town Okakwei in *Ayiwasu*. He was killed during the war between Gã Mashie and Akwamu in 1660 in Nsawam.[24] After the war, some of the Gã Mashie people left the hilly town of *Ayiwasu* to settle along the coast.[25] The Europeans described *Gã Mashie* on the hill as Greater Accra and those at the coast as little Accra.[26] The brother of Okai Kwei, Ayi Frimpong became the first Asɛrɛ chief.

The *wulɔmɛi* and the *gbalɔi* (prophet or foreteller, plural of *gbalɔ*) played significant roles in the socio-political and religious life of the Asɛrɛ

---

21. Field, *Social Organization*, 209.

22. Cited in Watson-Quartey, "Origin of the Gã".

23. Field, *Social Organization*, 142.

24. Watson-Quartey, "Origin of the Gã".

25. Marion Kilson, *African Urban Kinsmen: The Gã of Central Accra* (London: C. Hurst & Company, 1974), 6.

26. Watson-Quartey, "Origin of the Gã".

clan. Field[27] posits that, when the immigrant Gãs arrived in Accra, they inter-married with some of the *Kpeshi* Gã people; and, as time went by, *wulɔmɛi* of the *Kpeshi*e lagoon could not be found. Lomotshokona, an Asɛrɛ fisherman once caught a strange creature during fishing in the lagoon and threw it back into the lagoon. He caught the same creature the next day, but this time he decided to take it to a traditional priestess. The priestess told him that it was the spirit of the *Kpeshi*e lagoon that came to him in the creature and that the spirit of the lagoon had come to help the people of Asɛrɛ. Even though there was no *wulɔmɔ* for the lagoon at the time, there were (*Gbatsui*) sacred places for the lagoon. One day Lomotshokona looked into one of the pots containing water in the sacred places and amazingly, he could hear the voice of the lagoon deity speaking to him without being possessed. Any question that he asked was answered clearly. Thereafter, he was made *gbalɔ* (prophet or foreteller).

PROPHETISM IN GBAWE TRADITIONAL AREA

Gbawe is located in the Gã South Municipal Area (GSMA). It is one of the most densely populated areas in GSMA. The indigenes of Gbawe were from the Asɛrɛ division of Gã Mashie. Prophetism influenced the naming of Gbawe in Gã Tradition. Gã Traditional Prophetism refers to the means of receiving oracular messages from the deities/spirits. "Gbawe" is a *Gã* word meaning prophet's home, town or residence. The prefix "*Gba*" has religious and secular meanings: religiously, it means to prophesy (foretell). Secularly, it refers to telling stories of the past that has relevance for contemporary times (forthtell). The suffix "*We*" means a home, town or residence.

The term *Gbalɔ* in Gã language refers to a prophet, one who prophesies. According to Mr. Solomon Nii Atutu Quartey, Gbawe Kwatei family secretary, the founder of Gbawe was a prophet and a hunter, which is why the palace was called Gbawe *Gborbilor*, and the town named *Gbawe*,[28] which means the prophet who is also a hunter's home, town or residence. Hunting in some communities in Africa/Ghana is not just a zoological art of bravery in trapping game, it is also a prophetic art to 'see' and 'discern' accurately which game to go for, since some spirits could manifest in game form.

---

27. Field, *Social Organization*, 152–153.
28. Solomon Nii Atutu Quartey, interviewed by author, Mallam 28th February, 2014.

Prophetism in Gã Traditional Religion

Hunters could also meet spirit beings in the forests. The origin of the *Kundum* dance and festival can be traced to an encounter a hunter had during one of his hunting expeditions in the night. The hunter, who was a native of Aboadze, was reported to have been taught how to dance *Kundum* by the leader of the dwarfs called Afoakye for a period of one month.[29] The ability of the hunter to communicate with the dwarfs who were considered to be spirit beings, but could also appear physically, is a prophetic art. Normal or persons without prophetic prowess in traditional religion could hardly communicate with spirit beings like dwarfs and undergo a month's training for the *Kundum* dance. Quartey asserted that during the nineteenth century, Gbawe was where leaders of the Gã State came to inquire of the deities or spirits through the *Gbalɔ* of the prospects of an impending war before embarking on same. He also added that many of the wars that the Gã State emerged victorious in, had a prophetic input of *Gbalɔi* from Gbawe. An example is the Katamanso war during the reign of Nii Taki Kome I, 1825–1856.[30]

According to Gbawe Kpoboo Mantse and secretary to the traditional cabinet, Nii Abbey Okanfani,[31] during the early to middle 1900s, people from all walks of life came to Gbawe due to the visible presence of *Gbalɔi* to ask for guidance before taking important decisions. However, the presence of Churches and their subsequent condemnation of traditional prophetism, coupled with derogatory remarks, such as Christians referring to them as "demonic", have rendered the ministry of *Gbalɔi* unpopular. Insight gathered from Gã terms for the word "prophet" and the significance of oracular messages to political, economic, and social life of some Ghanaians cannot be overstated. It can be concluded that, in primal religions, a prophet is someone who has access to the spiritual world of the deities or spirits and uses it to benefit his or her solicitors and non-solicitors alike regardless of one's religious or ethnic affiliation. It is purely a foretelling enterprise where the *Gbalɔ* speaks of happenings in the present and future. It is significant to mention that solicitors do not need to convert to traditional religion as a requirement to consult with the deities through the *Gbalɔ*.

---

29. Stephen Sintim-Koree, *The God Who Answers by Thunder: An Account of Christian Persecution in Nzemaland During the Ban on Drumming 1993-1996* (Accra, Ghana: SonLife Press, 2013), 15–17.

30. http://gadangme.weebly.com/kings-of-the-ga-state.html. Accessed 5/4/2014.

31. Nii Abbey Okanfani, interviewed by author, Mallam, 28th February, 2014.

Biblical, Traditional, and Theological Framework

Many solicitors did not need to tell the *Gbalɔ* the challenges that brought them to the shrine. As a sign of the ability of the *Gbalɔ* to communicate with the deities promptly, he or she narrates some important and personal issues that had happened in the life of the solicitor. In some cases, the *Gbalɔ* prophetically mentions the main issue that compelled the solicitor to come and consult with him or her so that the solicitor would believe in the potency of the solution to be given by the *Gbalɔ*. This act also signified the active presence of the ancestors, spirits, and deities that are believed to be living in the community, and who also participate in daily activities of their subjects or relations.

The prophetic instincts of the *Gbalɔ* to reveal secrets from the spiritual realm authenticate his/her ministry. As J. K. Asamoah-Gyadu rightly notes "religious functionaries are basically persons of sacred power with the ability to 'see' into and 'discern' developments within the realms of the supernatural".[32] It implies that prophetism in primal religions is a continuous exercise where the *Gbalɔ's* prophetic antennae are set high and strategically to receive oracular messages from the deities, ancestors, and spirits that possesses him or her.

The significance of prophetism in traditional religions could be attributed to the lack of sacred scriptures[33] in African/Ghanaian Traditional Religions. This situation has contributed in making the prophetic ministry of *Gbalɔ* indispensable in some traditional religions. Since human nature is dynamic, prophetism in primal religions also helps to adapt to new circumstances synchronically.

There is another *Gã* religious designation—*wulɔmɔ* that needs to be commented upon as a prophet's title and the role of *Gbatsui* (shrines/sacred places, plural of *Gbatsu*) in *Gã* primal religions. According to Numbo Akrama,[34] the *wulɔmɔ* (high priest)[35] of Gbawe, all *wulɔmεi* of

---

32. J. Kwabena Asamoah-Gyadu, "Spirit and Spirits African Religious Traditions" in Veli-Matti Kärkkäinen, Kirsteen Kim, and Amos Yong (Eds.), *Interdisciplinary and Religio-Cultural Discourses on a Spirit-Filled World: Loosing the Spirits* (New York: Palgrave Macmillan, 2013), 46.

33. John S. Mbiti, *Introduction to African Religion* 2nd Rev. Ed. (Oxford: Heinemann Educational Publishers, 1991), 17.

34. Numbo Akrama, interviewed by author, Gbawe, 1st March, 2014. He was enthrone as *wulɔmɔ* in 1994.

35. A *wulɔmɔ* is a spiritual head of a *Gã* community. He is the foremost person before the *Mantse* (chief/king).

Prophetism in Gã Traditional Religion

Gã communities have individual *Gbatsui*.[36] They usually live in a house either built around a *Gbatsu* or near a *Gbatsu*.[37] It suggests that the location of *Gbatsu* determines were a *wulɔmɔ* lives. There is an inseparable relationship between *Gbatsu* and *wulɔmɔ*. P. T. Laryea translated *wulɔmɔ* as "priest".[38] However, it is significant to note that, functionally and prophetically, *wulɔmɔ* should be translated to mean the biblical "high priest" rather than simply "priest".

The Levitical high priest, as part of his liturgical dress, has "*Urim* and *Thummim*"[39] in the breast plate as a sign to bear Israel up in the presence of Yahweh (Ex. 28:30). Commenting on Numbers 27:21, C. F. Keil and F. Delitzsch posited that *Urim* and *Thummim* was a "medium" given by Yahweh for the high priest to access divine direction for Israel when they were in a dilemma.[40] David seemed to have used Abiathar's *Urim* and *Thummim* to inquire from Yahweh (1 Sam. 23:1–14). This makes Levitical high priesthood a prophetic type whereby, by the use of *Urim* and *Thummim*, the high priest could inquire from Yahweh at will. Comparing the cultic dress, the cultic songs and rituals of *wulɔmɛi* during the process of receiving oracular messages from the ancestors and spirits, it can then be concluded that *wulɔmɔ* should better be translated as "Levitical high priest".

Gbatsui is the plural of *Gbatsu*, which literally means "sacred room for receiving prophecies". *Gba*, as indicated earlier, has both secular and religious meanings. *Tsu* has two secular meanings: it means "a room", and also "work". Therefore *Gbatsu* is a sacred room dedicated to petitioning and inducing the spirits to receive prophetic messages for the community or prominent person(s) in the community. Akrama asserts that *Gbatsu* plays two major functions in the life of *wulɔmɔs* and the community. Firstly,

---

36. *Gbatsu* is built in various sizes and shapes. In Gbawe, the *Gbatsu* is a cylindrical plastered block work room of about 1.5m in radium, painted white with a conical roof of zinc roofing sheets. The height of the room is about 2.2m with a wooden door measuring 0.900m wide and 1.5m high. It has no windows. Refer to appendix 4.

37. Harry Nii Koney Odamtten, "They Bleed but they Don't Die: Towards a Theoretical Canon On Ga-Adangbe Gender Studies" in *The Journal of Pan African Studies*, vol.5, No.2, (April 2012), 110–127.

38. Philip Tetteh Laryea, *Yesu Hɔmɔwɔ nuŋtsɔ* (Akropong-Akuapem, Ghana: Regnum Africa, 2011), 135.

39. *Urim* and *Thummim* in Hebrew refers to "Lights and Perfections". The exact shape, size and make of it are yet to be known.

40. C. F. Keil and F. Delitzsch, *Keil & Delitzsch Commentary on the Old Testament Vol. 1, the Pentateuch* (Peabody, Massachusetts: Hendrickson Publishers, 1989), 199.

prior to the *hɔmɔwɔ*[41] festival, the *wulɔmɔ* will enter the *Gbatsu* to pray for the community for forgiveness of the sins of the community and inquire about happenings in the New Year and the way forward. This is reminiscent of the "Day of Atonement" in the Old Testament (Lev. 16).

Secondly, when calamity befalls the entire community, or a prominent person in the community is terminally/fatally ill, and the ancestors and spirits did not speak to the *wulɔmɔ* or *Gbalɔ* expressly concerning the matter, which may be due to the sins of the community, or the individual in question or failure to perform mandatory rituals. If this is believed to be the case, then the *wulɔmɔ* will enter the *Gbatsu* at night for a vigil to pray to the ancestors and the spirits for them to speak to him concerning how to avert the present situation. In the case of Akrama, he usually enters the *Gbatsu* at 11pm for a vigil till 4am by which time the ancestors and spirits would have spoken to him about the matter. The Gbawe *Gbatsu* does not have any ritual object or image in it. The room is physically empty. However, it houses myriads of spirits that communicate expressly with the *wulɔmɔ* whenever he enters. This points to the fact that prophetism in primal religions has been the main source of communication between the material and the immaterial worlds.

CONCLUSION

Prophetism exists in many traditional religions in Ghana. *Gbalɔ* and *wulɔmɔ* were religious intermediaries that were held in high esteem in Gbawe traditional religion. The ability of *Gbalɔ* and *wulɔmɔ* to communicate both vertically and horizontally coupled with the belief in soliciting the assistance of spirit beings for solutions in existential issues have made their roles indispensable in traditional religious life. This could also be due to the lack of sacred scripture in primal religions.

Due to the absence of sacred scripture in many traditional religions the position of the *Gbalɔ* and *wulɔmɔ* is indispensable and therefore makes it an office because there is no alternative scripture that could give guidance. This phenomenon of over reliance on *Gbalɔ* and *wulɔmɔ* in many religious issues is parallel to the Pythia and other cults in Corinth. Just as the Holy Spirit could use any Christian to prophesy, in Gbawe traditional

---

41. *hɔmɔwɔ* is a festival of the Gã people of Ghana. It means hooting at hunger. For further studies, refer to Philip Tetteh Laryea, *Yesu Hɔmɔwɔ nuŋtsɔ* (Akropong-Akuapem, Ghana: Regnum Africa, 2011).

area, the deities or spirits mostly use the *Gbalɔ* and *wulɔmɔ*; this is the same in the oracular cult of the Pythia and other cults in Corinth. In the absence of prophets and prophecies, Christians have the Bible as a guide in any matter of human existential needs. However, in Gbawe traditional area and oracular cults in Corinth, one could hardly find a known alternative.

Chapter Three

Early Christian Prophetism in Ghana

INTRODUCTION

THE PROPHETIC MINISTRIES OF the founders of the African Initiated/ Indigenous/Independent Churches (AICs) were considered as pioneers of prophetic ministry in Ghana's Christianity. Prior to the period of the AICs, there were elements of prophetism in the Historic Mission Churches but it was minimal and did not claim centre stages of charismatic renewals and influence. The chapter briefly discusses the emergence of prophetism in Ghana's Christianity. The goal is to identify the beginning of prophetism in Ghana's Christianity, which has gradually led to contemporary prophetic ministry in Ghana today. Early prophetism in Ghana was dominated by the ministry of prophets from the AICs. The form of prophetism was based on Africanism: the desire to be a Christian prophet without losing the African identity and cultural values. Significantly, it is apt to investigate its ethos and impact on Christianity in Ghana.

Factors Contributing to the Emergence of Prophetism in Ghana's Christianity

The Western missionary societies, who founded Churches in Ghana, began to hand over leadership roles to Ghanaians in the early twentieth century. The Evangelical Presbyterian Church and The Presbyterian Church of

Ghana were given autonomy in 1923.[1] Soon afterwards, some members of the churches found the need for a revival because the Ghanaian world-view needed to be considered in religious life. Consequently, it led to the establishment of various prayer groups in many denominations of the Christian Church in Ghana.

THE BEGINNING OF PROPHETISM IN GHANA'S CHRISTIANITY

In Ghana, the prophetic ministries of Prophet William Wadè Harris, Prophet John Swatson, and Prophet Sampson Oppong have attracted scholarly acceptance as known pioneers of prophetic ministry or pioneers of Pentecostalism in Ghana.[2] Although there may be unanswered questions concerning aspects of the ministry of the pioneers, it is an undeniable fact that prophetism in Ghana's Christianity has been largely influenced by non-Western elements of the pioneers of prophetic ministry in Ghana's Christianity. This is evident in African Christian identity and "pneumatic Christianity" especially.[3]

The charismatic experience of the pioneers of prophetic ministry in Ghana have affected and changed the face of Christianity, which used to be predominantly Western. Many of the missionaries represented Western forms of Christianity, which some Ghanaian Christians found difficult to relate to. The demand for non-Western Christianity was a demand for the gospel to be made incarnational to them. The pioneers of the prophetic ministry in Ghana's Christianity engaged socio-cultural elements as tools for hermeneutics and emphasis on pneumatic experience that resonated with the Ghanaian world view in Christian worship.

---

1. Omenyo, *Pentecost Outside Pentecostalism*, 63.

2. Christian. G. Baëta, *Prophetism in Ghana: A Study of Some 'Spiritual' Churches* (Achimota, Ghana: Africa Christian Press, 2004), 8–11. J. Kwabena Asamoah-Gyadu, *African Charismatics: Current Developments within Independent Indigenous Pentecostalism in Ghana* (Leiden, The Netherland: African Christian Press under Licence from Koninklijke Brill NV, 2005), 19. And Bartels, *The Roots*, 174, 188.

3. J. Kwabena Asamoah-Gyadu, *Contemporary Pentecostal Christianity: Interpretations from an African Context* (Oxford, U. K.: Regnum Books International, 2013), 1.

Biblical, Traditional, and Theological Framework

Prophet William Wadẻ Harris (c.1860-c.1929)

Prophet William Wadẻ Harris has attracted the attention of many scholars and ecumenical bodies as an influential prophet who converted many to the Christian faith. His preaching manners and theology of the Spirit also informed revival in the "Traditional Western Mission Churches" (TWMC).[4] Reference to William Wadẻ Harris as Prophet or Evangelist by some scholars is based on the writer's knowledge of aspects of Harris's work that he/she is acquainted with or aspects of Harris's work that are being discussed. There is no consensus among scholars concerning the birth date of Prophet William Wadẻ Harris. Some scholars postulate that he was born around 1860;[5] others suggest 1865 or an earlier date of 1850.[6] We can only conclude that Harris was born between 1850 and 1865 at Cape Palmas, Liberia. He was a Kru of Grebo tribe,[7] and the son of an illiterate non-Christian father and a mother who was believed to be a Christian because she lived among the inhabitants of a Christian village near the lagoon at Half Graway.[8]

While serving a treasonable prison sentence, Harris claimed to have had a vision in which the biblical angel Gabriel visited and anointed him to be a prophet (like the biblical Daniel and Elijah). He became an itinerant prophet soon after his release.[9] Liturgically, Prophet Harris was dressed very differently from the conventional clergy dress, as Kofi Asare Opoku puts it:

---

4. Cephas N. Omenyo, Pentecost *Outside Pentecostalism: A Study of the Development of Charismatic Renewal in the Mainline Churches in Ghana* (The Netherlands: Boekencentrum Publishing House, 2002), 37; Asamoah-Gyadu, *African Charismatic*, 30. And Kwame Bediako, *Christianity in Africa: The Renewal of a Non-Western Religion* (Edinburgh: Edinburgh University Press and New York: Orbis Books, 1995), 91.

5. David A. Shank, "Wadé Harris, William c. 1860 to 1929 Harrist Church (Église Harriste) Liberia/Ghana/Côte d'Ivoire" in G. H. Anderson et al (eds.), *Dictionary of African Christian Biography*. 1994. http://www.dacb.org/stories/liberia/legacy_harris.html. Accessed 6/6/2014.

6. John Zarwan, "William Wade Harris: The Genesis of an African Religious Movement" in *Mission: An International Review*, 431–450, http://www. mis.sagepub.com. Accessed 21/5/2014.

7. Bartels, *The Roots*, 174.

8. Shank, "Wadé Harris."

9. Peter B. Clarke, *West Africa and Christianity* (London: Edward Arnold (Publishers) Ltd, 1986), 179. And Kofi Asare Opoku, "A Brief History of Independent Church Movement in Ghana Since 1862" in *The Rise of Independent Churches in Ghana* (Accra: Asempa Publication, 1990), 16.

> Dressed in a white gown with a turban on his head, he held a bamboo cross, a calabash for baptism, and a Bible, and went about preaching to the people to abandon "fetishism", to believe in God and the cross, to be baptised, to organise Christian congregations under church leaders called Apostles, to keep Sundays holy, to respect the Bible and to wait for missionaries.[10]

We must state that the New Testament has no specific description for clergy vestment. It is a matter of denominational preference. Harris vestment was new to Christian clergy but it was not so for adherents of traditional religion. Describing how the Ivorians perceived Harris' regalia and manner of service, P. B. Clarke writes:

> ...nothing completely new to Ivorians in Harris's manner, style of dress, and methods, or in much of what he had to say. Prior to Harris conversion campaign in the Ivory Coast, traditional priests from Liberia who also wore white garments had brought what they claimed were more powerful spirits for the protection and the well-being of the Ivorians. And though Harris differed from these traditional priests or prophets in as much as he claimed to be sent by the only true God, he nevertheless resembled them in this and in many other aspects. For example Harris' form and style of worship which included the playing of the gourd rattle and singing and dancing resembled the traditional manner of worship. Indeed, Harris is said to have told his converts who asked him how they should worship that they were 'to dance as they had for the indigenous spirits and to sing their own songs adding the name 'God.'[11]

It is probable that Harris was dressed just like the traditional priests/prophets of his day, not like the clergy, probably because he was not ordained. His dress was reminiscent of spiritually powerful people in the African society at the time, who were not necessarily Christian. Moreover, non-Christian African people could more easily relate to Prophet Harris' dress and manner of worship than to Christians. Harris perhaps adopted what the people knew in traditional religion, and modified it to serve the living God in a non-Western manner.

The use of bamboo to make a cross was not strange in Harris' day. Some houses and churches were built with bamboo. It was the most available building material.[12] The cross was also analogous of the staff of office

---

10. Opoku, "A Brief History", 16.
11. Clarke, *West Africa*, 182–183.
12. Watson A. O. Omulokoli, "William Wade Harris: Premier African Evangelist" in

and power that traditional priests/prophets usually held in their hand and the centrality of the cross to the Christian faith. However, Prophet Harris's staff did not represent any deity but Christ. Again his use of a gourd as a bowl for baptism was to emphasize his affinity with traditional Africa. During his day, the gourd was used to fetch water from streams to homes and also used as a cup for drinking. Prophet Harris was said to have experienced the coming of the Holy Spirit upon him as "ice descending on his head and all over him" and began to speak in tongues.[13] He was gifted in many ways and demonstrated the power of God far above all the powers of traditional priests or prophets. G. M. Haliburton, as captioned in the writing of Omenyo, opined thus:

> Harris claimed to be a prophet with all the special powers that he bestows on those He chooses. These powers enabled him to drive out demons and spirits, the enemies of God. He cured the sick in body and in mind by driving out the evil being preying on them. Those who practised black magic had to confess and repent or he made them mad. He had all the powers of the fetishmen and more: with his basin of holy water he put God's seal on those who repented and accepted baptism. If after that they fell into old wickedness, they died or went mad. He believed God had given him other powers, more dramatic asserting of their relationship, notably the power to call down fire and rain from heaven.[14]

Harris' reference to himself as a prophet was to identify himself as an African Christian prophet. The African would more easily relate to the title "Prophet" than to Reverend Minister. Moreover, non-performing gods were usually neglected and in exchange support was given to high performing ones. Therefore, Harris' demonstration of power, which was over and above that of traditional priests or prophets, would be held in high esteem and their gods discarded.

From Ivory Coast, Harris crossed over to Apollonia (now Jomoro) in Nzema in the Western Region of the Ghana in 1914. He spent three months in the district, which led to the conversion of about 8,000 people to the

---

Africa Journal of Evangelical Theology (21. 1. 2002), 17.

13. Cephas O. Omenyo, *Pentecost Outside Pentecostalism: A Study of the Development of Charismatic Renewal in the Mainline Churches in Ghana* (The Netherlands: Boekencentrum Publishing House, 2002), 67.

14. G. M. Haliburton, *The Prophet Harris: A Study of an African Prophet and his Mass Movement in the Ivory Coast and the Gold Coast, 1913-1915* (London: Longman, 1971), 3.

Christian faith, and he tried to Christianize over 52 villages.[15] It is suggested that Harris was converting an average of 89 persons a day in Nzema, which no missionary had equalled in the mission history of Ghana. Notable among his converts in Ghana were John Nackabah a native of Essuawa near Enchi, and Grace Tanne who hailed from Ankobra Mouth: they were a former traditional priest and priestess respectively. Harris did not found a church. He directed his converts to join the established churches, namely The Roman Catholic Church and The Methodist Church. Where there were no existing churches he urged the converts to meet and fellowship as Christians and wait for missionaries to come and teach them the Bible. It implies that Harris ministry "transcended denominational barriers".[16]

Upon Harris's return from the Gold Coast to Ivory Coast, he was arrested by the French government for insubordination. His cross and gourd were broken and he was imprisoned. After his release, Harris returned to his home in Liberia in late 1915. He continued with the preaching work but at a slower pace.[17] He also traveled to Sierra Leone thrice in 1917, 1919 and 1921.[18] In 1925, he had a stroke from which he did not fully recover, and died in 1929 in Spring Hill, Liberia in abject poverty.[19] John Nackabah and Grace Tanne later founded Churches to perpetuate the ministry of Harris.

Prophet John Swatson (c.1855-c.1925)

Prophet John Swatson was a contemporary of Prophet William Wadė Harris. His ministry in Asante recorded massive conversion and mighty works. Swatson was born at Beyin in Apollonia (now Jomoro) Nzema to a European father who was attached to the ɔmanhene Amakye I of Beyin and a Ghanaian mother from a royal family.[20] He had basic and elementary education at a local Methodist School at Beyin and Cape Coast respectively. According to Omenyo, Swatson thereafter became a teacher-catechist of the local Methodist Church[21] at Beyin. He married a daughter of a Methodist

---

15. Omulokoli, "William Wade Harris", 13. Also Opoku, "A Brief History", 16.

16. Omenyo, *Pentecost Outside Pentecostalism*, 69.

17. Omulokoli, "William Wade Harris", 14. See also www.irr.org/pdfs/aic-chap6. Accessed 6/6/2014.

18. Shank, "Wadé Harris",

19. Omulokoli, "William Wade Harris", 14.

20. Larbi, *Pentecostalism*, 63.

21. Omenyo, *Pentecost Outside Pentecostalism*, 69–70.

Biblical, Traditional, and Theological Framework

pioneer in Beyin and worked as a clerk in a commercial house at Axim. He was not very successful and left to Benin City in Nigeria where he worked as a civil servant.[22]

Swatson later traveled to Ivory Coast and became a catechist in a local Methodist Church at Aboisso. It was during this period, between 1912 and 1913, that he probably met Prophet William Wadė Harris.[23] He became Harris' disciple and "begged him to teach him his powers of baptism". Harris responded in the affirmative. After that, he experienced the power of the Holy Spirit just as Harris did. Haliburton observed that "from that moment, Swatson believed that the Holy Spirit, so manifest in Harris, had fallen on him. He abandoned his personal possessions, dressed like him in a white robe and carried a cross swathed in white calico and the indispensable bowl of baptismal water".[24] He later claimed that he had 'angelic visitations and he exercised the gift of healing and exorcism comparable to Harris. Moreover, Swatson referred to himself as "Bishop" and his movement was called 'Christ Church Mission'.[25]

E. D. Martinson, an Anglican priest from Larteh, was so impressed with the work of Swatson that he remarked: "An extraordinary man named Swatson, (a mulatto) has been evangelizing and baptizing the remote heathen villages of the Western Province of the Colony. He has told many of his converts to become 'Church of England.'"[26] He was later commissioned and licensed by Bishop O'Rorke and put in charge of all the branches of the Church in Nzema.[27] The Anglican Church benefited from the ministry of Swatson, in that he directed his converts to join the Church. Swatson translated the Anglican Prayer book and Hymns into the Nzema language. He also preached in the local languages and was able to penetrate where the SPG could not succeed.[28] According to Larbi, Swatson became morose and eccentric as an old man. This situation led to mental challenges in 1924.[29]

---

22. Larbi, *Pentecostalism*, 64.

23. Debrunner, *A History*, 276.

24. G. M. Haliburton, "The Anglican Church in Ghana and Harris Movement in 1914" in *The Bulletin of the Society of African Church History* I (1964), 101–106. Quoted by Larbi, *Pentecostalism*, 64.

25. Omenyo, *Pentecost Outside Pentecostalism*, 70.

26. Missionary Reports, SPG Archives, London: 1916 quoted by Haliburton, "The Anglican Church", 104 cited from Larbi, *Pentecostalism*, 65.

27. Larbi, *Pentecostalism*, 64–65. See also Debrunner, *A History*, 277.

28. Omenyo, *Pentecost Outside Pentecostalism*, 70.

29. Debrunner, *A History*, 277. See also Larbi, *Pentecostalism*, 66.

Early Christian Prophetism in Ghana

Prophet Sampson Oppong (c.1884-c.1965)

Sampson Oppong, as he was popularly known, was a contemporary of Harris and Swatson. His ministry was characterized by wonders and mass conversions, just like Harris and Swatson. Sampson Oppong was born in the Brong Ahafo Region in Ghana. He was a native of a slave family called Gurunsi in Burkina Faso. He was illiterate and was taught the practice of magic by his uncle.[30] Unlike Harris and Swatson who had some Christian background, Oppong was a traditional priest without any Christian background.

While serving a jail term for embezzlement in Ivory Coast in 1913, he claimed to have had a vision in which he was instructed to burn all his idols, make a wooden cross and to preach the gospel and that the name Sampson was given to him in the vision.[31] He began preaching in Bompata in the Asante Region. He accused a woman of being a witch and in proving her case of innocence she held Oppong's cross and then run into the forest. This led to the breaking of Oppong's cross by the District Commissioner and subsequent imprisonment.[32] According to Haliburton, Oppong claimed to have been shown a white stone in the vision he had in prison. Though an illiterate he claimed that he could look on the stone, mention a Bible quotation and read the passage from the surface of the stone.[33]

Oppong was said to have been baptized into the Christian faith by a Minister of The African Methodist Episcopal, Rev. Fosuhene, and was introduced to the Methodist Church by Rev. Bart Plange and Rev. W. G. Waterworth at Kumasi in 1920.[34] Oppong converted about 110,000 people including some prominent persons in society. About 20,000 of the converts joined the Methodist Church in Ashanti.[35] Oppong claimed to have been called directly by God and that he could not submit himself to human

---

30. Andres F. Walls, "Sam(p)son Oppong c. 1884–1965 Methodist Ghana" in *Dictionary of African Christian Biography*. http://www.dacb.org/stories/ghana/opon_sampson2.html 6/6/2014.

31. Omenyo, *Pentecost Outside Pentecostalism*, 70. See also Larbi, *Pentecostalism*, 66. And Walls, "Sam(p)son Oppong".

32. Omenyo, *Pentecost Outside Pentecostalism*, 70.

33. G. M. Haliburton, "The Calling of the Prophet" in *The Bulletin of the Society for African Church History*, Vol. 2, (1965), 84–96. Cited from Omenyo, *Pentecost Outside Pentecostalism*, 71.

34. Larbi, *Pentecostalism*, 66.

35. Omenyo, *Pentecost Outside Pentecostalism*, 71. And Larbi, *Pentecostalism*, 66.

Biblical, Traditional, and Theological Framework

discipline.[36] Even though the Methodist Church accepted Oppong initially, they did not hesitate to caution him to submit to the disciplinary measures of the Church: a measure that he declined and this ran him into trouble with the Church. Oppong's uncle who taught him how to practice magic early in his life managed to lure him into drinking very excessively. He lost his preaching abilities and could not read the white stone. In 1929, he was convicted of a "sexual offence in a traditional court".[37] Oppong afterwards retired to his home town and continued with evangelistic work at a slow pace and was a crop farmer until his death in 1965.[38]

COMMENTS ON THE MINISTRY OF PIONEERS OF PROPHETIC MINISTRY IN GHANA'S CHRISTIANITY

The three prophets discussed above were admired by many early in their ministries, including missionaries. Their approach to evangelism was unique at the time because their message was "this worldly" but their charismatic manifestations were in doubt. They were later rejected by the missionaries on doctrinal issues and their end was miserable. The three forerunners have some similarities: firstly, they claimed to have been called in an angelic encounter when they were in difficult life situations — imprisonment and economic challenges; secondly, they used vestments that resonate more with traditional religion than with Christianity; thirdly, their work started declining during their old age and continued after their demise; and fourthly, the end of their lives were not generally befitting for men of God. This may have been due to very limited or no theological education prior to ministry. This does not suggest that theological education alone is able to immune one against challenges in ministry but it could limit mistakes and build the ministers' capacity to control and overcome challenges more easily.

In many religious movements or New Religious Movements (NRM), there are external factors that impel and attract adherents and internal factors that establish the adherents in the faith or influence their exit. As J. K. Asamoah-Gyadu aptly puts it: "In contradistinction to an 'emic' viewpoint, which results from studying behavior 'as from inside a system' like a religious movement, 'etic' is used to refer to attempts to study behavior using

---

36. Larbi, *Pentecostalism*, 66. And Omenyo, *Pentecost Outside Pentecostalism*, 71.
37. Walls, "Sam(p)son Oppong".
38. Larbi, *Pentecostalism*, 66.

criteria that are 'external to the system' under study".[39] There were external factors such as political, economic and religious that aided the success of the work of the forerunners of prophetic ministry in Ghana. Politically, one could argue that the deportation of the Bremen and the Basel missionaries during the First World War, coupled with the quest for independence, contributed partly to the success of the forerunners of the prophetic ministry in Ghana.[40] Their manner of ministry projected "African life and thought", which supported the need for independence. Economically, cocoa, the spine of Ghana's economy, was not doing well in the world market and, as Debrunner cited from Gold Coast Methodist Synod Minutes in 1917:

> Our people everywhere are beginning to realize the ill effects of the titanic struggle in Europe. Cocoa crops have been more than plentiful, but the market has been so glutted that planters have terribly burned their fingers over their business transactions. In one way or the other, this has affected our finance and the spiritual tone of some of our churches.[41]

On the religious front, there was an emergence of an anti-witchcraft cult between 1900 and 1950[42] because the indigenous people thought that their economic gains were being destroyed by witches. People trouped to these cults for spiritual assistance and to settle disputes there, more so than the traditional courts headed by the ɔmanhene (chief). Between 1894 and 1930, the Colonial government managed to suppress them by legislation.[43] Whilst the anti-witchcraft cults were becoming extinct, a new traditional cult "Tigare" emerged in 1940, which posed a threat to the survival of TWMCs Christianity in Ghana, because the shrine was attracting Christians. According to James Annorbah-Sarpei, it was the emergence of these prophets that helped control and eventually tamed the activities of the Tigare shrines.[44]

---

39. J. Kwabena Asamoah-Gyadu, *African Charismatics: Current Development Within Independent Indigenous Pentecostalism in Ghana* (Leiden: African Christian Press, 2005), 20–21.

40. Debrunner, *A History*, 269.

41. Debrunner, *A History*, 279.

42. James Annorbah-Sarpei, "The Rise of Prophetism — A Socio-Political Explanation" in *The Rise of Independent Churches in Ghana* (Accra: Asempa Publication, 1990), 27.

43. Annorbah-Sarpei, "The Rise of Prophetism", 29.

44. Annorbah-Sarpei, "The Rise of Prophetism", 30–31.

Biblical, Traditional, and Theological Framework

Internal factors that mainly attracted many to the forerunners of the prophetic ministry in Ghana were their charisma, language, and vestment. The forerunners demonstrated their powers to heal, exorcise demons and even cause opponents to go mad or die. They also professed to have the power to protect converts from being attacked by witches. In communicating their message, they used the local language which the indigenous person could easily understand. They were dressed like the traditional priests/prophets, which the converts could relate to. Their ministry made them the sole authority thereby making their prophetic ministry an office that did not continue effectively after their demise. Having mentioned all these, it is also significant to mention that the forerunners of the prophetic ministry in Ghana's Christianity failed in some regards. Most of their beliefs and practices, which they claimed to be biblical did not have strong theological backing. Their hermeneutics were not informed by any philosophical and rational exposition, but were basically founded on common theology that evolved with the people and the converts were moved by emotions as they saw the wonders. The forerunners could not establish the converts in the Christian faith, since some of them were morally and theologically weak.

CONCLUSION

Prophetism is not new to Ghana's Christianity. The ministries of Prophet William Wadė Harris, Prophet John Swatson, and Prophet Sampson Oppong were considered as pioneers of prophetic ministry in Ghana's Christianity. Unfortunately, there were many doubts concerning their spiritual endowments. Their ministries seemed to resonate with prophetism in some Ghanaian traditional religions more than with Christian prophetism in Pauline literature. The prophetic ministries of the forerunners of prophetic ministry in Ghana's Christianity seem to have been the combination of traditional prophetism and Old Testament prophetism: this is evident in their dress, ritual objects used, observance of holy days among others. It is obvious that Pauline instruction concerning prophetism in the church, particularly in 1 Corinthians 14:26–40 was not part of their guiding principles in ministry.

Chapter Four

Phases of Neo-Prophetism in Ghana's Christianity

INTRODUCTION

PROPHETISM IN GHANA HAD gone through phases. Each phase had its unique characteristics, which demonstrates its strength, weakness, and impact. Indeed C. G. Baëta postulated that prophetism is a "perennial phenomena",[1] which resurfaces with renewed hopes and aspirations. Prophetism here refers to speaking through divine inspiration that reveals the past, gives insight into present happenings and predicts the future. Joseph Quayesi-Amakye identified five phases[2] of prophetism in Ghana's Christianity. This chapter examines the factors that gave rise to each phase, its theology and emphasis on supernatural activities.

Phase 1

In Ghana, the prophetic ministries of Prophets William Wadé Harris (c. 1860–1929), John Swatson (c.1855-c.1925) and Kwame Sampson Oppong (c.1884-c.1965) are considered as the phase one or pioneers of prophetism in Ghana. They were the founders of the AICs, who have attracted scholarly

---

1. Christian G. Baëta, *Prophetism in Ghana* (Achimota, Ghana: African Christian Press, 2004), 6.

2. Quayesi-Amakye, *Prophetism in Ghana Today*, 26–28.

Biblical, Traditional, and Theological Framework

acceptance as forerunners of prophetic ministry or forerunners of Pentecostalism in Ghana. The AICs are also referred to as *sunsum sorè* (spiritual churches) and are similar to the Aladura Churches in Nigeria and the Zionist Churches in South Africa.[3] The phrase *sunsum sorè* is ambiguous and lacks precision. *Sunsum* refers to spirit or being spiritual, *sorè* can be used to refer to two related phenomena:

(i) It is derived from the word ɔsɔreɛ (worship or adoration) as used in John 4:24 (*Asante Twi* version); and (ii) it is also used to refer to a Church (*asɔre*) or a Christian denomination. It is probable that scholars who use *sorè* refer to a Christian denomination. However, to be precise, *asafo* (church, assembly, gathering) is a better option to *sorè* as used in Matthew 16:18; 18:17; in the book of Acts, the epistles and in the book of Revelation. Therefore *sunsum asafo* is better translated as spiritual Church than *sunsum sorè*. The name point to their emphasis on the activities of the Spirit in worship services as the antithesis to that of the Western led missionary Churches.

Phase one is popularly referred to as the emergence of prophetism in Ghana's Christianity.[4] It started in Axim and Apollonia in Nzima in 1914 by Prophet Harris[5] and was later supported by Prophets Swatson and Oppong after being influenced by Prophet Harris. J. K. Asamoah-Gyadu postulates that this form of prophetism was partly a reaction "against the over-cerebral and rationalistic nature of Western forms of being Christian. The inability of Western Christianity to integrate Charismatic experiences, particularly healing and prophecy, into worship in Africa, led in time to the rise of a plethora of independent, indigenous church movements under various local charismatic figures".[6] Because they were founded by indig-

---

3. J. Kwabena Asamoah-Gyadu, *African Charismatics: Current Developments within Independent Indigenous Pentecostalism in Ghana* (Leiden, Koninklijke Brill NV, 2005), 21.

4. Joseph Quayesi-Amakye, "Let The Prophet Speak: A Study On Trends In Pentecostal Prophetism With Particular Reference To The Church Of Pentecost And Some Neo-Pentecostal Churches In Ghana" An MPhil Thesis submitted to the Department of Religion and Human Values of the Faculty of Arts, *University of Cape Coast* (July 2009), 55. See also Daniel Nii Aboagye Aryeh, "Socio-Rhetorical Exegesis of 1 Corinthians 14:26–40 for an Understanding of προφητης in Pauline Corpus and its Implications for Contemporary Prophetic Ministry in Ghana" A Master of Theology Thesis submitted to *Trinity Theological Seminary*, Legon Ghana (May 2015), 77.

5. James Anquandah, "The Ghana Independent/Pentecostal Movement" in *The Rise of Independent Churches in Ghana* (Accra: Asempa Publishers, 1990), 22.

6. J. Kwabena Asamoah-Gyadu, "Pentecostalism and the Missiological Significance

enous individuals who were not deeply exposed to or disagreed with the missionaries' ways of worship service, local music and instruments, dancing, language, manners and Ghanaian world-views were used in Christian worship services in the midst of the activities of the Spirit.[7] J. Annorbah-Sarpei asserts that the prophetic activities of these prophets between 1900 and 1950 curtailed the activities and popularity of *Tigare* shines that were highly patronized in those days.[8] In other words, they served as a Christian alternative to *Tigare* shines. They used prophylactics such as oil, florida water, incense, candles, just to mention a few, to aid miracles. They also observed "holy days", ritual cleansing or bath.

Their activities were mainly concentrated in the rural areas. This may be due to the low levels of education by their leaders or the desire to eradicate idol worship, which is more rampant in rural areas. However, the pioneers of prophetism in Ghana's Christianity began to decline after about fifty (50) years of existence and popularity. Research in 1986 and 1991 by Ghana Evangelism Committee (GEC), has shown that the AICs began declining in membership in the 1970s.[9] Deducing from the works of G. C. Baëta and A. Hastings, Asamoah-Gyadu argues that the decline began in the 1960s.[10]

There were three main reasons associated with their decline: derogatory remarks, charisma and succession, and hermeneutics. (i) P. Mwaura asserts that, in view of their rootedness in African religio-cultural worldview, they were demonized by the newer Pentecostal Churches.[11] Simply put, they were derogated as ritualistic and occultic; (ii) Asamoah-Gyadu postulates that, in view of the fact that it is the charisma of the founders that attracts members, the death of the founder without commensurate

---

of Religious Experience in Africa Today: The Case for Ghana 'Church of Pentecost' in *Trinity Journal of Church and Theology*, Vol. XII, No 1&2 (July/December 2002), 30–57.

7. Anquandah, "The Ghana Independent/Pentecostal", 22.

8. James Annorbah-Sarpei, "The Rise of Prophetism—A Socio-Political Explanation" in *The Rise of Independent Churches in Ghana* (Accra: Asempa Publishers, 1990), 27, 30.

9. Frederick Mawusi Amevenku, "Mother Tongue Biblical Interpretation and the Future of African Instituted Christianity in Ghana" in *Trinity Journal of Church and Theology* Vol. 18, No. 1 (March 2014), 133–148.

10. Asamoah-Gyadu, *African Charismatics*, 29–30.

11. Cited in Cephas N. Omenyo & Abamfo O. Atiemo, "Claiming Religious Space: The Case of Neo-Prophetism in Ghana" in *Ghana Bulletin of Theology*, New Series Vol. 1, No. 1 (July 2006), 55–68.

replacement in the area of charisma contributed to the decline;[12] and (iii) Amevenku holds that leaders of the AICs perceive theological education as a form of Westernization and therefore prefer the mentorship form of training over formal theological training. This has relegated biblical interpretation to the popular level. Hence, the primary purpose of hermeneutics that seeks to understand the original intended meaning of a passage and delineate it to contemporary audience was not followed.[13]

However, the contributions of the AICs to Ghana's Christianity cannot be ignored. (i) The AICs considered gender issues in the clergy by involving women among the leaders of the Church. The qualification is the exhibition of charisma. This has made way for women like Grace Tani to join the evangelistic team of Harris;[14] (ii) they encouraged the use of indigenous mother tongue as the main *lingua franca* in Christian liturgy, hence the use of local choruses, drumming and spontaneous dancing in worship services; and (iii) they encouraged pneumatic Christianity that lead to the provision of existential needs of worshipers.[15]

Phase 2

Neo-prophetism in Ghana started with the Classical Pentecostals (CPs) led by Apostle Peter Newman Enim (1890–1984) in the 1950s. This phase of prophetism was mainly "championed by Brother Gilbert Ablorh Lawson and Prophet John Mensah through the leadership of James McKeown. Lawson and Mensah later broke away to form the Divine Healers Church and Church of Christ (Spiritual Movement) respectively".[16] This phase of prophetism emphasized divine healing. Prophets were perceived to have the divine power to heal the sick instantly. Many of the instant healings took place during crusades, revivals, and night vigils after the prophet had prayed. Very much has not been said about this phase of prophetism,[17]

---

12. Asamoah-Gyadu, *African Charismatics*, 65–66

13. Amevenku, "Mother Tongue Biblical Interpretation" in TJCT, 138–142.

14. Christian G. Baëta, *Prophetism in Ghana: A Study of Some 'Spiritual' Churches* (Accra: African Christian Press, 2004), 8.

15. For further discussion see Christian G. Baëta, *Prophetism in Ghana: A Study of Some 'Spiritual' Churches* (Accra: African Christian Press, 2004); The Rise of Independent Churches in Ghana (Accra: Asempa Publishers, 1990).

16. Aryeh, "Socio-Rhetorical Exegesis of 1 Corinthians 14:26–40", TTS, 74.

17. For further discussion on the ministry of Brother Lawson see Emmanuel Kingsley

therefore there is the need to undertake an in-depth study on this neo-prophetic group.

Phase 3

Revival of Christian fellowships in tertiary institutions expressed a certain level of prophetism, although it was limited to tertiary institutions. A. O. Atiemo suggests that this prophetism was mostly found among students who had experienced the fellowship of the Scripture Union (SU) at the secondary school level.[18] Reporting on prophetic activities of these fellowships at Kwame Nkrumah University of Science and Technology (KNUST), S. Adubofour postulates that 'prophecy was the excitement of the day'.[19] Many worship services were characterized by prophesy. Beside the leader, many of the members could equally prophesy. During prayer, some members "fall under the anointing" and began to prophesy. The majority of these persons were young, hence, it was believed to be a continues fulfilment of Acts 2: 17. It also resonates with Pauline expose that all believers can prophesy (1 Cor. 14: 31). However, some of these young people prophesied in an ecstatic mood. This may be due to the lack of theological training and experience in ministry by its leaders.

Phase 4

The fourth phase of prophetism in Ghana's Christianity was vivid in the prayer camps of the Church of Pentecost (CoP). Quayesi-Amakye asserts that there are two kinds of prophets in the CoP:[20] (i) grassroots prophets are very difficult to define because many of them have not been trained and officially recognized by the Church as such; and (ii) the official or institutionalized prophets are those trained and accepted by the Church. These prophets have established prayer camps from where they operate. Examples include Prophetess Grace Adu's Adumfa Prayer Camp located in the Central Region. Mama Grace's Agape Prayer Camp located at Ablekuma in

---

Larbi, *Pentecostalism: The Eddies of Ghanaian Christianity* (Accra: SAPC, 2001), 367–379.

18. Abamfo O. Atiemo, *The Rise of the Charismatic Movement in the Mainline Churches in Ghana* (Accra: Asempa Publishers, 1993), 30.

19. Cited in Quayesi-Amakye, "Let The Prophet Speak" UCC, 40.

20. Joseph Quayesi-Amakye, *Prophetism in Ghana Today: A Study on Trends in Ghanaian Pentecostal Prophetism* (n.c.: n.p., 2013), 59–81.

Accra. These prayer camps serve as a place for seeking God's intervention in existential needs.

Asamoah-Gyadu states that, "by this form of prophetisms in the CoP, demystified Ghana's prophetism; its 'centralized administration structure... strict moral ethics, very high standard of pastoral care'[21] attracted many to the CoP thereby contributing to the decline of the AICs".[22] During this period, many members of the church were encouraged to be receptive of the Spirit of prophecy. Consequently, during worship service, a quiet moment is observed during which some member bust forth speaking in tongues, which is followed by prophecy. The speaking in tongues during a quiet moment was seen as a prelude to prophecy. These prophesies were usually general. In other words, it does not often point to or is directed towards a particular person in the congregation.

It is the lay who often prophesy during the quiet moment. Usually, these persons are the most prayerful people in the Church, which is why the prophesies are preceded by praying/speaking in tongues. The quiet atmosphere provided for prophecies has the potential to present God as one who only speaks when all are silent or the individuals who prophesied could not hear the voice of God in a noisy environment.

Phase 5

The fifth phase of prophetism begun in the 1990s by indigenous charismatic Ghanaians. It is what Paul Gifford partly referred to as *Ghana's New Christianity*.[23] Many Christian programs or statements were linked with the word "prophetic" or "prophet" in order to attract and maintain seekers/members in the Church. The word "prophetic" means that seekers or members would receive personal prophecies. Apostle Kwamena Ahinful suggests that many members were forcing their pastors to prophesy.[24] The powerful pastor is the one who prophesies and whenever he or she laid hands on any seeker or member he or she falls under the anointing.

Although some of the programs could be labelled or described as "prophetic", Prophet Bill Hamon noted that some of the programs were only

---

21. Asamoah-Gyadu, *African Charismatics*, 88.
22. Aryeh, "Socio-Rhetorical Exegesis of 1 Corinthians 14:26–40", TTS, 75.
23. Paul Gifford, *Ghana's New Christianity: Pentecostalism in a Global African Economy* (Bloomington & Indianapolis: Indiana University Press, 2004), 90–112.
24. Cited in Gifford, *Ghana's New Christianity*, 90.

prophetic in name; the organizers were more "interested in drawing people in to pay large seminar fees to bolster the finances of their church than to minister prophetically to the people".[25] Prophets Bernard Opoku Nsiah, Elisha Salifu Amoako, Isaac Anto, Eric Nana Kwasi Amponsah and Isaac Owusu-Bempah, among others are progenitors of this neo-prophetism. They gradually position themselves as religious mediators in the Ghanaian society.[26] It could be argued that this phase of neo-prophetism, which was initially characterized by issuing of prophecies is gradually evolving into giving "spiritual directions" and selling of ritual objects.

Prophetism during this period upheld the interpretation and categorization of the gifts of the Holy Spirit (1 Cor. 12:1–11) by the Charismatic Ministries (CMs) and emphasized that each member of the Church must possess. The CMs categorized the nine gifts of the Spirit into three (3) and gave them certain interpretations: (i) revelational gifts—the gift of utterance of wisdom, utterance of knowledge, and discerning of spirits; (ii) power gifts—the gift of faith, working of miracles, and healings; and (iii) vocal or inspirational gifts—the gift of prophecy, speaking in tongues, and interpretation of tongues. A prophet is expected to possess and demonstrate at least two revelational gifts and the gift of prophecy. This is not based on biblical principles, particularly Pauline epistles, but a certain interpretation of the revelational gifts, which was adopt from charismatic preachers from North America.

The gift of utterance of wisdom was interpreted as having knowledge of a future event by the aid of the Spirit.[27] Utterance of knowledge was interpreted as having knowledge of past and present events by the Spirit.[28] Discerning of spirits was understood as the empowerment by the Spirit to identify various rages of spirits. The categorization and the interpretations did not consider the context of the text. It may be hinged on some charismatic experiences that these charismatic leaders experience. It is

---

25. Bill Hamon, *Prophets and the Prophetic Movement: God's Prophetic Move Today* (Shippensburg, PA: Destiny Image, 1990), 138.

26. Michael Perry Kweku Okyerefo, "The Role of Pentecostal Churches as an Influential Arm of Civil Society in Ghana" in *Ghana Social Science Journal* Vol. 11, No. 2 (2014), 77–101.

27. Kenneth E. Hagin, *The Holy Spirit and His Gifts* (Tulsa, Ok: Faith Library Publications, 2007), 101–107. See also Richard Oswald Commey, *Ministry Gifts: Apostles, Prophets, Evangelists, Pastors, and Teachers* (Summerville, U.K: Holy Fire Publishing, 2008), 68–71.

28. Commey, *Ministry Gifts: Apostles, Prophets, Evangelists, Pastors, and Teachers*, 35.,

significant to mention that, in the Old Testament, there was no mention of the gifts of utterance of wisdom, knowledge, and discernment of spirits. However, prophets such as Elijah, Elisha, and Samuel were able to tell future events, diagnose present happenings, and discern spirits, all under the umbrella of prophecy. The gifts captioned under "revelational" may have some meanings other than what the Pentecostal and Charismatic Ministries interpret. This will be explored in another research.

Phase 6

There was a re-emergence of a new form of prophetism in the 2000s in Ghana. The prophetic ministries of some indigenous Ghanaians: Ebenezer Opambour Yiadom's Ebenezer Miracle Worship Centre located at Kokoben, a suburb of Kumasi, in the Asante Region; Bishop Daniel Obinim's International God's Way Church located at Tema, in the Greater Accra Region; Bishop Daniel Bonigas' Great Fire Pentecostal Ministry located at Tuba, a suburb of Accra , and Prophet Gabriel Akwasi Sarpong's Cross of Miracle Evangelistic Ministry located at Taifa, a suburb of Accra, can be referred to as the sixth phase of neo-prophetism in Ghana's Christianity.

Even though some of them may claim to have begun ministry prior to the year 2000, they gained popularity and influence from the 2000s. They are the most criticized phase of neo-prophetism due to: (i) the demand for money from seekers or members before receiving the services of a prophet and the sale of prophylactics at exorbitant rates;[29] (ii) immoral acts; (iii) extravagant lifestyle; and (iv) lack of financial accountability, just to mention a few. This phase of prophetism is the loudest due to the use of the media. This phase of prophetism is largely urban centred, they have polluted the airwaves with "this worldly" message and are visible on giant bill boards. Many of them have services throughout the days of the week coupled with all-night vigils. The use of prophylactics can be compared to that of the pioneers of prophetic ministry in Ghana's Christianity—the AICs. However, the AICs do not sell prophylactics, it is given or used for the members of the Church during worship services.

---

29. Daniel Nii Aboagye Aryeh, "A Study of 'Prophetism in the Gospels and Ga South Municipal Area: A Way Forward for Contemporary Prophetic Ministry in Ghana's Christianity" in *Journal of Applied Thought* Vol.4, No. 1 (January 2015), 196–221.

CONCLUSION

We can deduce from the burgeoning discussion that prophetism in Ghana's Christianity is a "perennial phenomenon"[30] which seeks to replicate or re-enact and maintain biblical prophetism especially in the book of the Acts of the Apostles and in the Early Church in the context of the socio-religious world-view of Ghana. Each phase emerged at the time when the existing phase seemed to be losing relevance and members or seekers were looking for quick and better means of having solutions to their needs. Neo-prophetism usually promises better services than previous or existing prophetic ministries. They have succeeded in making time to meet the pastoral needs of their members or seekers. However, seekers or members are not usually satisfied with the outcome of encountering a prophet.[31] Their teachings emphasized the work of Satan to frustrate the success of believers and that the power of the Holy Spirit must be engaged through the charisma of a prophet to destroy the works of Satan and his co-horts.[32]

---

30. Baëta, *Prophetism in Ghana*, 6.
31. Aryeh, "A Study of 'Prophetism'" JAT, 214.
32. Omenyo and Atiemo, "Claiming Religious Space" GBT, 62–63.

Chapter Five

Contemporary Prophetic Ministry in Ghana

INTRODUCTION

THIS CHAPTER EXAMINES CONTEMPORARY prophetic ministry in Ghana and the perception of Ghanaians concerning contemporary prophets. It examines factors that gave rise to contemporary prophetic ministry. A case of the contemporary prophetic ministry of Prophet Dr. Eric Nana Kwasi Amponsah's Hope Generation Ministry International is presented. He was chosen for the study because his ministry came to prominence in the early 2000s just like other prophets such as Isaac Anto and Elisha Salifu Amoako. He also accepts general Pauline instructions concerning prophetism in the church, therefore he was chosen as being representative of contemporary prophets and their ministries. General Ghanaian perception concerning contemporary prophetic ministry is discussed and the impact of contemporary prophetic ministry analyzed. A way forward is then suggested for contemporary prophets. The terms neo-prophetism and contemporary prophetism are used interchangeably. The goal of this chapter is to understand contemporary designation of "prophet".

FACTORS THAT GAVE RISE TO CONTEMPORARY PROPHETIC MINISTRY

Many religious movements came about as a response to certain demands by society and the belief that one has the solutions to the demands or needs of society. There are both internal and external factors that gave rise to contemporary prophetic ministry in Ghana. These factors are critical to the understanding of the theological emphasis that is expressed.

EXTERNAL FACTORS

There are external factors such as political, economic, religious, social and health that gave rise to contemporary prophetism in Ghana.

Political Factors

Politically, prior to 2000, Ghana was preparing for general elections. President Jerry John Rawlings would finish serving two terms as President, and thereby could not present himself for re-election for the third time. President John Adjekum Kufuor had lost the 1996 election to Rawlings. Since he would not be competing with Rawlings, but rather the then candidate, John Evans Atta Mills, Kufuor was bent on winning the 2000 general elections. This situation led to accusations of corruption and intimidations between the ruling party, National Democratic Congress (NDC) and the main opposition New Patriotic Party (NPP).

Ghana Catholic Bishops' Conference issued a communiqué urging eligible Ghanaians "to vote for political parties and individuals whose policies were sound and who they knew were not deceiving them for the sake of winning votes".[1] Due to comments made by leaders of some Church denominations regarding electoral matters in Ghana, they were labelled "false prophets suffering from mental disorder"[2] by leaders of the ruling party. Subsequently, it led to the followers of particular political parties declaring support for some churches[3] thereby seeking protection and direction

---

1. A Communiqué Issued by the Ghana Catholic Bishops' Conference at their Annual Plenary Assembly Held in Cape Coast from 10th to 15th July 2000.

2. Elom Dovlo, "Religion and Politics of Fourth Republican Elections in Ghana (1992, 1996)" in *Ghana Bulletin of Theology*, New Series Vol. 1, No. 1 (July 2006), 3–19.

3. Dovlo, "Religion and Politics", 15.

from their pastors in order to win the election. The outbreak of civil wars in African countries such as Burundi,[4] Angola, Rwanda, Liberia and Sierra Leone, generally created fear among Ghanaians that there may be civil war in Ghana. It led to increased prayer for the nation, and the desire to know the future created the atmosphere for the springing up of new Churches and Ministries. The founders and leaders of these Ministries used the title "Prophet", they presented "themselves as offerers of spiritual panacea to the Ghanaian lack, and exploited the traditional desire to probe into the unknown."[5]

Economic Factors

Economically, structural adjustment and economic recovery programs embarked upon by governments did not really seem to have had deepening impact on the economy. The nation was heavily indebted to its development partners. A National Economic Dialogue was organized from 14th to 15th May, 2001 in Accra to deliberate on the way forward for Ghana's economy.[6] The Heavily Indebted and Poor Country (HIPC) initiative was adopted so that savings could be made regarding debt servicing,[7] and that some debts could be cancelled.

The Government then embarked on a "Golden Age of Business" where the private sector was considered as the engine of growth. The economic challenges coupled with a high level of inflation, "energy crisis, bribery and corruption"[8] led to an alarming brain drain[9] in search of greener pastures abroad. Since some Ghanaians preferred a religious solution in the face of very difficult and challenging situations,[10] those who could not travel

---

4. "Coup in Burundi" *Daily Graphic* (19th April, 2001), 1,3.

5. Quayesi-Amakye, *Prophetism in Ghana Today*, 122.

6. "Economic Dialogue Next Month" *Daily Graphic* (6th April, 2001), 1,3.

7. "HIPC Shows Positive Signs" *Daily Graphic* (13th June, 2001), 1.

8. A Communiqué Issued by the Ghana Catholic Bishops' Conference at their Annual Plenary Assembly Held in Koforidua from 2nd to 10th July 1998.

9. Isaac Anto, *The Office*, 37–38. *Daily Graphic* (13th April, 2001), 1. 3.

10. Daniel Nii Aboagye Aryeh, "Mission and Culture: An Expositional Analysis of Acts 1:8 and Mission in Some Ghanaian Market Places" a paper presented at *Valley View University, School of Theology and Mission*, 1st International Conference, (7th to 11th April, 2014), 30.

Benedict T. Viviano, 'The Gospel According to Matthew' in Raymond E. Brown, Joseph A. Fitzmyer, Roland E. Murphy Eds, *The Jerome Biblical Commentary* (London:

outside Ghana began to seek out prayer centres whose leaders promised a financial break - through and a diagnosis of misfortunes. This confirms Asamoah-Gyadu's assertion that "prophecy helps in diagnoses for the ailing African, who is familiar with the methods of the traditional diviner, prophecy is important for establishing the *cause* of one's condition".[11]

Although there may be testimonies as a result of meeting contemporary prophets, many seekers were not satisfied with the outcome of their engagement with some contemporary prophets. Many of the personal prophecies issued to seekers or members did not come to pass.[12] The desire to know the cause of misfortunes and hardships had opened "them up to the exploitative whims of 'self-proclaimed men of God' . . . who promise to hold the supernatural want to unlock the recesses of the unknown".[13] Often the diagnoses led to confusion in families because seekers/members were being told that their misfortunes were caused by close relatives. Many Ghanaians are yet to find enduring solutions to their economic woes. The problem could be partly attributed to "prophets and pastors making declarations in the name of God, supposedly under the influence of the Spirit when God may not have spoken".[14]

Religious and Social Factors

On the religious and social front, there was the re-emergence of shrines that were competing with the church for members and adherents. Some of them had erected signs and bill boards advertising their services. Nana Kwaku Bronsam, a popular traditional priest and many others advertized their services in the electronic and print media. People who patronized the services of these shrines were not satisfied because they later came into conflict with the priests at the shrine that led to illnesses and sometimes

---

Burns & Oates, 2007), 652.

11. Asamoah-Gyadu, "Pentecostalism and the Missiological", 43. Italicized in original

12. Daniel Nii Aboagye Aryeh, "A Study of 'Prophetism' in the Gospels and GA South Municipal Area: A Way Forward for Prophetic Ministry in Ghana's Christianity" in *Journal of Applied Thought (A Multidisciplinary Approach)* Vol. 4, No, 1 (January, 2015), 196–221.

13. Quayesi-Amakye, *Prophetism in Ghana Today*, 123.

14. Asamoah-Gyadu, "Pentecostalism and the Missiological", 43.

death of the adherents.[15] This was due to failure to perform certain rituals or not going back to thank the deity with gifts after getting good results.

T. N. O. Quarcoopome comparatively observes that " ... the biblical gods may be powerless and dysfunctional, but not the African gods. They are active and ever active. Countless devotees testified to various help .... The divinities punish those who disobey the norms ... with sickness and misfortune".[16] By biblical gods, Quarcoopome was referring to gods mentioned in the Bible. Nonetheless these gods were powerful but powerless in the presence of the Almighty God. Since the leaders of contemporary prophetic ministries were very vocal in advertising their endowments, they automatically became the alternative for people who had once patronized the services of traditional shrines.

Socially, there was poverty that virtually weakened individual family responsibilities.[17] The extended family had been neglected due to very limited economic resources thereby creating disintegration. Family planning to limit the number of children, which was not an African/Ghanaian norm, has been accepted by many couples. This is contrary to J. S. Mbiti's assertion that "the more children a person has, the higher is his status in society".[18] It suggests that a key prerequisite for elevating potential leaders in some Ghanaian communities have been tampered with. Hence the fewer children one has qualifies him/her for consideration for a leadership position in society, so that he/she can have some left over resources for the poor in society.

Health Factors

Health is a major concern in every human society. The spread of Human Immunodeficient Virus/Acquired Immune Deficiency Syndrome (HIV/AIDS)[19] partly boosted the re-emergence of the prophetic ministry in

15. "Deal with Nogokpo Shrine Now" *The Mirror* (26th June, 1999), 2.

16. T. N. O. Quarcoopome, *West African Traditional Religion* (Ibadan: African University Press, 1987), 73.

17. A Communiqué Issued by the Ghana Catholic Bishops' Conference at their Annual Plenary Assembly Held in Koforidua from 5nd to 9th July 1999. See also *Daily Graphic* (13th July, 2002), 1, 3.

18. John S. Mbiti, *Introduction to African Religion* 2nd Ed.(Oxford, Melbourne, Johannesburg, Ibadan, Chicago: Heinemann Educational Publishers, 1991), 111.

19. A Communiqué Issued by the Ghana Catholic Bishops' Conference at their Annual Plenary Assembly Held in Cape Coast from 10th to 15th July 2000.

Ghana because contemporary prophetic ministry claimed to have powers to heal all illnesses especially those that defied scientific and traditional remedies. This resonates with Asamoah-Gyadu's assertion that "the emphasis on healing in particular encouraged masses of people to seek refuge in those churches . . . as Christian alternatives to traditional shrines".[20]

According to the Concise Oxford English Dictionary (eleventh edition), AIDS is a disease that is caused by a transmission of a virus into body fluid "in which there is severe loss of cellular immunity that leaves the sufferer susceptible to infection and malignancy." Venereal diseases especially HIV/AIDS does not only bring discomfort to the patient but also to the family as well because the family are considered as immoral and carriers of AIDS. HIV was first reported in Ghana in 1986.[21] A survey jointly conducted by the World Health Organization (WHO) and United Nations Program on HIV/AIDS (UNAIDS) in December 1998 showed that, since the disease was reported in sub-Saharan Africa, a total of 34 million persons were infected. About 11.5 million died out of which 3 million were children. The report indicated that the rate of infection was rising with 2.38 of the population infected by HIV/AIDS in Ghana. The report attributed the quick spread of the disease to lack of public awareness to prevent the disease and the scarcity of antiretroviral drugs.[22]

At a function to release the report concerning the spread of HIV/AIDS for the year 2013, Dr. Stephen Ayisi Addo, Acting Programme Manager of the National AIDS Control Programme of the Ghana Health Service said the prevalence rate of HIV/AIDS had declined from 1.37 percent in 2012 to 1.30 percent in 2013. The report largely credited the decline to efforts by the Ghana Health Service and Ghana AIDS Commission to give education on HIV/AIDS and prevention of mother to child infection.[23] The report did not recognize religious contributions made to the decline. Probably the educational outreach of the church and healing did not attract the attention of the researchers since many who sought religious healing were encouraged

---

20. Asamoah-Gyadu, *Contemporary Pentecostal Christianity*, 131.

21. Ghana Aids Commission, Country Aids Response Progress Report - Ghana (January 2012—December 2013), 29.

22. Cited in Samuel Acquaah Arhin, "HIV/AIDS, the Church and Pastoral Care: African Perspectives" in J. Kwabena Asamoah-Gyadu (Ed.) *Christianity, Mission and Ecumenism in Ghana, Essays in honour of Robert K. Aboagye-Mensah* (Accra: Asempa Publishers, 2009), 251.

23. Ghana's HIV Prevalence for 2013 Declines on http://www.ghanaweb.com/Ghana-HomePage/health/artikel.php?ID=314325 Accessed 22/03/2015.

to believe that they had been healed after prayer without going for retesting. In other words, they were not encouraged, as a matter of verification, to subject themselves to empirical investigations.

According to J. Moltmann, 'healing vanquishes illness and creates health'.[24] Although healing vanquishes illness, sometimes it is not permanent in the sense that some other sickness may show up. F. J. Gaiser observed that the goal of healing is to draw the individual close to Jesus and that healing in the name of Jesus is not an option.[25] It does not suggest that sick persons have no good standing with God; sickness could be caused by evil spirits, lack of personal and collaborate hygiene, poverty or for generic reason. God uses healing to draw us closer to Him for a better relationship. This resonates with P. N. Mwaura's assertion that "healing becomes a means of communicating with God and the community".[26] Contemporary prophets use prophecy to diagnose illnesses[27] that on many occasions, are said to have been caused spiritually by some relative of the patient. The result of the diagnosis determines the approach to be used for healing.

"'Faith healing' is an anti-medicine doctrine that regards the use of medicine and prophylactic substances for the healing of sickness and disease as sin".[28] 'Faith healing' is what Opoku Onyinah called 'divine healing' where faith and healing are inseparable.[29] The patient needed to express "strong faith" in the healing power of God in order to appropriate healing. It implies that, although the prophet may be gifted or claimed to have the gift of healing, the faith of the patient is indispensable for healing.

The role of faith is to expel doubts and hope for immediate healing, therefore sceptics can hardly receive healing because they do not express

---

24. Cited in Frederick J. Gaiser, *Healing in the Bible: Theological Insight for Christian Ministry* (Grand Rapids, Michigan: Baker Academic, 2010), 103.

25. Gaiser, *Healing in the Bible*, 113.

26. Philomena Njeri Mwaura, "Spirituality and Healing in African Indigenous Culture and Contemporary Society" in Gillian Mary Bediako, Benhardt Y. Quarshie and J. Kwabena Asamoah-Gyadu (Eds.) *Seeing New Facets of the Diamond: Christianity as a Universal Faith*, Essays in Honour of Kwame Bediako (Oxford: Regnum Africa, 2014), 328.

27. Asamoah-Gyadu, "Pentecostalism and the Missiological", 43.

28. Asamoah-Gyadu, "Pentecostalism and the Missiological", 37.

29. Opoku Onyinah, "Faith, Healing and Mission: Perspectives from the Bible" in J. Kwabena Asamoah-Gyadu (Ed.) *Christianity, Mission and Ecumenism in Ghana*, Essays in honour of Robert K. Aboagye-Mensah (Accra: Asempa Publishers, 2009), 213.

faith in God and the prophet's healing endowments.[30] The patient is prayed for by the laying on of hands; sometimes they are given directions with oil for gradual healing. The 'anointing oil' is seen as a symbol of the Holy Spirit and means of healing. In the words of L. Tetteh, the anointing:

> ... is the power of God and the manifestation of God's presence. The anointing is 'God with us,' *Immanuel*, or the *Christos*, 'Christ with us'. It is Shekinah glory of the Lord bestowed on the saints and it creates divine favour. It is the Messiah, which means the rubbing of God's divine nature on us to separate us unto good works for the manifestation of His power and gifts in our lives. The anointing is life, and the glory of God, imparted to the lives of believers in order to equip them for divine service.[31]

Stating the importance of the anointing with 'oil' for empowerment for fulfilling ministry task and healing, D. Heward-Mills had this to say: "if more ministers could see what the anointing does, they would desire it and seek it above everything else. If the anointing had such an effect on David's life, you must expect the anointing to have the same effect on your life and ministry.... The anointing will remove all sorts of weaknesses from your life and ministry".[32]

INTERNAL FACTORS

There were internal factors such as charisma, extensive use of the media and the use of vernacular that supported the rise of contemporary prophetism in Ghana.

Charisma

Some contemporary prophets claimed to have had certain endowments that are analogous with the giftings of the original apostles of Jesus as demonstrated in the book of Acts.[33] In other words, they sought to restore a

---

30. Mwaura, "Spirituality and Healing", 329.

31. Lawrence Tetteh, *Benefit of the Anointing* (London: LT Media Ministries, 2002), 1.

32. Dag Heward-Mills, *Steps to the Anointing* (Wellington, South Africa: Lux Verbi (Pty) Ltd., 2008), 8–9.

33. J. Kwabena Asamoah-Gyadu, "Pentecostalism and the Missiological Significance of Religious Experience: The Case of Ghana's 'Church of Pentecost' in *Trinity Journal of Church and Theology* Vol. XII, No. 1&2 (July/December, 2002), 30–57.

Biblical, Traditional, and Theological Framework

"lost concern of the Early Church",[34] therefore "prophet and apostle" were preferred ecclesiological titles. Some Ghanaians generally believe that a prophet in the traditional context is a religious intermediary with "sacred power"[35] to manipulate the spirits for the benefit of the inquirer(s). Although charismatic prayer groups and some individuals who claimed to have had some charisma were given some room to operate in the TWMCs, "most of them operated without the official approval of their churches and often found themselves in conflict with the official church hierarchy".[36]

The charisma of prophets attracted both Christians and non-Christians to their meetings. This partly confirms the title of C. P. Wagner's book: *Your Spiritual Gifts Can Help Your Church Grow.*[37] This growth refers to numerical growth. Pentecostalism is an experiential movement; and, as a stream of Pentecostalism highly encourages experience with the Holy Spirit, especially the experience of its leaders with the Holy Spirit, which leaves an indelible mark of the gifts of the Spirit[38] in their lives. Therefore, the demonstration of some charismata becomes a qualification for a prophet. However, W. W. Menzies and R. P. Menzies posited that spiritual giftedness does not necessarily suggest spiritual maturity or leadership endowments. Possession of charismata should not be used as the major criterion for leadership in the church.[39]

Pentecostals and CMs usually categorize the gifts of the Spirit as found in 1 Cor. 12:8–11 into three parts that have been inherited by NPMs: revelational gifts - the gifts of utterance of wisdom, utterance of knowledge and discerning of spirits; power gifts - the gifts of faith, working of miracles and healings; and vocal or inspirational gifts - the gifts of prophecy, speaking in

---

34. Keith Warrington, *Pentecostal Theology: A Theology of Encounter* (London and New York: T&T Clark, 2008), 265–266.

35. J. Kwabena Asamoah-Gyadu, "Spirit and Spirits in African Religious Traditions" in Veli-Matti Kärkkäinen, Kirsteen Kim, and Amos Yong (Eds.) *Interdisciplinary and Religio-Cultural Discourses on a Spirit-Filled World: Loosing the Spirits* (New York: Palgrave Macmillan, 2013), 47–49.

36. Abamfo O. Atiemo, "The Evangelical Christian Fellowship and the Charismatization of Ghanaian Christianity" in *Ghana Bulletin of Theology*, New Series, Vol. 2 (July 2007), 43–65.

37. C. Peter Wagner, *Your Spiritual Gifts Can Help Your Church Grow* (California: Regal Books, 2005).

38. Asamoah-Gyadu, *Contemporary Pentecostal Christianity*, 139.

39. William W. Menzies and Robert P. Menzies, *Spirit and Power: The Foundation of Pentecostal Experience* (Grand Rapids, Michigan: Zondervan Publishing House, 2000), 181.

tongues and interpretation of tongues.[40] There is convention among contemporary prophets that a prophet must possess at least two revelational gifts, in addition to the gift of prophecy and sometimes healing.[41]

Quayesi-Amakye observed that in the CoP, institutionalized prophets were expected to manifest "revelational gifts or vocal gifts of prophecy, speaking in different kinds of tongues and interpretation of tongues and should maintain a certain standard as becomes of 'a prophet'".[42] Prophet Anto affirms the categorizations of the gifts and the prerequisite gifts that makes one a prophet.[43] It is generally explained by many who believed in prophetic ministry that the gift of utterance of wisdom reveals future events, utterance of knowledge reveals past and present happenings, and therefore these gifts were very important in the life of a prophet.[44]

> If that is so, then what is the gift of prophecy? There is no evidence in Paul's epistles to the Corinthians to support such claims. We are yet to discover anything like the giving of utterance of wisdom which is [a] revelation concerning the future and the giving of utterance of knowledge which is a revelation concerning the past and present. The gift of prophecy has the potential to reveal past, present and future events (1 Cor. 14:23–25).[45]

Many Pentecostals and Charismatics give considerable attention to "experience over theology".[46] Therefore, the categorization may emanate from the ministry experiences of those who subscribe to such categorizations and definitions. Although these authors illustrate some biblical passages to ra-

---

40. Kenneth E. Hagin, *The Holy Spirit and His Gifts* (Tulsa, Ok: Faith Library Publications, 2007), 101–107. And Richard Oswald Commey, *Ministry Gifts: Apostles, Prophets, Evangelists, Pastors, and Teachers* (Summerville, U. K.: Holy Fire Publishing, 2008), 68–71.

41. Richard Oswald Commey, *Prophecy and Prophets* (Summerville, SC: Holy Fire Publishing, 2007) 130–139.

42. Quayesi-Amakye, *Prophetism in Ghana Today*, 77.

43. Isaac Anto, *The Office of the Prophet* (Accra: Nobles Multimedia, 2011), 31–32.

44. Richard Oswald Commey, *Ministry Gifts: Apostle, Prophets, Evangelist, Pastors and Teachers* (Summerville, SC: Holy Fire Publishing, 2008), 68–69. See also Lester Sumrall, *The Gifts and Ministries of the Holy Spirit* (New Kensington, PA: Whitaker House, 1982), 57.

45. Daniel Nii Aboagye Aryeh, "Exegetical Analysis of 1 Cor. 12:1–11: Manifestations of the Gifts of the Holy Spirit in some Ghanaian Churches" in *Journal of Applied Thought (A Multidisciplinary Approach)* Vol. 3, No. 3 (November, 2014), 194–215.

46. William W. Menzies and Robert P. Menzies, *Spirit and Power: Foundations of Pentecostal Experience* (Grand Rapids, Michigan: Zondervan Publishing House, 2000), 209.

tionalize their definitions, the context is usually ignored. For example, the prophets in the Church in Antioch, the daughters of Stephen and Agabus (Acts 13:1–3; 21:1–16) were said to have prophesied concerning the future of Paul, not giving utterance of wisdom. It is undoubtedly certain that the gifts of utterance of wisdom and utterance of knowledge are not easy to define because Paul did not give enough clues to their meanings and operations.

Extensive Use of the Media

Contemporary prophets' use of the media has contributed to their popularity and momentum. They engage every available opportunity created in the media to advertize[47] their services, endowments and testimonies in order to attract others to their services. They are visible on bill boards situated at strategic locations in urban areas. The use of the media to advertize the ability to heal, exorcize demons and prophesy contributed to the popularity and the patronage of the services of contemporary prophets. Complemented by "this worldly" message (prosperity gospel) that some contemporary prophets preach, this suggests that every available means will be used and if possible "contortionist hermeneutics of Scripture",[48] which is usually preaching a passage out of context for a desired result, will be engaged to make seekers/members prosper. This notion is reinforced by the desire and acceptance of the Bible as power to effect changes[49] rather than ideological precepts.

Some contemporary prophets hold worship services in uncompleted buildings, houses, sheds, football pitches, in the forest, ware houses,[50] and public and school buildings[51] that do not necessarily require any elegant ecclesiological features. In other words, they do not need a well-furnished

---

47. Asamoah-Gyadu, *African Charismatics*, 31. See also Quayesi-Amakye, *Prophetism in Ghana Today*, 117–118. Cephas N. Omenyo, "The Spirit-Filled Goes to School": Theological Education in African Pentecostalism in *Ogbomosho Journal of Theology* Vol. XIII, No. 2, 2008), 41–55.

48. Wesley Granberg-Michaelson, *From Times Square to Timbuktu: The Post-Christian West Meets the Non-Western Church* (Grand Rapids, Michigan/Cambridge, U.K.: William B. Eerdmans Publishing Company, 2013), 142.

49. Asamoah-Gyadu, "Pentecostalism and the Missiological", 31.

50. Aryeh, "A Study of 'Prophetism'", 213.

51. *The Ghanaian Times* (21st January, 2015), 4. See also *Daily Graphic* (2nd December, 2014), 55.

auditorium and liturgical codes before a worship service could be held. In his article: "'On the "Mountain" of the Lord' Healing Pilgrimages in Ghanaian Christianity", Asamoah-Gyadu comparatively argues that, just as in primal religions, shrines were not decorated and these meeting places of some contemporary prophets were meant for healing, deliverance and miracles for seekers or members.[52]

The liberal approach to worship services is likely to draw people to their services. One would sometimes hear continuous adverts in the media for an upcoming program, but when seekers or members later get to the venue, one is likely to discover that the meeting place is not commensurate to the adverts. In other words, the cost of running adverts could be used to upgrade meeting places. Analyzing the role of the media, R. I. J. Hackett pointed out that, the media is 'a stool of expansion' and 'a reflection of globalizing aspiration'.[53] Okyerefo asserts that, by extensive use of the media, contemporary prophets seek to take the church, which is confined to its walls to the public sphere in order to have distant members[54] who would visit the church in the future.

Use of Vernacular Language

Christianity is a religion that transcends language and cultural barriers without losing the core message and value of the salvific work of Jesus. Alternatively put, the Christian faith is not limited to the language of the founder; and is dominant outside the geography of the founder. Therefore, there is a need for the faith to be expressed in other languages and still remain authentic. After Vatican II in 1965, the Catholic Church encouraged the use of native language in worship services.[55] In Ghana it led to the adoption of some *Akan* (Akwapim, Akim and Fante) cultural and social manners into Asante Catholicism.[56] It signifies that some socio-cultural elements of *Akans* could be used to worship God. B. Y. Quarshie contended

---

52. J. Kwabena Asamoah-Gyadu, "'On the "Mountain" of the Lord' Healing Pilgrimages in Ghanaian Christianity" in *Exchange Journal of Missiological and Ecumenical Research* Vol. 36 (2007), 65–86.

53. Cited in Asamoah-Gyadu, *African Charismatics*, 99.

54. Okyerefo, "The role of Pentecostal", 85.

55. Philip Jenkins, *The Next Christendom: The Coming of Global Christianity* (New York: Oxford University Press, 2007), 134.

56. Pashington Obeng, *Asante Catholism: Religion and Cultural Reproduction Among the Akan of Ghana* (Leiden and New York: E. J. Brill, 1996), 119.

that the use of mother-tongue partly contributed to the rise of the AICs because they discovered that the emphasis of the missionaries during preaching demonized the Ghanaian culture and did not take cognisance of the Ghanaian world-view.[57]

Although translations had some political and ideological influences, and there may have been some variations compared to the initial language in which the scriptures were first written, they were inconsequential. Commenting on colonial influence on translations and beneficiaries of the translated scriptures, Lamin Sanneh observes as follows:

> Vernacular Bible outdistanced and outlasted the forces of ephemeral colonial rule. Where they could, administrators tried to forestall mother-tongue development by sequestering mission policy and imposing a mandate for the exclusive use of European languages in schools and other educational establishments. Language was key to the outcome of Europe's encounter with the non-European world, and Bible translation favoured non-European languages.[58]

According to J. D. K. Ekem, attempts to translate the Bible into Ghanaian languages by the Wesleyan Methodist Missionary Society as an evangelistic project received a further boost in 1835 when issues of grammar and orthography were agreed upon.[59] Sanneh notes that in 1887, some educated Ghanaians found the need for the vernacular to be used in liturgy and preaching in church. This led to the phenomenal work of Rev. Carl Christian Reindorf: *The History of the Gold Coast and Asante* that was initially written in Gã and was published in Switzerland in 1889.[60] A. M. Howell noted that, as at December 2010, the whole Bible had been translated into thirteen principal Ghanaian languages, and the New Testament was exclusively available in twenty-six Ghanaian languages.[61] We posit that

---

57. Benhardt Y. Quarshie, 'Doing Biblical Studies in the African Context-the Challenge of Mother-Tongue Scriptures,' in *Journal of African Christian Thought*, Vol. 5, No. 1 (June 2002), 4–14.

58. Lamin Sanneh, *Translating the Message: The Missionary Impact on Culture* (Maryknoll, New York: Orbis Books, 2009), 163.

59. John D. K. Ekem, Wesleyan Methodist and Bible Translation in the Gold Coast in J. Kwabena Asamoah-Gyadu (Ed.) *Christianity, Mission and Ecumenism in Ghana*, Essays in Honour of Robert K. Aboagye-Mensah (Accra: Asempa Publishers, 2009), 81.

60. Sanneh, *Translating the Message*, 161.

61. Allison M. Howell, "Beyond Translating Western Commentaries: Bible Commentary Writing in African Languages" in Gillian Mary Bediako, Benhardt Y. Quarshie

the translation projects embarked on by missionary societies and biblical scholars have become very useful and important Bible versions preferred by contemporary prophets, especially the *Akan* versions.

It is imperative that Christianity be owned in all native languages for a better understanding of the Bible. Many of these prophets use the *Akan* language, which many Ghanaians understand for liturgy and preaching. In other words, *Akan* language is the main language used while interpretation is sometimes conducted into English language. This is directly opposite to what happens in the CMs where English language was the principal language for communication.[62] Writing on the subtitle: Liturgy and vernacularization in Pentecostalism with special reference to the CoP, Asamoah-Gyadu observed as follows: "Pentecostals are thus able to make room for participatory worship in which people are able to worship God in languages that come naturally to them . . . .the vernacularization policy creates the space and atmosphere for the Spirit to operate . . . and the expressions of emotional sensibilities".[63] To communicate in a language that the audience understands very well "is to influence others with our feelings and ideas which means that the importance of language cannot be overemphasized".[64]

Contemporary prophets do not follow the concepts of mother-tongue biblical hermeneutics that sought to understand scripture passages from the "original" languages in which they were first written into a mother-tongue.[65] They generally rely on the translated versions to preach in the *Akan* language. This phenomenon partly attracted many to their meetings even though a few of them had begun to use the English language as the

---

and J. Kwabena Asamoah-Gyadu (Eds.) *Seeing New Facets of the Diamond: Christianity as a Universal Faith*, Essays in Honour of Kwame Bediako (Oxford: Regnum Africa, 2014), 225.

62. Asamoah-Gyadu, *African Charismatics*, 31.

63. Asamoah-Gyadu, "'The Promise is for you'", 20–21.

64. Jonathan Aremu Yayi, "Language Barrier: A Serious Handicap for Theologizing and Mission Input in West Africa: A Case Study of French in Nigeria" in *Ogbomosho Journal of Theology* Vol. XV, No. 2(2010), 179–186.

65. John D. K. Ekem, "Early Translators and Interpreters of the Judeo-Christian Scriptures on the Gold Coast (Ghana): Two Case Studies," in *Journal of African Christian Thought*, Vol. 13, No. 2 (December 2010), 34–37. See also Benhardt Y. Quarshie, 'Doing Biblical Studies', 8. Daniel Nii Aboagye Aryeh, "The Relevance of Mother-Tongue Biblical Hermeneutics in the Ghanaian Context" in *Journal of Applied Thought (A Multidisciplinary Approach)* Vol. 3, No, 2 (May, 2014), 282–301.

Biblical, Traditional, and Theological Framework

principal language for preaching: examples are Prophet Amoako (who never had formal education) and Prophet Anto.

If one has not acquired the skills and proficiency in English language, he or she is considered to be illiterate.[66] At the onset of contemporary prophetic ministry in the year 2000, the literacy level in Ghana was 70%.[67] In a report on literacy levels in Ghana in 2012, the Food and Agricultural Organization (FAO) stated that the literacy level in Ghana was generally high especially among women. It showed that the literacy level among women was 46% and 67% among men.[68] There is a dichotomy between the use of *Akan* mother-tongue in TWMCs and that of contemporary prophets.

The use of mother-tongue by TWMCs was a theological decision to raise the level of mother-tongue literary and encourage Ghanaians to understand the Bible in their own language and culture. Hitherto, English was the main language for liturgy and preaching in the TWMCs. Contemporary prophets probably use the *Akan* mother-tongue for worship service in order to firstly appeal to a wider audience; secondly, although some contemporary prophets have begun to use the English language for worship services, they generally perceive the use of the English language for worship service as the promotion of "clericalism that sacrifices vital religious experience as fundamental to discipleship".[69]

Thirdly, it is probable that the extensive use of the *Akan* language by some contemporary prophets could be attributed to the fact that some of them are illiterates or semi-literate in the use of English language. Notwithstanding, a major challenge of using a particular mother-tongue is that it only appeals to a section of the audience and undermines the global outlook of Pentecostalism. We are not therefore arguing that mother-tongues should not be used but that one language should not be used to the detriment of others.

---

66. Yankah, *Education, Literacy and Governance*, 15.

67. Gifford, *Ghana's New Christianity*, 4.

68. http://ghananewsagency.org/human-interest/illiteracy-rate-among-women-still-high-in-ghana-fao-54631 Accessed 22/03/2015.

69. Asamoah-Gyadu, "The Promise is for you", 17.

CONTEMPORARY PROPHETIC MINISTRY: THE CASE OF PROPHET DR. ERIC NANA KWASI AMPONSAH'S HOPE GENERATION MINISTRY INTERNATIONAL

Prophetic ministry is the single most popular and most chastised ministry in Ghana today. Some contemporary prophets complain of being misinterpreted by some Ghanaians. Prophet Dr. Eric Nana Kwasi Amponsah is a contemporary prophet who is popular among some inhabitants of Accra in the Gã South Municipal Area (GSMA). He is the founder and general overseer of Hope Generation Ministry International (HGMI) located at Oblogo, Weija near the Oblogo Health Centre. Prophet Dr. Amponsah was born on December 1, 1966 in the Ashanti Region of the Republic of Ghana, the son of Mr. Joseph Amponsah and Mrs. Janet Amponsah. He had his primary school education at Abuakwa in the Ashanti Region. He continued to secondary school in Bechem in the Brong Ahafo Region. Prophet Dr. Amponsah had his sixth form education at Kumasi Workers College in the Ashanti Region after which he gained admission to read Political Science at Kwame Nkrumah University of Science and Technology (KNUST). He later pursued a Master's program in the United Kingdom (U.K) from 1995–1996, and was later enlisted into the Ghana Armed Forces (GAF).

Apparently whilst he was in his mothers' womb, an unknown prophet prophesied to the mother at Ayirakwa in the Brong Ahafo (BA) Region that the child in her womb would be used by the Lord to draw many to Christ. Prophet Anto also reports a similar phenomenon. According to him, when he was about eight months' "gestation, his mother fell into a trance twice where she was given the name Isaac as the name of the yet to be born child by an angel and that God would use the child mightily.[70] These prophecies and supernatural experiences resonate with the biblical stories of Jesus and John the Baptist (Lk. 1:5–38). However, they do not suggest automatic success in ministry. They have the potential to influence parents to be biased towards such children. By this, we are not intimating that prophecies and supernatural experiences prior to delivery should be discouraged but that parents must not be biase, based on such experiences, and must not be seen as major criterion for ministry success.

Prophet Dr. Amponsah was a member of the Church of Pentecost (CoP) Mamprobi District, Salem Assembly. When the time came for the fulfilment of the prophecy, a renowned Pentecostal musician, Elder Mireku's

---

70. Isaac Anto, *The Office of the Prophet* (Accra: Nobles Multimedia, 2011), 109–110.

father, Kofi Mireku, prophesied concerning his calling and ministry as a prophet during an annual convention in Mamprobi on 13th October, 1997. He then resigned from GAF and the CoP in order to pursue his calling and ministry as a prophet. Many contemporary prophets were initially members of TWMCs or Classical Pentecostal Churches (CPCs) but left to form their own Churches after receiving the prophetic grace probably in the TWMC, CPCs or other Christian denominations. For example, although Prophet Anto was born a Presbyterian, he later moved to United Pentecostal Church (UPC) where he was a deacon.[71] He left after receiving the prophetic grace to start his own Church—Conquerors Chapel International located at Dansoman, a suburb of Accra. Prophet Atsu Manasseh who was born Evangelical Presbyterian (EP), moved to Miracle Assemblies of God at Jasikan and finally left to establish his own Church - Watered Garden also at Dansoman.[72] The phenomenon of leaving the parent Church to form one's own Church is not unique to contemporary prophets. Prophets in the AICs and CMs do the same. Prophet Joseph William Appiah was a catechist in the Methodist Church, Ghana. He left to form Musama Disco Christo Church (MDCC).[73]

There are varying reasons why some prophets and pastors leave their mother Churches to form their own Churches. According to Prophet Dr. Amponsah, there was no room for lay persons to use their prophetic gifts to help the members. Even where opportunities had been created, the human impediments were so intimidating that one could not minister according to the dictate of the Spirit.[74] It is likely that others may leave based on missionary decision (God sending the prophet to accomplish a particular task) just as was the case of Prophet Anto.[75] In view of economic situations in Ghana today and the quest to "get rich quick", some of them might leave for egocentric and economic reasons. According to Prophet Dr. Amponsah, upon resignation, he said to God "as I drop the gun, no sickness will come to my meetings without healing"[76] and since that time till now, God has been faithful. It implies that the gun has been converted into the gift of healing.

71. Anto, *The Office*, 110–111.

72. Quayesi-Amakye, *Prophetism in Ghana Today*, 92.

73. See Baëta, *Prophetism in Ghana*, 26. See also Ekem, *Priesthood in Context*, 21–23.

74. Eric Nana Kwasi Amponsah, interviewed by author at the Church office at Oblogo, Weija. 22/10/2014.

75. Anto, *The Office*, 112–113.

76. Amponsah, interviewed by author at the Church office at Oblogo, Weija.

The Import of the Name "Hope Generation Ministry International" and Prophetic Manifestations

The name "Hope Generation Ministry International" (HGMI) was revealed to Prophet Dr. Amponsah in a vision. The name reveals the task given to him to give hope to the hopeless by the ministration of healing and prophetic gift to his generation. It implies that the kind of prophetic ministry that emanates from Prophet Dr. Amponsah is geared towards giving hope and restoration rather than despair and discouragement. This confirms the norm of naming or renaming in some CMs for missional reasons. Preaching on the title 'change of name' Most Rev. Dr. Charles Agyinasare said the change of name from Word Miracle Church International to Perez Chapel International was to make missionary inroads into nations who do not easily open doors for the Christian faith.

He further elaborates that the core values and objectives of the Church remained the same.[77] Consequently, it is probable that, if objectives are reviewed the name of the Church/Ministry will also be reviewed accordingly. Naming and renaming to reflect ministry objectives, aids the fulfilment of prophecy or hopes and aspirations and, to a large extent, agrees with the Pentateuchal narratives concerning the naming of Benjamin (Gen. 35:16–26); renaming of Abram and Sarai and Jacob (Gen. 17; 32:22–32) just to mention a few. There is a challenge in obtaining a permanent place for worship services in urban areas in Ghana. Even when one finds a place for worship services there are financial challenges for new Ministries because they have to pay exorbitant rent advances. Prophet Dr. Amponsah moved from one place of worship to the other and finally the current permanent place at Oblogo, Weija near the Oblogo Health Centre. He started at Kaneshie behind the market in 1999, to Palas Town in 2004, Atico Junction in 2005 and to the current location in 2006, all in Accra.

Many contemporary prophets give considerable attention to music. Music seems to be the spine of the prophetic grace in the life of some prophets. Prophet Dr. Amponsah is gifted in the area of music. He launched his maiden album of nine tracks titled: "*Onyame wɔ hɔ daa*" ("God lives perpetually") in March, 2009. According to him, even though music gives life and entertains the church, any time he sings, "Angels come close to me and

---

22/10/2014.

77. http://www.ghanaweb.com/GhanaHomePage/religion/artikel.php?ID=276602 Accessed 28/03/2015.

Biblical, Traditional, and Theological Framework

give me directions".[78] In that regard, any time the church has a program, musicians and songs are meticulously selected.

During "moment of worship" where songs are sang slowly and solemnly at Faithway International Chapel, late coming seekers or members were kept at the rear of the auditorium until the worship moment is over so that they would not interrupt with the service.[79] R. G. McCutchan argues that 'religion is a matter of both words and music, and the music is more important than the words, . . . the music of religion is its life of love . . . '[80] H. A. Asiedu argues that Rev. Gaddiel Robert Acquaah was one of the progenitors of vernacular choruses, commonly referred to as *Ebibindwom*, which was used for evangelism in the Methodist Church, Ghana. People are stimulated when they hear songs being sung in their mother-tongue - *Mfantse*.[81]

Asamoah-Gyadu contends that spirituality in the context of Pentecostalism relies heavily on oral theology, which is expressed in music.[82] These are short, sometimes repetitive and easy to memorize songs that have the Spirit or God's promise of miracles as its theme. Singing these songs devotionally leads to Spirit possession and the manifestation of charisma for the benefit of seekers/members. The use of music to arouse Spirit possession is not an innovation by contemporary prophets. In the AICs, singing local choruses was spontaneous with Spirit possession.

Spirit possession sometimes leads to the release of angels. In the words of A. E. Dyer, "The basic term 'angel' means 'messenger' and it implies God sends a 'heavenly agent' to communicate with humans".[83] P. J. Budd

---

78. Personal interview by author. 22/10/2014.

79. Participant Observation by author 1/2/2015.

80. Cited in Casely B. Essamuah, "Heart Music as Identity Marker: Ebibindwom and Ghanaian Methodism" in J. Kwabena Asamoah-Gyadu (Ed.) *Christianity, Mission and Ecumenism in Ghana, Essays in honour of Robert K. Aboagye-Mensah* (Accra: Asempa Publishers, 2009), 15.

81. Henry Ampaw Asiedu, "Gaddiel R. Acquaah and the Hermeneutics of Vernacular Hymns" in Kwabena Asamoah-Gyadu (Ed.) *Christianity, Mission and Ecumenism in Ghana, Essays in honour of Robert K. Aboagye-Mensah* (Accra: Asempa Publishers, 2009), 23, 32–33.

82. Asamoah-Gyadu, "The Promise is for you", 18.

83. Anne E. Dyer, "Angels and Pentecostals: An Empirical Investigation into Grassroots Opinions on Angels among Assemblies of God, UK Members" in Veli-Matti Kärkkäinen, Kirsteen Kim, and Amos Yong (Eds.) *Interdisciplinary and Religio-Cultural Discourses on a Spirit-filled World: Loosing the Spirits* (New York; Palgrave Macmillan, 2013), 113.

intimated that angels come from the "immediate presence" of God to proclaim good news and reassurance to God's people.[84] Dyer advised that since we cannot deny the fact that there are evil angels, the gift of discerning of spirits must be engaged in order to distinguish between godly and ungodly angels.[85] Many contemporary prophets have nick names that depicted the endowment(s) of the prophet. Prophet Dr. Amponsah could not be left out of this phenomenon. He is popularly referred to as "computer man". The name came about as a result of detailed prophecies he gives concerning past, present and future happenings. A member of the Church also said that whenever Prophet Dr. Amponsah called a seeker or member to prophesy unto him/her, he does it so uniquely beginning from his or her birth date, early life, education, career/profession, hopes and aspirations for the future.

Therefore, the name "computer man" is very appropriate for him. Just as what one puts in the memory of a computer is what he or she gets back, upon observation,[86] one could contend that many seekers or members at HGMI believe that Prophet Dr. Amponsah accurately delivers prophecies as revealed to him by God without editing or being affected by a virus, and the prophecies come to pass exactly as prophesied. Notwithstanding, the chanting of the name "computer man" stimulates prophecies.

"Emergency" Counselling Session in HGMI

The issue of "emergency" has been misinterpreted by many to suggest that prophets charge for their services. During counselling, Prophet Dr. Amponsah usually dresses in a simple and casual outfit in order that the counsellees can easily approach him and air out their problems freely. It is significant to state that there are two forms of counselling in HGMI: normal and "emergency" counselling. Normal counselling is where counsellees were not expected to necessarily give money or pay any fee in the form of offering to God. They were sometimes asked to buy "miracle water" at Gh¢ 10.00 (approximately $ 2.88), bring toffees (candies), water, handkerchief, or any substance(s) as directed by the prophet. On the other hand, "emergency" counselling is a process of meeting a prophet during a counselling

---

84. P. J. Budd, "Γαβριήλ" in Colin Brown (Ed.) *The New International Dictionary of New Testament Theology* (Grand Rapids, Michigan: Zondervan Publishing House, 1975), 104.

85. Dyer, "Angels and Pentecostals", 119.

86. Observer participation by author 15/3/2015 and 17/3/2015.

session where a counsellee is expected to "sow a seed"[87] in return for water or oil of the prophet that is expected to produce a miracle in less than seven days for the counsellee. "Emergency" fees range between Gh¢ 200.00 and Gh¢ 500.00 (approximately $ 58.00 to $ 147.00).

The two take place at the same time. It is the counsellee who would indicate the kind of counselling he or she has come for. The prophet sometimes recommends "emergency" counselling for seekers/members because the results are almost immediate. The "emergency oil" given by Prophet Dr. Amponsah has been labelled "special emergency oil" to distinguish it from other "emergency oils" by other prophets. "Special emergency oil" is contained in a sprayable plastic bottle cover which had his picture, HGMI, location of the ministry, petitionary Psalm 61 and contact telephone numbers pasted on it as indicated in Appendix Six. The composition of the oil is not stated for fear that some other prophets may reproduce the same oil to serve as an alternative. However, manual examination suggests that it is a mixture of olive oil, some kind of grounded seeds and some kind of perfume.

Responding to a question by the author concerning the rationale behind "emergency", its scriptural support and what monies realized from "emergency" are used for, Prophet Dr. Amponsah explains that, firstly, newer churches are always struggling to pay for long term rent advance for places of worship and maintaining permanent places for worship services. Secondly, these churches do not receive any financial support from any organization or a parent church abroad. Thirdly, the pain of it is that many of the members are not very punctual and honest. Some of them may promise to support the church financially if they should receive a miracle through the ministry of the prophet. After the miracle, they leave to other churches without honouring their pledges.

Fourthly, as new churches, there is the need to advertise their services and programs in the media for patronage by the general public. Offerings are generally not enough to cater for all the above mentioned and offerings are dwindling due to the economic situations in Ghana. There is the need to find additional means of income. He further adds that "emergency" is not compulsory, it is voluntary giving; those who do not have money to give during counselling were equally well attended to. Monies realized out of "emergency" are used for the construction of 1,050 seater capacity Church

---

87. Sowing seed is giving to "a man of God" with the understanding and inference that one had given to God.

building, media programs and philanthropic works. A research conducted by D. J. Hesselgrave and published in 1988, indicated that the cost of mission is always rising at an escalating rate. According to him, a Ph.D. holder field missionary, married with two children, bound for Europe was to receive $ 36,000.00 as yearly salary and $ 23,000.00 for outgoing outfit (wardrobe). In his words:

> Many missions build the cost of health insurance, retirement plan, children's education, and even a vacation allowance into their support structure. (At least one mission even allows candidates to raise monies required to pay off debts incurred in the process of getting their education!) Then too, the cost of maintaining a home office and staff, and of promoting the work of the mission, must be taken into consideration.[88]

It is absolutely clear that the cost of mission in any form, continent and country is expensive. Prophet Dr. Amponsah stated that the philosophy that underpins the concept of "emergency" is that when Hannah and Elkanah gave out their only treasured son Samuel to the Lord to serve in His house, God blessed Hannah and Elkanah with three other sons and two daughters without sweat (1 Sam. 2:21). Therefore, anyone who gives something precious to God receives multiple blessings. According to him, "Emergency" is organized for a few who need the services of a prophet urgently. He argues that the services of a prophet cannot be quantified in financial terms; what is given for "emergency" should better be described as offering to God.[89]

The Future of Prophetism in Ghana's Christianity

As a church, every pastor wants his or her work to abide or live after his or her demise. Therefore, the need for perpetuity is paramount in the minds of many founding prophets. Commenting on the future of contemporary prophetic ministry, Prophet Dr. Amponsah lamented that some of the so-called prophets are motivated by money and characterized by snatching other men's wives. If this is not checked, it is likely that in two years from now, it will be difficult for someone to believe in a prophet, because their

---

88. David J. Hesselgrave, *Today's Choices for Tomorrow's Mission: An Evangelical Perspective on Trends and Issues in Missions* (Grand Rapids, Michigan: Zondervan Publishing House, 1988),165–166.

89. Personal interview by author. 22/10/2014.

moral lives are not compatible with the teachings of the Bible. To sustain and improve on contemporary prophetic ministry, the moral and financial life of some prophets must comply with the Bible.

CONTEMPORARY PROPHETIC MINISTRY: PERCEPTION OF SOME GHANAIANS

In the estimation of contemporary prophets, they are doing so well and must be commended. However, Ghanaians are not enthuse with some activities of contemporary prophetic ministries. In that regard, they have been labelled false prophets whiles others were referred to derogatedly in the media.

Claims by Some Contemporary Prophets and the Decline in Membership

The prophetic ministry is the loudest of all Christian ministries in Ghana's media today. Contemporary prophets have arrogated some positions to themselves in order to make themselves indispensable in the lives and minds of seekers or members and to make the ministry of the prophet look like the most important of all other ministries. The negative remarks about some prophets in the media seem not to deter some Ghanaians from patronizing their services. Recently, the former President Rawlings asked: what at all do these prophets have that Ghanaians easily follow them without scrutiny? He described some of them as magicians who use the name of Jesus for money.[90] Asamoah-Gyadu suggested that the traditional understanding of the functions of a prophet contributed to their patronage. He rightly states that:

> In the context of healing, prophecy helps in diagnosis, and for the ailing African, who is familiar with the methods of the traditional diviner, prophecy is important for establishing the *cause* of one's condition. Many a vulnerable patient have fallen prey to the devices of prophets and pastors making declarations in the name of God, supposedly under the influence of the Spirit, when God may not have spoken.[91]

90. "Rawlings Jabs Obinim, Kumchacha Calls them False Prophets" *Daily Guide* (12th November, 2014), 3.

91. Asamoah-Gyadu, "Pentecostalism and the Missiological", 43.

Some contemporary prophets usually claim to be the mouth piece of God and mediators of spiritual issues between God and humans, thereby advocating the need for prophets in all Christian denominations. Prophet Anto stated that "a prophet is a human vessel chosen and commissioned by divine grace to function as God's mouth piece. Simply put, he is a 'messenger'".[92] These arrogations are not exclusive to contemporary prophetic ministry in Ghana. Writing from the American view point, Prophet Hamon posits that "prophets are special and precious to God. Yes, prophets are very near and dear to the heart of God".[93] It is true that prophets communicate revelations concerning current issues to seekers or members, but to make such claims for the prophet may imply that other ministries are not as important as prophetic ministry.

However, it can be argued that, in the quest to make one's ministry more important and powerful than another, ministers or pastors take up certain titles such as Apostle General, Apostolic Prophet etc. in order to point out to the masses that they are so close to the mouth of God and hear his voice. For example, in his book titled *Constitutional Amendment in Heaven: Why the Lord Jesus Christ, the Anointed One, did not Use Oil*, Pastor Lawrence K. Ayerh referred to himself as God's Public Relations Officer.[94] The phenomenon is likely to stir-up egocentric desires and inferiority complexes among ministers/pastors. All ministries are unique, it is significant to state that all ministries are important and dear to God's heart. Paul mentioned the purpose for the ministries "to equip the saints for the work of ministry, for building up the body of Christ, until all of us come to the unity of the faith and of the knowledge of the Son of God, to maturity, to the measure of the full stature of Christ" (Eph. 4:12–13). As far as all ministries preach the word of God (Bible), they are the mouth piece of God.

The assertion by contemporary prophets that their ministries have a large following (members) cannot be sustained. Some of the participants at their meetings can hardly be referred to as members due to the problem solving approach to winning souls. Some people seen at their meetings could better be described as seekers or inquirers. They are members as far

---

92. Anto, *The Office*, 18

93. Bill Hamon, *Prophets and Personal Prophecy* (Shippensburg, PA: Destiny Image Publishers, 1987), 38.

94. Lawrence K. Ayerh, *Constitutional Amendment in Heaven: Why the Lord Jesus Christ, the Anointed One, did not Use Oil* (Accra: Forever Grateful Ministries International Publishing, n.d.), cover page.

as their problems remain; as soon as they have a solution to their problems[95] or the solution for the problem is unduly prolonged, they leave to shop for a solution elsewhere. Seekers were not ashamed to still identify themselves as Catholic, Anglican, Presbyterian, Methodist, and so forth.

Impact of Contemporary Prophetic Ministry

The influences of contemporary prophetic ministry on some Ghanaians cannot be ignored. Although seekers or members sometimes have to wait for a long time or pay fees before meeting a prophet, contemporary prophets have not done badly in the area of making time to meet their members. Prophet Dr. Amponsah is mostly available at the Church premises to attend to troubled persons in counselling. Apart from Sundays and Tuesdays which are usual church service days, all the other days are counselling days. Even after Church service on Sundays and Tuesdays, he still sits for counselling. One cannot tell the motivation for making time to meet counsellees. It is likely that, since the ministry is oriented towards problem solving, time must be made for seekers/members. It is also probable that they are motivated by the love of money since "emergency oil", "miracle water" among others are sold during counselling sessions.

As the AICs provoked the acceptance of charismatic inclinations in the TWMCs in Ghana, contemporary prophetic ministry has contributed in reminding the TWMCs to sustain the charismatic activities. This is done unconsciously by their visible presence in the media and on bill boards. They have also served as clients to media houses thereby keeping them in business. Furthermore, the Ghanaian world-view has been taken along in Christian worship. Some Ghanaians may read certain meanings into miracles performed by contemporary prophets as being from other sources than God. However, it cannot be denied that some seekers/members have received healings, some "have experienced supernatural interventions in their crisis moments, received guidance, encouragements, revelations and the ministry of the word".[96]

---

95. Asamoah-Gyadu, *African Charismatics*, 81.

96. "The Prophetic Ministry in Ghana: A Quandary" *Daily Guide* (13th November, 2014), 4.

A Way Forward for Contemporary Prophetic Ministry

Pentecostals generally prefer spirituality (experience with the Spirit) over scholarship. There should be a balance between the two. Due to the over-emphasis of spirituality, there are no ecclesiastical structures to manage seekers or members; everything seemed to revolve around the founding prophet. Many of the founding prophets do not have any formal theological training. Experience has shown that over-emphasis on the non-rational aspect of religion to the detriment of the rational aspect has not been helpful and sustaining. This phenomenon is one of the factors that contributed to the numerical decline of the AICs.[97] Yet, contemporary prophets continue to prefer the mentorship form of training over and above formal theological training. Prophet Dr. Amponsah advocates for training that would help prophets' life style conform to the teaching of the Bible. However, by training, he meant mentorship under senior prophets like himself.

The popular notion among some contemporary prophets that formal theological education does not support spiritual formation is not true. J. K. Agbeti writes that "Appropriate academic and spiritual formation of the lecturers are the bedrocks of the formation of the students, ... teachers at Trinity College, Legon, Ghana ... are highly qualified academically and subtly spiritually".[98] It is not only lecturers from Trinity College (now Trinity Theological Seminary) that have both academic and spiritual impetus, but lecturers of other accredited theological institutions also have these dispositions that contemporary prophets could benefit from.

J. S. Pobee and J. N. K. Kudadjie stated that the purpose of theological education was to 'conscientize, mobilize and motivate the people at the grass-roots levels for social change, and to work with them in identifying their needs, setting their own priorities and the standards and recognizing the resources that are available to them for use in development'.[99] The lack of formal theological education by many contemporary prophets does not make them identify the actual needs of the people in their congregation.

---

97. Asamoah-Gyadu, *African Charismatics*, 80–81. See also Frederick Mawusi Amevenku, "Mother-Tongue Biblical Interpretation and the Future of African Instituted Christianity in Ghana" in *Trinity Journal of Church and Theology* Vol. 18 No.1 (March 2014), 132–148.

98. J. K. Agbeti, "The Need for Scholarship in the Training for the Christian Ministry" in *Trinity Journal of Church and Theology* Vol. 1 No.1 (June 1991), 25–34.

99. Cited in Emmanuel Asante, "The Relevance of Theological Education in the 21st Century" in *Trinity Journal of Church and Theology* Vol. XIII No.03 (July 2003), 77–82.

Biblical, Traditional, and Theological Framework

Most of the problems that seekers or members present have been explained to have been caused spiritually by someone else. Quayesi-Amakye succinctly puts it thus: "It is always the 'other', the evil person who does not want one's prosperity and success who is behind it all . . . which means that 'misfortunes' are rooted in the *other from outside*".[100] Asamoah-Gyadu contends that the challenge for the Christian faith is not the pluralistic nature of the Ghanaian religious landscape "but that its supposed adherents have become the proselytizing target of other faiths". He further elaborates this call for serious theological education to move away from the 'Bible School approach' to "ministerial formation" that take cognisance of the salvific work of Jesus in the midst of religious pluralistic society.[101]

The belief in the infallibility of the revelation of some prophets makes them resist "wise counselling" from other Pastors.[102] Charismatically endowed persons usually attract people who are reluctant to give them counsel. They also surround themselves with persons who could not criticize them because they believe that the Holy Spirit is their counsel. It is absolutely true that the Holy Spirit is their counsel. However, the Holy Spirit is the counsel of all believers not only Prophets. The Council of the Holy Spirit does not immune prophets from the council of other senior pastors.

CONCLUSION

We have attempted to discuss contemporary prophetic ministry in Ghana's Christianity. By contemporary prophetic ministry, we refer to the fifth phase of neo-prophetism in Ghana's Christianity since the decline of the AICs. There were numerous external and internal factors that gave rise to the phenomenon: political, economic, health, charisma, the use of vernacular language and the extensive use of the media among others. Many contemporary prophets received the prophetic grace in either TWMCs or CPCs. They claimed that, after the grace had been bestowed upon them, conditions in the mother churches did not make it comfortable for them to stay. They were therefore forced to move out to establish their own

---

100. Quayesi-Amakye, *Prophetism in Ghana Today*, 130.

101. J. Kwabena Asamoah-Gyadu, "Theological Education and Religious Pluralism in Ghana" in J. Kwabena Asamoah-Gyadu (Ed.) *Christianity, Mission and Ecumenism in Ghana, Essays in honour of Robert K. Aboagye-Mensah* (Accra: Asempa Publishers, 2009), 158–159.

102. Quayesi-Amakye, *Prophetism in Ghana Today*, 141.

Churches. However, it is likely that some of them did not want to submit to the authority of the mother Church or they moved out for egocentric and economic purposes. We cannot also deny the fact that some of them moved out for missionary reasons to win souls for the Lord.

The so-called "prophetic acts" by some contemporary prophets have been criticized as ritualistic and occultic. In May 2011, the CoP prayer camp at Edumfa was sanctioned for indulging in such ungodly practices. Prophets do everything possible to perform miracles in order to be referred to as powerful. They see the performance of miracles as that which authenticates one's ministry rather than the appropriate preaching of the word. Therefore experience is preferred over theology. Notwithstanding, contemporary prophetic ministry has had an impact on the Ghanaian society. Contemporary prophetic ministry has taken on board the Ghanaian worldview in Christian worship although they sometimes sound ambiguous. They are a very good client to many media networks because they sustain them in business. Moving forward, contemporary prophets need to subject themselves to formal theological education in order to remain relevant to society. In addition, they must also take wise counsel from other persons and not to be surrounded by sycophants. It is obvious that contemporary prophets' designation of "prophet" is similar to that of the prophetic forerunners of the AICs, and the function of the *Gbalɔ* and *wulɔmɔ* in *Gbawe* traditional prophetism. Bearers of the title "prophet" are seen as the direct mouth piece of God rather than the titles "pastor", "reverend minister" etc. despite them preaching from the Bible, which contained the word of God.

Chapter Six

Contemporary Prophetic Ministry

A Case of *Gã* South Municipal Area

INTRODUCTION

This chapter discusses contemporary prophetic ministry, a case of *Gã* South Municipal Area. The *Gã* South Municipal Area (GSMA) was derived out of the then *Gã* West District, in February, 2009 in pursuance of the government's decentralization and local government reform policy as enshrined in the LI 1867.[1] Weija is the capital of the Municipal Area . According to an unpublished 2010 Head Count Population Census by the Municipal Assembly, there are 101,931 people living in 289 communities in the municipality.[2] The most populous localities in the municipal area are Weija, Gbawe, Awoshie and Anyaa, with the main religious groupings being Christianity (dominant), Islam and African Traditional Religion.[3] According to a 2010

---

1. Republic of Ghana, *Local Government Act, 1993 (Act 462)* (Accra: Ghana Publishing Corporation (Assembly Press), 1993), 4–6.

2. Unpublished 2010 Head Count Population Census of Ga South Municipal Assembly, Source: GSMA

3. http/www.Ghanadistricts.com/gasouthmunicipalassembly

Census of Churches in the municipality, there are about 119 Churches out of which about 84% are 'prophetic' churches/ministry.[4]

RESEARCH FINDINGS

In this research, a total of 297 persons, from various Christian denominations as illustrated in Table 1, responded to the questions:

Roman Catholic Church	14	4.71%
Presbyterian Church	16	5.38%
Methodist Church	16	5.38%
Pentecostal and Charismatic Ministries	79	26.59%
Seventh Day Adventist	13	4.37%
Jehovah Witness	22	7.40%
Prophetic Churches/Ministries	137	46.12%

Table 1. Source: 2013 field research by the Author

Figure 1 below indicates that 297 respondents gave their views on belief in prophetic ministry and prophecy; 229 respondents representing 77.10% of the total respondents believed in prophetic ministry and prophecy; 56 respondents representing 18.85% do not believe in prophetic ministry and prophecy; and 12 respondents representing 4.04% of total respondents were undecided.

---

4. Unpublished census of Churches in the Ga South Municipal Assembly, source: GSMA

Biblical, Traditional, and Theological Framework

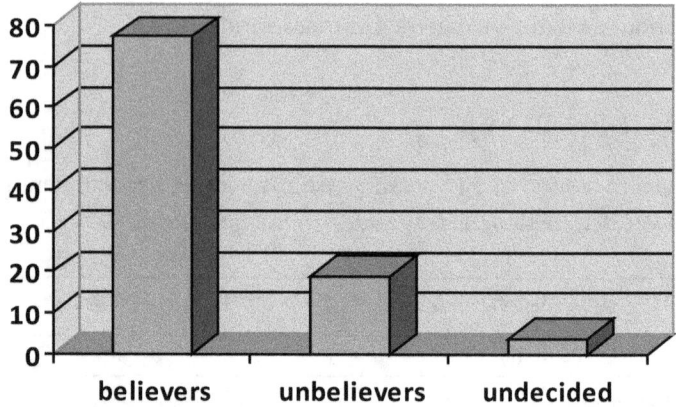

Figure 1. Source: 2013 field research by the Author

On fulfillment of prophecy, 176 respondents said they have receive prophecy; 120 respondents representing 68.18% said the prophecy came to pass; and 56 respondents representing 31.81% said the prophecy did not come to pass. This is illustrated in figure 2.

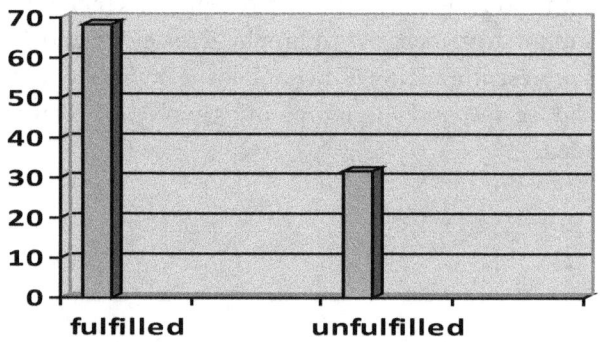

Figure 2. Source: 2013 field research by the Author

During this research, 109 respondents said that they received spiritual direction *sunsum akwankyere*; and 84 respondents representing 77.06% of the total respondents in this category said that they had to pay an amount ranging between GH¢ 50.00 to 3,000.00 (12.5 to 750 USD) before they were given some concoction with green, blue, and red oil or bottled water to be administered by themselves at a specific time given by the prophet. The determination of the fee was based on the number of issues that one tables and their gravity. Others were asked to buy wrist bands and chains for protection. The remaining 25 representing 22.93% said they were asked to fast and pray without being charged.

Figure 3 below illustrates these findings.

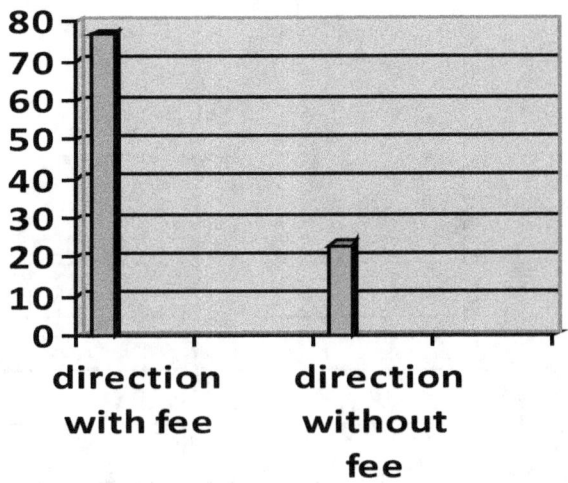

Figure 3. Source: 2013 field research by the Author

Biblical, Traditional, and Theological Framework

Figure 4 deals with the issue of general overview of respondents concerning prophets and prophecy. Out of 98 respondents, 40 respondents representing 40.82% said prophetic ministry and prophecy is true and should be encouraged; and 58 respondents representing 59.18% said there are too many false claims and that it must be regulated and screened.

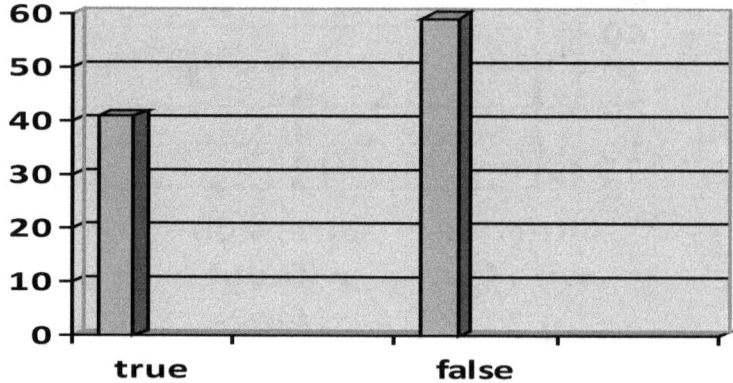

Figure 4

A woman who attended one of the prophetic churches/ministries said she went to see her 'prophet' on the issue of barrenness. The 'prophet' asked her to buy water in a bottle to be taken at mid-night, after which she would be pregnant the following month. The woman was given *sunsum akwankyere*. The process of diagnosing the problem, prescription and administering the prescription is usually called *sunsum akwankyere* literally, meaning spiritual direction, and a moderate fee is mostly charged. The woman said she over slept and when she woke up at 1:20 am, she noticed a living creature like a little snake in the water. According to her, she noticed that, if she had taken the water at mid-night as prescribed by the prophet, the creature would have developed in her stomach. She added that she was made to believe that after receiving prophecy, one needed to have *sunsum akwankyere* before that prophecy could be fulfilled.

One of the 'prophets' we listened to on a private radio station in Accra said that, if someone came to consult with him, he would give the person spiritual direction *(sunsum akwankyere)* that would make the person dream of lotto numbers, which if he/she staked, would win. This act is reminiscent of Roman incubation oracles, where the inquirers were asked to sleep at the temple in order to have dreams about their challenges and the solutions.[5]

ANALYSIS OF FINDINGS

According to table 1 above on the presence of church denominations in *Ga* South Municipal Area, it was realized that the prophetic churches/ministries are dominant at 46.12%. Some of them meet in classrooms, uncompleted buildings and sheds. It could mean that the services of prophets are patronized in the municipality. However, figure 2 and 3 indicate that some of the people who patronize the services of these prophets are not satisfied due to the demand for money and unfulfilled prophecies.

In figure 2, 31.81% of the total respondents on fulfillment of prophecy, indicated that the prophecies received from the prophets did not come to pass. For these respondents, since the prophecy did not come to pass, the prophets are false. This assertion may be correct in view of Deuteronomy 18:22. In addition, if the prophecy comes to pass or not, there must be evidence of the prophet leading the client to worship other gods (Deut. 13:1–5), before we can conclude that the prophet is false.

5. Aune, *Prophecy in Early Christianity*, 25–26.

Biblical, Traditional, and Theological Framework

The issue of *sunsum akwankyere* is gaining popularity in Ga South Municipal Area. Figure 3 indicates that 77.06% of the total respondents in this category had to pay a fee before being given *sunsum akwankyere*. The respondents also indicate that they were made to believe that one needed *sunsum akwankyere* in order to have a prophecy fulfilled. The assertion that one necessarily needed *sunsum akwankyere* in order to have prophecy fulfilled is not in agreement with biblical teachings on prophecy. There are some conditional prophecies that demand the input of the recipient in order to be fulfilled. For example, Samson was instructed not to trim his hair in order to maintain the power of Yahweh in his life (Judges 13–16). However, the prophecy concerning the birth of John the Baptist and Jesus did not require the input of their parents in order for the prophecies to be fulfilled (Luke 1:5–38).

Is it that members of the prophetic churches/ministries do not give enough offering that is why a fee is charged for *sunsum akwankyere*? If this is true, on the basis of the biblical theology concerning giving, we suggest that the better thing to do by the prophetic churches/ministries is to teach the members about giving rather than imposing a fee, which the poor cannot pay. *Sunsum akwankyere* is ambiguous. One may ask, what kind of *sunsum*? Is it God's *sunsum* or the Devil's *sunsum*? The practices of the prophets are in some respects related to African Traditional Religious practices and manticism rather than the New Testament practices of prophets and prophecies. For example, the selling of assorted oils, water, stones, and sand to be spread where one lives, cannot be seen in the Bible. Wrist bands and chains to be worn for protection can be traced to the amulets worn around the neck, wrist, waist etc. in African Traditional Religion.[6] Can we then say that they are leading the members to worship other gods or they are acting ignorantly? The mere fact that someone reveals a past life of a person does not make that person a prophet of God and that revelation does not necessary constitute prophecy, because Traditional Priests and/or Seers can equally do the same. Jesus prophetically reveals the past life of the Samaritan woman at the well which ended up in the salvation of the woman (John 4:1–42). The question here is: do the revelations of those prophets lead to the total salvation of the human person?

---

6. Mbiti, *Introduction to African*, 144.

Contemporary Prophetic Ministry

PROPHETS AND PROPHECY IN GHANA TODAY

The Church of Jesus Christ has existed on earth for more than two thousand years along with its challenges of leadership and charismatic gifts: what is the role of 'prophets and prophecy' in the Church today; is 'prophecy' still relevant to the Church today? Ghana is blessed with many Church denominations. The Christian community in Ghana did not experience the activities of 'prophets and prophecy' during the missionary periods of the 18th and 19th centuries. During the period of the emergence of the African Initiated Churches (AIC's) and the rise of Pentecostalism and Charismaticism in Ghana, there were spasmodic occurrences of the prophetic phenomenon.[7] The AIC's express the Christian faith in African/Ghanaian culture and more; and, sometimes their ritual practices can be relative to African Traditional Religion (ATR). They claim to take justification from worship practices of the Old Testament (OT).

Since the coming of the Pentecostal and Charismatic Churches, there have been many claims by its charismatic leaders concerning the prophetic ministry. Many of the leaders of the charismatic Churches claim to be prophets or apostles. And even now there is a group of Churches that call themselves prophetic Churches/ministries, which are different from the AIC's and the Charismatic Church. The majority of them are founded by Ghanaians and their liturgy is similar to the charismatic ministry, however they place more emphases on the prophetic ministry than do the Charismatic Churches. According to Abraham Akrong, the rise of prophetic churches/ministries is as a result of the inability of the Historic Mission Churches, the AIC's, the Pentecostal Churches and the Charismatic Churches to meet the soteriological needs of the African person.[8] To the African, salvation must lead to total wellbeing in this present life. The quest for wellbeing[9] gave rise to the evolvement of the prophetic churches/ministries. Certain claims are made concerning the prophetic churches/ministries: (i) by the 'prophets' themselves concerning their gifts of prophecy; (ii) by persons who patronize their service; and (iii) others who advertize for them in the media.

---

7. Emmanuel Kingsley Larbi, *Pentecostalism: The Eddies of Ghanaian Christianity*, (Accra: SAPC, 2001), 57–93.

8. Abraham Akrong, 'Salvation in African Christianity'.*Legon Journal of the HUMANITIES*, Volume 12,1990–2001.

9. John S. Mbiti, *Introduction to African Religion, Second Edition*, (Oxford: Heinemann Educational Publishers,1991), 139.

Biblical, Traditional, and Theological Framework

Practices engaged in by some of the prophets include collecting consultation fees from clients. If this is acceptable, can the poor enjoy the services of a prophet? Even though there is some evidence in the Old Testament (Num.22:7; 1 Sam.9:7, 8) concerning giving to prophets, we do not know if it was a fixed amount. The activities of some of these prophets have rendered their congregation poorer than before. They have succeeded in creating confusion and hatred among family members by accusing old persons and parents, who are poor, to be witches and wizards. Many of the prophetic churches/ministries are located in the urban areas of Ghana. This may be due to the economic activities in these areas. They do not belong to ecumenical bodies like the Christian Council of Ghana, Council of Pentecostal and Charismatic Churches etc. They are mostly independent. The prophetic phenomenon has become a very controversial issue in and outside the Church.

Generally, Pentecostal and Charismatic denominations believe in the manifestation of the gift of prophecy and prophets today.[10] For example, the Church of Pentecost in Ghana (CoP) believes in the ministry of women who are prophetesses and have allowed them to set up prayer camps. An example is Mama Grace at Edumfa prayer camp in the Central Region. Another example, is the Pentecost prayer camp at Ablekuma-Agape in the Greater Accra Region. Today, the phenomena of miracles and prophecy are also experienced, probably on a lower scale, in other Christian denominations that are not traditionally known for projecting the phenomenon. For instance, one may hear ministers from denominations, which are not known for the phenomena, narrating a dream to someone he/she has prayed for; or a direction God gave him/her in a dream. These are prophetic instincts in the 'historic mission Churches' and the quest to make religion respond to the daily needs of the Ghanaian Christian. As Turner suggests 'spiritually-minded Christians often seek God's guidance on decisions, which they know the Bible cannot settle for them; and many expect that God will sometimes give them a definite and direct indication . . . on a matter'.[11]

The prophetic churches/ministries are mostly referred to as 'one man church(es)' due to the overwhelming influence that the founder/leader has over decision making of the church. The founder/leader who is usually gifted charismatically, in many instances is the sole signatory to the account

---

10. Turner, *The Holy Spirit*, 336–337.
11. Turner, *The Holy Spirit*, 338.

of the church/ministry if they have one, and does not render accounts to anybody. These churches/ministries are mainly located in the urban areas of Ghana such as Accra, Kumasi, Takoradi, Sunyani etc. and have occupied most of the religious broadcast space in the media. For example, religious programs feature on Saturday mornings on Metropolitan Television (Metro TV) between 5:00 am and 11:00 am; religious programs on Television Africa (TV Africa) between 5:00 pm and 6:00 pm, from Monday to Friday, and on Saturdays between 5:00 am and 7:00 am. On radio, they are often found on Channel R, an Accra based radio station (now 3fm)..

CONCLUSION

The mere fact that someone reveals a past life story of a person does not make that person a prophet of God and that revelation does not necessary constitute prophecy because Traditional Priests and/or Seers can equally do the same. Jesus prophetically revealed the past life story of the Samaritan woman at the well, which ended up in the salvation of the woman (John 4:1–42). The question here is whether the revelations of those prophets lead to the total salvation of the human person. Prophesies must lead to the total salvation of the audience. There is the need for religious experiences to be subjected to the stipulations of scripture.

Chapter Seven

Prophetism in the Old Testament

INTRODUCTION: THE CALL OF A PROPHET

THE CALL EXPERIENCE OF Old Testament 'prophets' varies from one prophet to the other. Some of the charismatic pre-monarchy leaders of Israel and the prophets experience spiritual encounters with Yahweh that informed the individual about the objectives of the call and they were commissioned to undertake the task ahead. The prophets responded differently to the call events.[1] For example, the experience of Moses in the wilderness, when he saw the bush burning but the bush was not consumed followed by the voice of Yahweh that commissioned him to go and bring out Israel from Egypt. Moses initially was reluctant to accept going to Egypt, but after Yahweh had shown him some miracles he accepted Yahweh's call and commissioning (Ex. 3). In the *Akan* Traditional Religion, the prospective priest/priestess experiences an encounter with the deities that sometimes leads them into the forest or sometimes makes them partially insane until a seer is consulted and the necessary rituals are performed.[2]

Samuel A. Meier refers to the call event as 'divine council', mostly composed of supernatural creatures such as angels and the hosts of heaven (1 Kings 22:19). This council meets periodically and is described in a number of passages in the Bible (See Isaiah 6:2; Job 1:6; 2:1; Jeremiah 1:4–19;

---

1. Asante, *The Prophetic and Apocalyptic.* 19–25
2. Ekem, *Priesthood.* 48

Ezekiel 13). The prophet is sometimes present when God puts forth an issue and anyone present at the meeting could comment. Some of the prophets participate actively in the meeting; for example, prophet Mecaiah (1 Kings 22:19-28). Others just stand by and record what transpires at the meeting [3](see Habakkuk 1:2-4). However, all these supernatural events do not necessarily authenticate the work of the prophet to others: after all, this experience is exclusive to the prophet. No one was present as witness and therefore it is the testing of the prophet's word and fruitful and good moral life that give credibility to the prophet.[4] Even though there is no record in the Bible about prophets like Elijah, Elisha etc as having a supernatural encounter prior to their calling, they discharged their ministries with diligence and were held in high esteem. The 'divine council' experience convinces the prophet that God has called him/her and sets them apart for a special task.

CLASSIFICATIONS OF PROPHETS IN THE OLD TESTAMENT

Before we discuss the issue of classification of prophets in the OT, we would like to discuss certain persons who experienced visions and revelations and functioned in one way or the other as prophets in the OT, but who were not acknowledged as prophets in its classical sense. There were others who were acknowledged as prophets but could not be easily classified due to the multiple nature of their ministry.

Pre-monarchical Period

The Pre-monarchic period is from the ancestral period of Abraham, Isaac, Jacob etc (date uncertain) through to the period of the Judges (c.1200-1020).[5] Isaac, Jacob, Lot, etc. received visions, divine revelations and supernatural visitations but were not called prophets. Abraham, the father of the Jewish faith, was referred to as נָבִיא (prophet)–in Genesis 20:7. The passage did not bring out the meaning of נָבִיא very clearly. Perhaps the meaning is

---

3. Samuel A. Meier, *Themes and Transformations in Old Testament Prophecy*, (Illinois: InterVarsity Press, 2009), 19–27.

4. Jim & Carolyn Murphy, *Prophets and Prophecy in Today's Church*, (California: Hundredfold Press, 1994), 122,123.

5. Matthews and Benjamin, *Old Testament Parallels*, 361.

Biblical, Traditional, and Theological Framework

related to the spiritual endowment to pray (intercede) for someone or to communicate on someone's behalf with God.

Moses was a prophet to the very core of the meaning of נָבִיא. While some prophets received revelations from season to season and through dreams, Moses spoke to God 'face to face' (Numbers 12:6). Through Moses' prophetic prowess, God brought Israel out of Egypt.[6] The greater part of the Pentateuch is the prophetic communication between Moses and Yahweh resulting in the giving of the (torah)תּוֹרָה he was such a great prophet during the pre-monarchical period.

The Period of the Monarchy

This is the period spanning Samuel to Saul (c.1020–1000 BCE) to the divided kingdom of Israel in 720 BCE and Judah 587 BCE.[7] This period experienced a lot of prophets because Israel's religion was confronted with secularization or syncretism. One such issue was their request of a king to rule over them as the surrounding nations had (see 1 Sam. 8:1–18). The request for a king was not the will of Yahweh, and so the prophets drew Israel's attention to the covenant relationship that existed between them and Yahweh.[8] Prophetic activities during this period are very significant in the study of prophets and prophecy. Aune classified OT prophets into 4 main categories:[9] (i) shamanistic prophets; (ii) cult, temple and classical/literary prophets; (iii) court prophets; and (iv) freelance prophets.

Shamanistic Prophets

This prophetic group, made up of Samuel, Elijah, and Elisha demonstrated a kind of prophetic ministry that combines miracle working, and foretelling with strange life style or worship life and forth telling. Samuel functioned as prophet, priest and king maker (1 Sam.2:18–20; 3:1, 19–20). These prophets were referred to as 'father' by their trainees (1 Sam.10:12; 2 Kings 2:12; 6:21; 13:14). They were also in charge of group of trainee prophets called

---

6. Orelli, 'Prophecy, Prophets' in James Orr Ed., *The International Standard, Volume IV.* 2461.

7. Matthews and Benjamin, *Old Testament Parallels*, 361.

8. Asante, *The Prophetic and Apocalyptic.* 41–43

9. Aune, *Prophecy in Early Christianity.*83–85

'the sons of the prophets' who usually prophesied in groups (1 Kings 20:35; 2 Kings2:3,5,7,15; 4:1,38; 5:22; 6:1; 9:1; Amos 7:14).[10]

Cult, Temple and Classical/Literary Prophets

These prophets emerged during the exilic and post-exilic periods (Babylonian - 597–538 and Persian—538–332 BCE). They were called to speak against religious syncretism that was emerging as a result of the formation of Israel as a State. This class of prophets were inseparably associated with Judah and the city of Jerusalem. Ezekiel and Jeremiah were also linked to the priesthood, and may likely have played priestly functions. Amos went to the sanctuary at Bethel to prophesy (Amos 7:10–13); Isaiah's 'divine council' meeting or call experience took place in the temple (Isaiah 6), and particularly the prophecies of Jeremiah were delivered to the priest at the temple (Jer.26:2; 27:16–22; 28:1, 5).

'Haggai and Zechariah worked closely with Zerubbabel and the priest Jeshua ben Jozadak in the rebuilding of the temple' (Ezra 5:1–2). Aune argues that some of the Psalms that have prophetic undertones were as a result of the influences of these prophets (Ps.20; 21; 50; 60; 72; 75 etc.).[11] However, some of the pre-exilic literary prophets such as Joel, Nahum, Habakkuk and Zephaniah seem to have used the order of worship at the time to communicate their prophecies. Relative to the shamanistic prophets, there is no record in the Bible of these prophets performing miracles, except Isaiah (Isaiah 36–39) who was reported to have caused the sundial to move backward and a prescription for the healing of King Hezekiah. Some scholars think that this miraculous passage originated during the Deuteronomistic historical period.[12] It was copied into the book of Isaiah to depict that all prophets are miracle workers.[13] The literary/classical prophets were basically messengers who delivered the word of Yahweh concerning their covenant relationship and the restoration of the true worship required from Israel.

---

10. Aune, *Prophecy in Early Christianity*, 83.
11. Aune, *Prophecy in Early Christianity*, 84.
12. Meier, *Themes and Transformations*, 121.
13. Meier, *Themes and Transformations*, 123.

Court Prophets

There were another group of prophets who functioned in the courts of the kings. They delivered unsolicited oracles to the monarchs during a time of crises. King Ahab and Jezebel had a large group of Baal prophets in their court (1 Kings 18:19; 2 Kings 3:13). These prophets also functioned as counselors to the King: the prophet Gad was King David's seer (2 Sam.24:11; 1 Chro.21:9; 2 Chro.29:25); Nathan was also a prophet of King David (2 Sam.7:4–17; 12:1–17; 1 Kings 1:8, 10, 23–37); Asaph, Heman, and Jeduthun were all called the seers of King David (1 Chro.25:5; 2 Chro.35:15).[14] It seems that the Court prophets kept records of activities of reigning kings and their designations were official.

Freelance Prophets

As the name implies, they were prophets who were not affiliated to any cult/temple, or the court. They emerged at the time of political and economic struggles in the Ancient Near East. Examples include Amos and Hosea whose prophetic activities were concentrated in Israel, while Micah worked in Judah. The freelance prophets do not seem to be innovators but social and religious reformers. They acted independent of existing religious and political establishments and the liturgy of the day. They claimed their authority from Yahweh to call Israel to the covenant stipulations by interpreting the Law.[15] Their work centered on restoring Israel to the ancient theocracy.

TRAINING OF OLD TESTAMENT PROPHETS

Training into prophetic ministry was a very important and indispensable process during the period of the judges to the period of the monarchy. Samuel was the first prophet to have the 'school of the prophets' followed by Elijah and then Elisha. Young people who sensed the calling of Yahweh gathered around senior prophets who lived in colonies[16] with their families

---

14. Aune, *Prophecy in Early Christianity*, 85.

15. Aune, *Prophecy in Early Christianity*, 85.

16. Orelli, '*Prophecy, and Prophets*' in James Orr Ed., *The International, Volume IV*. 2462.

for training (1 Sam.10:12; 2 Kings 2:12; 6:21; 13:14). There is no biblical record of any training for would be prophets before or after this period.

The intention of these disciples was to receive, if possible, the double portion of their master's spirit (see 2 Kings 2: 1–12). They are mostly in an ecstatic mood that is contagious to others and prophesy in group. The first school of the 'sons of the prophets' was at Ramah (1 Sam.19:18; 20:1). The daily up keep of the group was dependent on the gifts that individuals, who benefited from the ministry of the senior prophet, gave him (2 Kings 5:22). It is not very clear from the biblical passages the content and duration of the training. However, on the basis of the role of the Torah and prophets in the socio-religious life of Israel, we argue that, no matter what the content and duration may have been, it would have included the tradition of the past prophets and the covenant relationship between Yahweh and Israel.

THE OLD TESTAMENT PROPHETS AND THE SPIRIT OF GOD

Different religious groups in the Old Testament had varied understandings of the ministry of prophets; nevertheless, it is important to discuss the main elements relating to the prophets and prophecy. The words 'in, with and on'[17] will be used interchangeably to mean the influence of the spirit over some one. The Hebrew word, רוּחַ means either wind (Gen.8:1; Numb.11:31), or breath (Job 12:10; 15:30). It was used for humans to refer to 'the seat of emotions', of mental and moral character (Ex.28:3; Ezekiel 11:19). The Spirit of God is the power of God on the prophets, and it signified the influence of God's spirit in the life of the prophet. When the Spirit of God stirred up a prophet to prophesy, then it is said that the Spirit of God or the hand of the Lord has come on the prophet[18] (1Sam.10:10; Judges 15:14; Ezekiel 37:1). The 'Spirit of Yahweh' is an indispensable topic in Old Testament studies. It is the power of God behind every good accomplishment of the prophets. Most importantly, it was the 'organ of communication' between God and the prophets.

In the OT, God anointed many priests, kings, judges and other individuals to accomplish specific tasks. Bezalel and Oholiab were anointed to

---

17. Max Turner, *The Holy Spirit and Spiritual Gifts: Then and Now*, (Cumbria: Paternoster Press, 1996), 5.

18. J.C.Lambert, '*Spirit*' in James Orr Ed., *The International Standard Bible Encyclopedia, Volume V* (Grand Rapids: Michigan, WM.B. Eerdmans Publishing Co., 1949), 2841.

Biblical, Traditional, and Theological Framework

work in gold, bronze, silver and furnishings for the Tabernacle (Ex. 31:1–11). To the prophets, and other persons who were called to minister in the Tabernacle etc. the manifestation of the Spirit is synonymous with prophecy. For example, the seventy elders (Numb.11:25–29; Saul (1 Sam.10:1–11); and mighty works by judges (Judges 15:14–16; 14:19–20). According to Max Turner, Judaism understands that the Spirit of God played the role of an intermediary between God and humans. We can then suggest that the 'Spirit of Yahweh' was using the prophets as intermediaries between God and humans through prophecy. Prophets were sometimes referred to as 'persons of the Spirit' (Isaiah 48:16; Zech.7:12). The Spirit of God was a seal of ownership of the prophets and other anointed persons by God. It comes upon prophets and leaders to fulfill a peculiar task. It was anticipated to come upon all flesh in the future (Joel 2:28; Jer.31:34).[19]

OLD TESTAMENT PROPHECY

Prophecy in the Old Testament is mostly predictive (foretelling) of future events publicly before they happen. It may comprise insight into the past and present happenings and a foresight of its future consequences. Prophecy is indicative of God's involvement and care for the happenings in the life of individuals and nations. It also strengthens the relationship that God always desires to have with His creation (Gen.2:8–10). God compels the prophets to prophesy and so it is not the initiative of the prophet but God. Some of the prophecies, especially by the literary prophets, were 'messianic' in nature. The messianic concept of Jesus Christ may not necessarily have been in the minds of the prophets at the time of the prophecy but was later understood as messianic by redactors.[20] Most of the prophecies were delivered/given orally and were later collected by others into scrolls[21] of various lengths and styles of writing.

The Gentile nations also practiced an analogous form of prophecy, which was 'necromancy and technical witchcraft'.[22] It is an art in which the practitioner calls upon the spirit of the dead, in order to enquire of the

---

19. Turner, *The Holy Spirit*, 8–18.
20. Orelli, *'Prophecy, Prophets'* in James Orr Ed., *The International, Volume IV.* 2464–2465.
21. Meier, *Themes and Transformations.* 94,95.
22. Orelli, *'Prophecy, Prophets'* in James Orr Ed., *The International, Volume IV.* 2464–2465

future or give meaning to present happenings for the living. Parts of sacrificial animals were also used by religious intermediaries for omen to know the future. False prophets also used mantic art to interpret dreams among the heathen. God cautioned Israel against these acts (Deut.18:10; Lev.19:26; 31:20).

FINE PROPHETIC SPEECH IN THE OLD TESTAMENT

Israel's prophetic speeches took various forms. Oracles could be solicited or unsolicited. Some of the oracles of the Temple and the court prophets did not survive due to wars. According to Meier, the information provided in the books of Samuel and Kings did not give extensive details concerning the ministry of prophets like Samuel, Elijah and Elisha and therefore the prophetic narrative in the Hebrew Bible, finds writing less important because the books did not tell how the information about these prophets were preserved, nor the concept of writing seen in the books but rather the 'allusions of writings in other context'[23] (2 Sam.1:18; 1 Kings 11:41; 14:19,29; 2 Kings 23:2–3,21,24).

Lindblom asserts that the prophetic writings, as we have them today have gone through many years of editing and enlargement by redactors or disciples of these prophets in accordance to the 'taste and the needs of the later times'.[24] This means that the prophetic writings have gone through interpretations and reinterpretations due to the changing fortunes of the recipients. Many critical scholars have tried to ascertain when a particular prophetic speech was prevalent; but their findings are so diverse that conclusions are difficult to agree upon. Meier buttresses this point when he posits that it is not easy to establish the purpose and the 'process of composition' of some of the books of the prophets in the Hebrew Bible, even though the art of writing was developed by the first millennium BCE.[25] In view of all these, one can find a number of formulas that occurred in prophetic speeches in the Old Testament, that in most cases, are in first person address by Yahweh and are mostly poetic in form.

---

23. Meier, *Themes and Transformations*, 96,97.

24. J. Lindblom, *Prophecy In Ancient Israel* (Oxford: The Alden Press, 1962), 149,239,279.

25. Meier, *Themes and Transformations*, 94.

Biblical, Traditional, and Theological Framework

The Messenger Formula

'Thus says the Lord' or 'Yahweh has said' are a common phenomenon that runs through most of the writings of the prophets. Aune refers to it as the 'messenger formula'.[26] This is the norm for transmitting oracular information from Yahweh to the people of Israel. The earliest record of this formula was in Amos 1:1, 6; but there is evidence that it was already in use in the 'Mari letters' (parallels of prophetic tradition in the books of Samuel and Kings in Syria) with slight variations.[27] The messenger formula is the most popular with the prophets and is indicative of the fact that the prophet was being portrayed as someone who received information from a higher authority. Meier suggests that the usage of this formula was dominant among the exilic and post-exilic prophets,[28] most of which can be dated. The importance of this formula is the effort to dichotomize the voice of Yahweh from the prophet and others. For example, 1 Kings 17:14-16 reads,

> 14 For thus says the Lord the God of Israel: The jar of meal will not be emptied and the jug of oil will not fail until the day that the Lord sends rain on the earth." 15 She went and did as Elijah said, so that she as well as he and her household ate for many days. 16 The jar of meal was not emptied, neither did the jug of oil fail, according to the word of the Lord that he spoke by Elijah (NRSV)

In the above passage, verse 14a used the messenger formula indicating the voice of God to Elijah. Verse 14b indicates Elijah paraphrasing what God had told him concerning the woman while verse 15 and 16 represent the voice of the narrator.

FALSE PROPHETS AND PROPHECY

False prophets who are also designated [29]נְבִיא is an important topic in 'prophetism'. Deut.13:1-5, indicates that the prophets who prophesy or tell a dream that, eventually came to pass but demanded that the recipient(s) of the oracle go(es) to worship other gods, or instructed them to practice

---

26. Aune, *Prophecy in Early Christianity*, 89.
27. Matthews and Benjamin, *Old Testament Parallels, Third Edition*, Xiv, 341–346.
28. Meier, *Themes and Transformations*, 70.
29. Leonard J.Coppes, *'Nabi'* in R. Laird Harris, Gleason L. Archer Jr. , Bruce K. Waltke (Eds), *Theological Wordbook Of The Old Testament, Vol.2*, (Chicago: Moody Press, 1980), 545.

acts that are contrary to the worship stipulations of Yahweh, were false. A true prophet of God was not measured by the number of miracles that he/she does, but by the truthfulness of the word of God spoken through him/her. According to the above scripture, God allowed the false prophets to rise in order to try the faith of the Israelites, because they were about to enter Canaan where they would be faced with issues of how to drive out the inhabitants, and possess the land. This is indicative of the fact that not all prophecies are from God. God wants His people to use their intellectual faculties judiciously at all times.

Even though the dreams, prophecies, signs and wonders of the false prophets may come to pass, the source may not be Yahweh but instead their own imaginations or their gods.[30] If fulfillment of an oracle authenticates the prophet to be of God (Deut.18:22) and non-fulfillment indicates otherwise, then we will suggest that it is a recipe for the in-flood of false prophets. And what can we say about Abraham when it was claimed that Yahweh told him that his descendants would be slaves in Egypt for 400 years, which eventually took 430years (Gen.15; Acts 7:6; Ex 12:40). Jeremiah prophesied concerning the exile to Babylon, saying, the exile will last for 70 years after which Yahweh will bring back Israel (Jer.25:11; 29:10-14; Ezra 1:1; Dan.9:1-2). Why should Daniel fast and pray for the fulfillment of what Yahweh had promised, since the prophecy was not conditional? Keil and Delitzsch suggest that the prayer of Daniel was motivated by the fact that Yahweh expected repentance from Israel, which had not been done. This can be deduced from the content of Daniel's prayer. And so the test for a true or false prophet cannot be based on fulfillment of prophecy only but also the character and teachings of the prophet after the oracle is delivered and fulfilled.

Prophecy was closely neated with religion in the Ancient Near East. It was one of the means of having knowledge of the future. The desire of the Israelites to know the course of future events, with the assumption that the future is determined, coupled with the fearful experience they had with Yahweh at Mount Sinai and requested that Adonai should not speak to them directly but rather through someone (Ex.19), motivated Moses to promise them another prophet, like himself, who will speak to them in the name of the Lord (Deut.18:15-18). Because Moses had been told by God that he would not lead the people to the Promised Land, and Israel was

---

30. C.F.Keil and F. Delitzsch, *Commentary on the Old Testament, The Pentateuch* (Massachusetts: Hendrickson Publishers, 1989), 363.

likely to embrace the false prophets due to the absence of Moses and the Israelites faith in prophets.

On the issue of false prophets and prophecy, except that the figure of 430 is a hyperbole, legendary or an epic to indicate and intensify the suffering of Israel in Egypt; one may argue that the prophecy was false. The Daniel story was told to point out the human effort in 'helping' God to fulfill what He had promised or else we are tempted to say that the prophecies of Abraham and Jeremiah on those occasions were false or, as human as they were, they are limited in their faculties when it comes to predictive prophecy. King Saul visited a diviner and all that the diviner told him (Saul) came to pass (1sam.28:3–25; 31:1–13). Balaam's prophecies were believed to have come from Yahweh and yet he was seen as an enemy of Yahweh and Israel and was killed (Num.22–24). Can we, as a matter of principle, say that the diviner's and Balaam's prophecies were from God?

DID PROPHECY CEASE?

Scholars are divided on the issue of cessation of prophecy from 400 BCE till the introduction of Christianity in the first century CE. Asante posits that, at the time when Israel was expecting prophetic messages to explain and give meaning to their present happenings, none came up and that there was a general belief that prophecy had ceased after the exile.[31] The scriptures used in support of this claim include: Ps.94:9; Zech.13:2–6; 1Macc.4:46. According to Aune, prophecy never ceased but rather it took a different form due to the *sitz im leben* of the people.[32] Aune's reasons included the suggestion that, since there is no evidence that the 'Spirit of Yahweh' was withdrawn, prophecy cannot be said to have ceased. Aune adds that, even though there are internal questions as to the legitimacy of prophecy in Israel, and seasons where prophecy is prevalent, prophecy never ceased in Israel at the time it was believed to have ceased. According to Meyer, post-exilic prophecy took the form of 'nomistic rationalism'.[33] The uniqueness of prophecy in Israel is that it is able to take different forms due to the changing fortunes of Israel.

It was also believed that Yahweh changed/varied His mode of communication with the prophets to the usage of the *bath qol*, which literally

---

31. Asante, *The Prophetic and Apocalyptic*, 57–58.

32. Aune, *Prophecy in Early Christianity*, 103.

33. Gerhard Kittel, Gerhard Friedrich, (Eds), *Theological Dictionary of the New Testament Vol.vi* (Michigan: WM.B. Eerdmans Publishing Company, 1968), 828.

means 'daughter of voice' or 'voice of a daughter'. In this, Yahweh is believed to have spoken through the occurrence of some natural phenomena like thunder, earth quakes[34] etc. (Job 37:4-5; Isa.30:30; Ps.18:14; 68:38; John 12:28-29). Aune appropriately describes the *bath qol* as 'a heavenly voice or sound which had both oracular and divinatory functions'.[35]

This heavenly voice may sometimes be subjected to interpretation due to the symbolic nature that it possesses. Prophecy in Israel was seen as the influence of the Holy Spirit on the prophets. Can we conveniently say that the Holy Spirit had ceased for a period in Israel? Secondly, persons like John the Baptist were referred to as prophets; Anna was called a prophetess; and Zachariah is said to have prophesied, all within the period where prophecy was believed to have ceased. The argument for the cessation of prophecy is difficult to sustain. Again Jesus' statement in Matthew 10:41 'whoever welcomes a prophet in the name of a prophet will receive a prophet's reward', is indicative of the fact that the idea of prophets and prophecy was still conscious in the minds of the people,[36] even though we cannot necessarily say that consciousness is equal to activity, it can be argued that Matthew's audience seem to have prophets among them.

OLD TESTAMENT PROPHECY AND APOCALYPTIC PHENOMENA

After Israel had returned from the Babylonian exile, coupled with activities of some wicked Emperors, gave rise to apocalyptic phenomena.[37] 'Apocalyptic' is from the Greek αποκαλυπτω, απο –(from or away from)[38] and καλυπτω –('possibly that of hiding, or burying, in the earth . . . . .or generally

---

34. Keil and Delitzsch, *Commentary on the Old Testament, Vol. 5.* 258, 369 . . .
Henry Alford, *Alford's Greek Testament: An Exegetical and Critical Commentary, Vol.1* (Michigan: Baker Book House, 1980), 835.
William Barclay, *The New Daily Study Bible, The Gospel of John, Vol.2* (Bangalore: Theological Publication in India, 2009), 147-148.

35. Aune, *Prophecy in Early Christianity*, 104.

36. Benedict T. Viviano, 'The Gospel According to Matthew' in Raymond E. Brown, Joseph A. Fitzmyer, Roland E. Murphy Eds, *The Jerome Biblical Commentary* (London: Burns & Oates, 2007), 652.

37. J. E. H. Thomson, 'Background of Apocalyptic' in James Orr Ed., *The International Standard Bible Encyclopedia, Volume V* (Grand Rapids: Michigan, WM.B. Eerdmans Publishing Co., 1949), 162.

38. Verbrugge Ed, *New International Dictionary of New Testament Theology*, 56.

to conceal').³⁹ Apocalyptic is a 'type of biblical literature that emphasizes the lifting of the veil between heaven and the earth and the revelation of God and His plans for the world'.⁴⁰

Scholars are divided over the issue of the origin of apocalyptic literature. One school of thought believes that it originated from 'the Jewish wisdom tradition', while others hold that it succeeded prophecy.⁴¹ Since it is revelational in nature, it is likely that it played the role of prophecy when it is predictive. Be it from wisdom tradition or prophecy, both hold that 'apocalyptic' is revelatory/visionary of the supernatural through the medium of angels or supernatural beings.

Even though there is apocalyptic literature embedded in a narrative framework in some Old Testament texts (cf. Isa.6:1–12; 24–27; Eze.30; 37–39; Zech.3:1–10; 9–14), the book of Daniel stands out as fully apocalyptic. Apocalyptic literature is mainly characterized by symbolic language and pseudonymity. It lays claims to what is believed to have been revealed to ancient patriarchs and made manifest concerning the end times, with its special feature of cosmic dualism (this age and the age to come) or the messianic expectation. It gained popularity during the time of severe suffering of the Jewish people in the hands of foreigners. Asante posits that apocalyptic literature tries to interpret and re-apply existing prophecies that are yet to be fulfilled.⁴² It is mainly predictive, but differs from prophecy in that, while prophecy claims it source from Yahweh, apocalypses claims it authenticity from a revelation that a revered ancient person had had, which may not ultimately be attributed to Yahweh.

OLD TESTAMENT PROPHECY AND ESCHATOLOGY

Eschatology is from the Greek εσκατον meaning 'the last event of a series'.⁴³ Eschatology is the study of the last events. Some of the prophets of the Old Testament used eschatological language to introduce a salvific message

---

39. Halle Otto Michel, 'kaluptw' in Kittel and Friedrich Eds, *Theological Dictionary of the New Testament Vol.iii* (Michigan: WM.B.Eedmans Publishing Company, 1965), 556-557.

40. Stephen Motyer, '*Apocalyptic and Revelation*' in Walter A. Elwell Ed, *Baker Theological Dictionary of the Bible* (Michigan: Baker Books, 1996), 28.

41. Asante, *The Prophetic and Apocalyptic*, 50–51.

42. Asante, *The Prophetic and Apocalyptic*, 67–68.

43. Verbrugge Ed, *New International Dictionary of New Testament Theology*, 210–211.

(e.g. 'in the last days')[44] (cf. Isa.2:2; Eze.38:16; Jer.23:20). One characteristic of Eschatology, which gained much popularity during the inter-testamental period, is the comparison between 'this age' and 'the age to come'. Lindblom postulates that, the prophets who spoke about 'this age' spoke of 'positive Eschatology',[45] and those who spoke concerning 'the age to come' spoke about 'negative eschatology'.[46] He adds that, due to the ambiguous, obscure, symbolic, diction and proverbial nature of some prophetic messages, it gave rise to reinterpretation that resulted in Eschatology. [47] For example, Isaiah chapter 9, if studied in context, was a direct prophecy for a son that will be born to Ahaz, but it has been eschatologically reinterpreted to point to the messianic expectation. Eschatology has the tendency of picking pre-exilic prophecy and reinterpreting it to include the future. The belief was that Yahweh has communicated future events to the earlier prophets.

On the other hand, Blenkinsopp postulates that the rise and need of Eschatology was the inability and failure of some earlier prophecies to 'solve certain crucial problems'[48] as expected. In other words, some prophecies were not fully fulfilled. For example, the restoration that was prophesied by Jeremiah concerning the return from exile did not fully materialize. The question of the communities that were the custodians of prophetic literature was how ancient documents that were relevant to their ancestors, whose *sitz im leben* was different from theirs, was relevant to their own days. The need for reinterpretation resulted in Eschatology.[49] For example, 'This was the word that the LORD spoke concerning Moab in the past. But now the LORD says ... (Isaiah 16:13–14a). This clearly shows that an earlier prophecy concerning Moab had been reinterpreted to make it relevant and significant for the present and future.

CONCLUSION

The Old Testament clearly shows that prophetism exists in Israelite's religion. There are various classes of prophets. The shamanistic, and the

---

44. Verbrugge Ed, *New International Dictionary of New Testament Theology*, 210–211.

45. Lindblom, *Prophecy in Ancient Israel*, 361–362.

46. Lindblom, *Prophecy in Ancient Israel*, 361–362.

47. Lindblom, *Prophecy in Ancient Israel*, 361–362.

48. Joseph Blenkinsopp, *A History of Prophecy in Israel: From The Settlement in the Land to the Hellenistic Period* (Philadelphia: The Westminster Press, 1983), 257.

49. Blenkinsopp, *A History of Prophecy in Israel*, 257.

Biblical, Traditional, and Theological Framework

freelance prophets belong to the main category of this study. The ministry activities of this group of prophets strike some similarities with certain activities of traditional African prophets in that the main objective is to minister for solution for existential needs of adherents or seekers. They are also involved in giving some directions (spiritual) based on the dictates of their God/gods. However, the Old Testament prophets were also social reformers: they are the enforcing officers of the stipulations of Adonai to keep a homogeneous society. There is the need to carefully explain the relevance of Old Testament prophetic activity for contemporary Christian society in Ghana. This will help reduce uninformed emulation of Old Testament prophetic activities as being biblical.

Chapter Eight

Prophetism in the Gospels

INTRODUCTION

PROPHETISM IN THE GOSPEL has been an issue of intensed discussion among gospel scholars. Majority of scholars argue that there is no prophetism expressed in the gospels while the minority scholars think otherwise. Prophetism in the Greco-Roman religions serves as the background to the understanding of prophetism in the gospels. This chapter attempts to examine prophetic ministry in the gospels. The role of prophets and their importance are discussed.

PROPHECY IN THE GRECO-ROMAN WORLD

The Greco-Roman period preceded the New Testament and even shaped the world-view of New Testament people. The art of receiving oracular messages from a god was very popular in Greek and Roman religions. The Pythia at Delphi was referred to as προφητης and also προμαντῆς. Her messages were not easy to understand, since she often spoke in an unknown language. Some officials of the shrine had to interpret the message into an intelligible language to the recipient(s).[1] A term that is most often used to describe the activities of knowing the future is μαντης which means a

---

1. Verbrugge ed, *New International Dictionary of New Testament Theology*, 499.

'diviner, soothsayer, seer or less appropriately prophet'.² A Christian prophet is not a mantis/diviner. 'Divination may be defined as the art or science of interpreting symbolic messages from the gods. Often these symbols are unpredictable or even trivial . . . '³. The settings for 'prophetism' in the Greco-Roman world are different from the gospels settings and the kind of prophetic practices in the Greco-Roman world did not metamorphose into prophetism in the gospels.

PROPHETS AND PROPHECY IN THE GOSPELS

John the Baptist

The record of the ministry of John the Baptist can be found mainly in the gospels and in the work of Josephus.⁴ John the Baptist's prophetic ministry/phenomena can be considered contemporaneous to the prophetic ministry in the New Testament. According to the Lukan account, he is the son of Elizabeth and Zachariah. His birth and mission were prophesied by an angel (Luke 1:5–25, 57–66). Jesus refers to him as 'Ἰωάννου τοῦ βαπτιστοῦ' (John the Baptist) (Matt.11:11), in order to differentiate him from other possible Johns and to give recognition to his ministry of baptism.

In addition, Jesus called him περισσότερον προφήτου (more than a prophet), but it is not so clear why Jesus would regard John the Baptist as such. John lived an ascetic life in the wilderness, possibly in Judaea, since his parents lived there. Bruce suggests John might have been trained by the Qumran or Essene community but this is difficult to substantiate,⁵ because the leaders of the Qumran community are referred to as 'Teachers of Righteousness' rather than 'prophets'. John's preaching was eschatological, proclaiming the end of humanity and the world at the coming of the Messiah. He identified Jesus as the Messiah, but when in prison, he sent his disciples to enquire further from Jesus whether He is the Messiah or if someone else is to be expected (Matt.11:2–6). Some scholars think that the question arose as John's disciples were doubting Jesus was the Messiah or

---

2. Aune, *Prophecy in Early Christianity*, 23.

3. Aune, *Prophecy in Early Christianity*, 23.

4. Flavius Josephus, *The New Complete Works Of Josephus* (Michigan: Kregel Publications, 1999), 594–597.

5. F. F. Bruce, "*John the Forerunner,*" *Faith and Thought* 94.3 (Autumn 1965), 182.

from the impatience of John. Since John's message was revolutional,[6] 'His winnowing-fork is in his hand, and he will clear his threshing floor ... (Matt.3:12) and so John would expect Jesus to do something about his imprisonment for him to be freed[7].

Upon careful examination of the text, it seems that, since John knew that he came to prepare the way for Jesus, the Messiah would 'keep the fire burning'. It did not seem to John that Jesus had begun ministry, which is why John sent his disciples to Jesus. Jesus' answer, '... go and tell John what you hear and see; the blind receive their sight, the lame walk, the lepers are cleansed, the deaf hear, the dead are raised and the poor have the good news ...,' confirms the assertion. In other words, Jesus was saying 'the Messiah has begun His work'.

The ministry of John as the Baptizer was a little strange to Jewish culture. Although there are religious washings in the תּוֹרָה: for example, when one comes into contact with what is unclean (Lev.15; Numb.19; Isa.1 15–16) - we do not really know the form of John's baptism be it immersion, aspersion or affusion even though immersion is probable, yet we know that it was once and for all life baptism that required repentance. Colin Brown posits that John's use of the Jordan River for baptism was significant, because it symbolized the entry into the promise land by Israel (Josh. 3; 4; 5,). In effect, John was sanctifying the new Israel to repossess the land in Christ,[8] even though the Fourth Gospel recorded another venue (Aenon) where John baptized, because there was much water there (John 3:23). It can be posited that John's 'prophetic' ministry included the ministry of baptism, preaching and asceticism.

Is Jesus a Prophet?

That Jesus was a prophet does not reduce Him from being the Son of God to a messenger as believed in some religions. Jesus is the Christ, whose function included prophetic activities; for example, His ability to predict His death and resurrection (Mark 8:31–9:1). In addition, His ability to predict His death and resurrection does not make Him any more of a prophet

---

6. William Barclay, *The New Daily study Bible, The Gospel of Matthew Vol.2* (Bangalore: Theological Publications in India, 2009), 2–4.

7. Barclay, *The New Daily study Bible*, 2–4.

8. Colin Brown, "What Was John The Baptist Doing?", *Bulletin for Biblical Research* 7 (1997), 45–47.

Biblical, Traditional, and Theological Framework

than the son of God. After all, the son of God 'knows the mind of God' more than a prophet (see John 16:4–15).

Jesus' prophetic ministry may have allowed Him to preach powerful, revolutionary sermons that were completely new (see Matt.5–7; Luke 4:18ff). Jesus' foresight to know that the enemy had planned to sieve Peter, for example is a prophetic act, which can be seen as aspects of the ministry of various Old Testament prophets. For example, Yahweh spoke to Samuel concerning Saul prior to Samuel's meeting with him (1Sam. 8; 9). Elisha had fore knowledge of what the King of Aram was planning, together with his counselors in his chamber, against Israel (1Kings 6:8–23). Due to the forth telling nature of prophecy in the New Testament, a person can be biblically deemed to be a prophet if his/her actions and inactions makes others see and recognize the involvement of God in human history and the divine purpose of God concerning humans without necessarily fore telling.

To say Jesus is a prophet is to discuss his function and work, not person or status. For instance, Daniel was a prophet but he functioned as adviser to the King of Babylon. Samuel was a prophet but also functioned as a king maker and priest. Ezekiel was a prophet but also functioned as a priest. Jesus referred to Himself as a prophet when His own people rejected Him (Matt.13:57). He also referred to Himself as prophet when He was about to enter Jerusalem in order to die (Luke 13:33). Many a time Jesus prefixed His message with 'truly truly I say to you'; or 'He who has an ear', which are similar to the messenger formula in the Old Testament. The difference is that He quoted Himself rather than Yahweh. The gospel writers believed Jesus to be a prophet.

The Gospels' Presentation of Jesus as a Prophet

In the gospels, the audience referred to Jesus as a prophet. In Mark 6:14–15, in view of the miracles and wonders that Jesus performed, Herod and other persons believed that Jesus was 'John the Baptist incarnate', 'Elijah' or 'other Old Testament prophet'.[9] Hill's assertion is that, it is important to note that the reference to Jesus as one of the prophets was made by non-disciples and that the rendering was an editorial redaction and that the appropriate rendering of the scripture text should be 'This is the prophet Jesus from Nazareth of Galilee'.[10]

9. Aune, *Prophecy in Early Christianity*, 154.
10. Hill, *New Testament Prophecy*, 51.

Prophetism in the Gospels

We have no record that John the Baptist performed any miracle as compared to Elijah or the other prophets. Morison observes that even, though Herod Antipas knew that John did not perform miracles when he was alive, he thought that, by dying, John had acquired some supernatural powers to perform miracles.[11] A similar situation arose when Jesus was on His way with His disciples to the villages of Caesarea Philippi. He asked the disciples, 'who do people say that I am'? The response of the disciples was that, some say 'you are John the Baptist, others say Elijah and again others say one of the prophets' (Matt.16:13-20). This assertion was made by the people because Jesus' ministry was closely synonymous with, but more than the ministry of the Old Testament prophets.

Again when Jesus was arrested and presented before the Council, He was blind folded and struck and was asked to identify (prophesy) who struck Him (Mark 14:65 cf. Matt.26:68 and Luke 22:64). The people were questioning the ability of Jesus, as a prophet to reveal secrets. Hill asserts that 'Jesus was accused before the Supreme Council of being a false prophet'.[12] Based on the above scripture passages, we think that the soldiers knew Him to be a prophet who revealed secrets. That is why He was asked to identify the one who hit Him.

We have a similar situation in Matthew and Luke where the onlookers said He was a prophet. Some scholars attribute it to the 'low Christology' of the crowd.[13] In Matthew 21:11, when Jesus entered Jerusalem and the news spread all over the town the people said 'This is the prophet Jesus, from Nazareth in Galilee'. This statement was further emphasized in Verse 46 'because they regarded Him as a prophet'. In Luke 7:15, the writer narrated a story from the L-source in respect of a miracle that Jesus performed and made the people claim He was a prophet. The crowd might have recalled the mighty works of Elijah and Elisha in relation to raising the dead[14] and categorized Jesus with them.

The Pharisees, however, did not acknowledge Jesus as a prophet. Their argument was based on the so-called sinner who Jesus accepted to anoint Him (Matt.7:39). They believed that if Jesus was truly a prophet as claimed

11. Marvin R. Vincent, *Vincent's Word Studies in the New Testament Vol.1* (Massachusetts: Hendrickson Publishers Inc, 2009), 192.

12. Hill, *New Testament Prophecy*, 52.

13. Viviano, 'The Gospel According to Matthew' in Brown, Fitzmyer, Murphy Eds, *the Jerome*, 664.

14. . Viviano, 'The Gospel According to Matthew' in Brown, Fitzmyer, Murphy Eds, *the Jerome*, 696.

by the crowd, He would have known that the woman was sinful and did not deserve acceptance by Jewish tradition. According to the Law, the touching of unclean persons made one unclean. They expected Jesus to shun the woman; but Jesus is a prophet who forgives sin. Luke 24:19 records a conversation between Cleopas and possibly a disciple/follower of Jesus; they refer to Him as 'a prophet mighty in deed and word'. Hill posits that the disciples saw the prophecy of Moses in Deuteronomy 18:15 being fulfilled in the ministry of Jesus.[15]

Jesus was again recognized as a prophet in the Fourth Gospel. The Samaritan woman at the well called Jesus a prophet because Jesus told her all her past marital challenges (John 4:19). After the miraculous feeding of the five thousand (John 6:14), the crowd identified Jesus as the 'promised prophet' by Moses (Deut.18:15), probably because Yahweh, through the hand of Moses, miraculously fed the Israelites with manna and quails in the wilderness. Again He taught in John 7:40, and the people easily said He was a prophet; but some doubted Him as a prophet because He was from Galilee (John 7:52).

Friedrich, as captured in the work of Hill, remarks that the title 'prophet' is not a self-designation but that Jesus was quoting a popular proverb at the time.[16] Aune added that there is no evidence of the significance of the death of a prophet in Jerusalem in "early Jewish and Christian literature".[17] It is a Christological issue to assert that Jesus is a prophet. It is also important to acknowledge that it is the influence of the Holy Spirit on the human person that makes Him/her a prophet/prophetess and so the prophetic ministry of Jesus emphasizes the fact that Jesus was human and divine.

PROPHETIC FEATURES IN JESUS' MINISTRY

Several prophetic features exist in the speech of Jesus. Aune called it "prophetic rhetoric",[18] which may be similar to the Old Testament prophetic speech: but this is not to suggest continuity between the Old Testament prophetic speech and that of Jesus.

---

15. Hill, *New Testament Prophecy*, 51.
16. Hill, *New Testament Prophecy*, 57.
17. Aune, *Prophecy in Early Christianity*, 156–157.
18. Aune, *Prophecy in Early Christianity*, 164.

Fine Prophetic Speeches

Aune identified five prophetic speeches of Jesus as recorded in the gospels: (i) "(Amen) I say to you"; (ii) "who among you"; (iii) the two-part structure of Jesus' sayings; (iv) pronouncement of sacral law; and (v) the eschatological correlative.[19] We will discuss the most popular of these sayings of Jesus. In the gospels, Jesus mostly introduces His speech with "ἀμὴν ἀμὴν λέγω ὑμῖν". It is comparable to the messenger formula of the Old Testament prophets "thus says the Lord", which authenticates the messenger's message as originating from Yahweh. The difference is that Jesus quoted Himself instead of Yahweh who his predecessors quoted.

The phrase 'ἀμὴν ἀμὴν λέγω ὑμῖν' is not a 'functional equivalent' of 'thus says the Lord' but it indicates the 'unique authority claimed by Jesus'.[20] Some scholars have critiqued the form of the phrase. V. Hasler thinks that the phrase 'ἀμὴν ἀμὴν λέγω ὑμῖν' was not coined by Jesus and that it develops in the liturgy of the Jewish-Hellenistic community, which was placed on Jesus' lips by the gospel writers.[21] Klaus Berger, as stated in the work of Hill, posits that ἀμὴν existed in the apocalyptic literature and was used to introduce oath speeches,[22] which was later found in an expanded form on the lips of Jesus and adopted into the New Testament document by the various evangelists.

CONCLUSION

The above discussion shows that, in comparison to the Old Testament, the activities of prophets and prophecy is limited in the Gospels. It may be due to the assertion that prophecy ceased during the intertestamental period, and Jesus, who is the main character in the gospels, did not present Himself as a prophet like those of the Old Testament, which the audience and authors of the gospels were familiar with. He presented Himself as a Messiah whose work includes prophetic activities. His presentation of John the Baptist as "more than a prophet" points to the fact that there is a ministry gift beyond that of the prophet. In other words, He was disabusing the Old Testament aura that has been attached to the ministry of the prophets.

19. Aune, *Prophecy in Early Christianity*, 164–169.
20. Aune, *Prophecy in Early Christianity*, 164.
21. Hill, *New Testament Prophecy*, 65.
22. Hill, *New Testament Prophecy*, 65.

However, His prefix to some significant statements agrees with the messenger formula used by Old Testament prophets.

Chapter Nine

Prophetism in Early Christianity

INTRODUCTION

PROPHETS AND PROPHECY PLAYED a significant role in early Christianity until the institutionalization of the Church in the second century CE.[1] Luke gave considerable attention to the work of the Holy Spirit in his gospel. It is not out of context that we see the work of the Holy Spirit in the life of the followers of Jesus in his second book, Acts. Acts is prefixed, in chapter two, with the pouring of the Holy Spirit on the believers on the Day of Pentecost. Peter's interpretation of the event was that it is the fulfillment of what Joel had prophesied in 2:28–29. One of the reasons for the Spirit is for the sons and daughters to prophesy. This means that a lot of prophetic activities would have been in operation, perhaps more than what is recorded in the Old Testament.

PROPHETS IN THE BOOK OF ACTS

David Hill refers to some individuals in the book of Acts as 'prophets', although they were not called prophets by the writer. For instance, Hill posits that Philip was a prophet because firstly, it was reported that he was full of the Holy Spirit; secondly, he performed miracles and signs in Samaria; and thirdly, he was carried by the Holy Spirit to Azotus to minister to the

---

1. Aune, *Prophecy in Early Christianity*, 189.

Biblical, Traditional, and Theological Framework

Ethiopian Eunuch.[2] The presence of the Holy Spirit in the life of the believer and the ability to perform miracles does not necessarily qualify someone to be a prophet, or else we will be compelled to say, then, that all believers are prophets, because the Holy Spirit lives in each believer (1Cor.3:16). We are also encouraged to be filled with the Holy Spirit always (Eph.5:18); and again each believer is expected to ". . . cast out demons; speak in new tongues; pick up snakes; and if they drink any deadly thing, it will not hurt them; they will lay hand on the sick and they will recover" (Mark 16:17–18).

Hill refers to Barnabas as a prophet[3] because of the meaning of his name (comforter or son of consolation). Except that we can prove that Barnabas lived to fulfill the meaning of his name, other than that it is not legitimate to call someone a prophet based on the meaning of his name. There are certain persons in Acts who had visions and revelations and consoled and comforted other people but were not called prophets. For example, the Apostle Peter had visions prior to the coming of the messengers of Cornelius (Acts 10:9–21); had the ability to know the secrets of other people's hearts (Acts 5:3). A disciple named Ananias in Damascus had a vision from the Lord concerning the call of Paul to the ministry and he was asked by the Lord to go and pray for the restoration of Paul's eyes and to baptize him. Ananias also comforted Paul.

The Apostle Paul had revelations concerning their voyage to Rome (Acts 27:21–24). He comforted and consoled most of the Churches he founded, when he was due to move on to other places (Acts 14:21–28). It is amazing to state that all these notable and influential individuals in the early communities of believers were not called prophets. Thus, in Acts, having visions and revelations, performing miracles and comforting others does not necessarily make one a prophet, therefore miracles and visions etc. is not the preserve of prophets.

Certain individuals were called prophets in the book of Acts, but we do not fully know the nature of their ministry. In Acts 11:27–30, we read that a company of προφῆται (prophets) came from Jerusalem to Antioch. One of them, Agabus (Ἄγαβος ἐσήμανεν διὰ τοῦ πνεύματος) predicted, through the Spirit, a severe famine that, indeed, came to pass. According to Johnson, this prophecy was fulfilled in the flooding of river Nile in 45 CE,

---

2. Hill, *New Testament Prophecy*, 100–101.
3. Hill, *New Testament Prophecy*, 101–103.

which led to the destruction of farm produce and affected the then known world.[4] Marshall also asserts that there was famine in Judea in c. 46 CE.

This prophecy lacks specificity in relation to time, and so Jeremias said that Agabus' prophecy was a mere coincidence, since the years 47–48 BCE were sabbatical years and famine was possible for those who did not plan.[5] This same Agabus was seen in Acts 21:10ff, where he prophesied concerning the arrest of Paul in Jerusalem. This prophecy was fulfilled in Acts 21:27–36ff. However, the prophecy did not tell Paul what he should do. It was open to the choice of Paul and so can we really suggest that Paul disobeyed/disregarded the prophecy? We can also say that Agabus' prophecy was not accurate because he is human and cannot understand everything of the Spirit of God.

In Acts 13:1, we read about five persons, including Saul and Barnabas who were called προφῆται καὶ διδάσκαλοι (teachers and prophets) in the Church of Antioch. It is not clear as to who among them is a teacher or a prophet or both. Some scholars argue that, taking into consideration the arrangement of the words in the verse i.e. προφῆται coming before διδάσκαλοι, it is likely that Barnabas, Simeon and Lucius were prophets and Manaen and Saul were teachers.[6] But by our definition, and looking at the work of Paul, he can better be described as a prophet.

Again in Acts 15: 32, it is recorded that two persons (Judas and Silas), who were προφῆται were sent by the Jerusalem Church to proclaim its decision to the Gentile believers in Antioch. These prophets also exhorted the Antioch Church to be steadfast in the teachings of Jesus Christ. From the above discussion, we can deduce that the prophets, together with the help of other persons in the Early Church, played significant roles in the establishment and growth of the Church. The coming of the prophets from Jerusalem to Antioch, where Agabus prophesied about the famine and the sending of prophets to announce the decision of the Council, is indicative that they played a missionary role, and were involved in giving guidance to missionaries. For instance, Agabus' prophecy to Paul concerning his arrest in Jerusalem and the prophecy to set apart Barnabas and Saul for missionary work (Acts 13:1–3), prepared Paul and Barnabas for the missionary

---

4. Dennis E. Johnson, *Let's Study Acts (Edinburgh*: The Banner of Truth Trust,2003), 146.

5. I. Howard Marshall, *Tyndale New Testament Commentaries: The Acts of the Apostles* (Michigan: Wm. B. Eerdmans Publishing Company, 1980), 204.

6. Henry, *Alford's Greek Testament Vol.II*, 138–139.

Biblical, Traditional, and Theological Framework

task ahead. This prophecy came with clear direction to those for which they were intended.

Other People who Prophesied in the Book of Acts

There were other persons who had prophetic revelations and prophesied in the book of Acts but were not called prophets. The disciples in Ephesus (Acts 19:6) were said to have spoken in tongues and prophesied. We do not know the content of their prophecy or who they prophesied to but we note that the gift of tongues served as stimulus for the manifestation of prophecy and there are references in the Bible suggesting that the gift of tongues and prophecy can be received through the laying on of hands (Acts 19:6); and in some cases it can be received through preaching the word of God (Acts 10).

In Acts 21:4, there were certain disciples in Tyre who prophesied concerning the arrest of Paul if he should go to Jerusalem. Their prophecy preceded Agabus' prophecy on the same matter. We are not told their number and probably one of them might have given the prophecy on behalf of the group. The prophecy was specific that Paul should not go to Jerusalem but no reasons were given. Again in Acts 21:9, we learn about four unmarried daughters of Philip, the evangelist, who had the gift of prophecy. Marshall posits that it is unclear if their unmarriedness had anything to do with the gift of prophecy[7] as was the ascetic life of John the Baptist and other Old Testament prophets. None of their prophecies were recorded.

We argue that the contrast between prophets and those who had the gift of prophecy is that the prophets were missionary minded in their role, while those who merely had the gift of prophecy were stationed in a Church setting. The above discussion, coupled with 1Thes.5:21, which is one of the earliest epistles where Paul is reported to have said that we should not despise prophecy, indicates that prophets and prophecy, prayer and the word of God were held in high esteem in the Early Church.

PROPHETS AND PROPHECY IN PAULINE LITERATURE

The word 'Pauline' will refer to both the disputed (deutero-Pauline) and undisputed[8] epistles of Paul. Paul dealt with issues of prophets, prophecy

---

7. Marshall, *The Acts of the Apostles*, 339–340.

8. Dennis C. Duling, *The New Testament: History, Literature and Social Context* 4th Ed. (Canada: Wadsworth, 2003). 140.

and their role in the Church community, which is relevant to this work. Pauline literature is mostly situational in nature. The epistles were written to address particular needs of particular congregations.[9] The book of Romans seems to be the general one among them. However, there are perceived issues Paul was dealing with in the letter. For instance, the rhetorical issues raised with the imaginary interlocutor such as marriage, sex etc. may have prevailed in the Roman Church at the time. This makes it implausible to use one epistle of Paul as a standard for others in a different *sitz im leben*.

No name of a prophet was mentioned in Pauline literature. However, Paul appears to define their activities in the Church. Some scholars see Paul as a prophet due to the prophetic features of visions and revelations that characterized his ministry. He often refers to himself as 'apostle' rather than prophet.[10] We suggest that he is both an apostle and a prophet. The rule that should regulate the activities of the prophets in the Church is best outlined in 1Cor. 14. In 1 Cor.14:29a, Paul says that two or three prophets should be allowed to speak in a church meeting. The restriction indicates that there must have been a lot[11] of prophets who would like to speak in a meeting. And there were also abuses in how the gift of prophecy was being practiced. Hill strikingly asserts that the interest to be called a prophet was very high in the Corinthian Church and this pushed Paul to ask the question μὴ πάντες προφῆται[12] (1 Cor.12:29). Paul added in verse 3, that when a prophet is speaking and a revelation is given to another prophet, who is sitting, the prophet speaking must make way for the one sitting to speak. The reason is for orderliness in the service.

While a prophet is speaking, the others sitting were ask to διακρινέτωσαν· (judge or evaluate) what is being said (1Cor.14:29b). Turner suggests that *diakrino* in the text actually refers to grading of the prophecy.[13] In other words, it concerns which prophecy is weightier, or more important than others and whether it was a true or false decision. Hill shares Grudem's position that, due to the subjection of New Testament prophecy to judgment by other prophets, New Testament prophecy is not as authoritative as their Old Testament counterparts.[14] We suggest that judgment of prophecy

9. Duling, *The New Testament*, 197–198.
10. Aune, *Prophecy in Early Christianity*, 248.
11. Turner, *The Holy Spirit*, 204.
12. Hill, *New Testament Prophecy*, 120.
13. Turner, *The Holy Spirit*, 207.
14. Hill, *New Testament Prophecy*, 135.

Biblical, Traditional, and Theological Framework

here is to check if the prophecy agrees with the teachings of Jesus or the Bible, since there were a lot of people who wanted to be heard.

If prophecies from prophets need to be judged then we are implicitly saying that somebody must exercise authority over the prophecies of the prophets. Secondly, if the sitting prophets will have to judge the prophecies of the speaking prophet, then the service is likely to take a long time, even though Paul directed that a maximum of three prophets should speak. Thirdly, if truly Paul's usage of διακρινέτωσαν means differentiating between true and false prophecies, then this is a recipe for confusion because each prophet would defend his/her prophecy. Paul teaches that God is not the author of confusion (1Cor.14:33). If modalities are properly defined and if the prophets are being led by the Holy Spirit, then there would be no confusion.

It can be argued that, if God, who is the author of prophecy, cannot prevent the speaking prophet from making mistake(s) in the delivery of prophecy, how sure are we that He will prevent the sitting prophet from making mistake(s)? We note that God's people can make mistakes. The interpretation of tongues into intelligible language (1 Cor.14:27) can be deemed to be prophecy, but we have not read about judging such utterances. Notwithstanding, we are urged to test every spirit (1John 4:1). Perhaps the judgment Paul was referring to was in relation to visiting prophet(s), whose activities were common in the Early Church. In Acts, we have records of a visiting company of prophets (see 11:27–30; 15:32). When these prophetic missionaries visited congregations they were given the opportunity to share the word of God, which may also lead to giving prophecy (see 13:15–16, 42; 17:10–15).

The prophetic ministry is recognized as offices in Pauline literature (1 Cor.12:28; Eph.4:11). In 1 Corinthians. 12:28, it seems Paul ranked the prophets next to the Apostle πρῶτον ἀποστόλους, δεύτερον προφήτας, τρίτον διδασκάλους, and Hill suggests that pastors and teachers were a later interpolation to indicate 'ecclesiastical unity' rather than charismatic endowment.[15] Listing ideas in points, say: (a), (b), (c) etc. does not necessarily suggest hierarchy, but systematization and logic. Paul urged the Corinthian Church to desire the gifts of the Holy Spirit, especially prophecy, so as to build the Church (1 Cor.14:1). This assertion is indicative of the fact that the gift of prophecy was crucial to the growth of the Corinthian Church at

---

15. Hill, *New Testament Prophecy*, 138–139.

Prophetism in Early Christianity

the time. It seems, in the thoughts of Paul, that the gift of prophecy is first among equals.

In Romans 12:6, Paul pointed out that prophecy should be given according to the proportion of faith. Barrett's comment on the statement is that the proportion of faith represents the Christian faith.[16] Dunn points out that 'proportion of faith' refers to a right relationship with the giver of the revelation (God).[17] The text under discussion suggests mathematics. One needs to reach a certain level of faith in order to either receive a prophetic revelation or deliver a prophetic message.

In 1 Corinthians.11:5, Paul permits women to prophesy in the Church if they fulfill the cultural requirements. Jewish law generally identified women with property. They were considered the property of the father or husband and were not counted among the required number of people needed to start a worship service.[18] If God had chosen these women to prophesy, who could deny them? Women were not recorded working miracles like their male counterparts in the New Testament, but when it came to prophecy, they were reported prophesying, just like their male counterparts, although most of them were not designated 'prophetesses'. It is surprising to realized that the NRSV refers to Anna as prophet instead of prophetess (Luke 2:36).

Paul teaches that predictive prophecy is to be a revelation that leads to repentance (1 Cor.14:24–25). He expected each member of the Corinthian Church to prophesy, and not only those who were called 'prophets.' This seems to be the fulfillment of Moses' desire (Numb.11:29) and the presence of the Holy Spirit in the heart of believers (1Cor.3:16). Aune asserts that most Early Church members were potential prophets or possessed the ability to prophesy.[19] The nature of prophetic revelation must not glorify the one who prophesies but must glorify and lead people to Christ.

---

16. C.K. Barrett, *A Commentary On The Epistle To The Romans* (London: Adam & Charles Black, 1957), 237–238.

17. James D. G. Dunn, *Word Biblical Commentary: Romans 9–16* (Texas: Word Book, Publisher, 1988), 726–727.

18. William Barclay, *The New Daily Study Bible: The Letter To The Corinthians* (Bangalore: Theological Publications In India, 2009), 116.

19. Aune, *Prophecy in Early Christianity*, 200–201.

Biblical, Traditional, and Theological Framework

DID PROPHECY CEASE?

There is no scripture passage that directly states that prophecy will cease apart from 1Corrithians 13:8. The statement '... when the perfect comes...', can be interpreted to mean (i) when the 'Church reached maturity';[20] (ii) Gentiles are included in the church; (iii) when the last apostle dies; (iv) when the canon of the Bible is completed; and (v) the second coming of Jesus.[21] It is difficult to settle on any one of the above interpretations. The argument is that prophecy and other gifts of the Holy Spirit will cease provided the interpretations above are correct since prophecy is partial knowledge. Hill's assertions that Christ/God who is transcendent from humans and therefore speaks through the prophets and other gifted persons, is now with us and so there is no need for prophecy.

Gifts and ministries are given for the perfecting of the saints (Eph.4:11). Some of the arguments on ceasationism are based on Ephesians 2:20; in that, if these gifts/ministries were used as the foundation for the Church, now that the Church is established, there is no need for them. The scripture does not suggest so, but rather, what is to be built on the foundation must conform to the materials used in the foundation or must also conform to the bearing capacity of the foundation. In other words, the foundation design is based on the feasibility study that has been done and the building must conform to it; and one needs expertise in feasibility studies in order to build the needed structure on the foundation.

Cessationists suggest that prophecy amounts to new revelations as based on the exploits of Montanism to add to the scriptures.[22] Since the scriptures have been canonized there is no need for any additions. This is true. However, New Testament prophecy is not intended to add unto scripture but to give personal and specific directions to individuals, which do not contradict the scriptures. For example, the caution to Timothy not to ignore a word of prophecy that was given to him personally (1Tim.4:14). Prophecy is meant to edify, exhort and comfort (1Cor.14:3) and the Church today needs them. Since genuine prophecy would have to conform to

---

20. Turner, *The Holy Spirit*, 287.

21. Hill, *New Testament Prophecy*, 136–137.

22. George Mallone, *Those Controversial Gifts: Prophecy, Dreams, Visions, Tongues, Interpretation, Healing* (Illinois: InterVarsity Press, 1983), 18–19..

Montanism is a second century prophetic group who claim to have new revelation that should be added to the Bible. They contributed to the canonization of the New Testament. It was later discovered that this group is not Christian.

scripture, it is possible to also receive 'prophetic direction' from a study of scripture. Because our definition of prophecy includes forth telling and fore telling, it is not necessary to prefix 'prophecy' with 'Thus sayeth the Lord' in order to give any authentication.

History has indicated that, since the death of the Apostles and their disciples, there has been a decline in the manifestation of the gifts of the Holy Spirit. Yet decline does not mean cessation or the withdrawal of the gifts of the Holy Spirit and silence does not necessarily mean absence.[23] The institutionalization of the Church did not make room for the operation of prophecy, because leadership was by apostolic succession and those who possess the gifts were ridiculed and described as practicing magic.[24] Ministry, conferred by ordination, was much more recognized than ministry through charismatic giftings,[25] because it led to chaos in Corinth. The institutionalization of the Church led to the decline of prophets and prophecy in the Church in successive years.

CONCLUSION

The book of Acts and some Pauline epistles clearly indicate that there were prophetic activities in the Early Church. The Spirit of prophecy that was believed to have ceased during the intertestamental period is believed to have been restored on the "Day of Pentecost" when the Holy Spirit was poured. Jewish theology closely associates prophecy with the presence of the Spirit of God. Hence, the restoration of prophecy was expected to probably establish the church and indicate to the Jewish community in which the church begun, that the God known in the Old Testament is the same God working in the New Testament.

---

23. Mallone, *Those Controversial Gifts*, 22.
24. Mallone, *Those Controversial Gifts*, 24–25.
25. Hill, *New Testament Prophecy*, 190–192.

Chapter Ten

Prophetism in *Corpus Paulinum*

A Case of 1 Corinthians 14:26-40

INTRODUCTION

THIS CHAPTER UNDERTAKES EXEGESIS of 1 Corinthians 14:26-40 from a grammatico-historical and religio-cultural perspective. J. S. Hafemann stated that "more than perhaps any other of the Pauline letters, the sociological characteristics of Corinth, together with the religious and philosophical milieu of the region, influence one's interpretation of 1 Corinthian...".[1] More specifically, it sought to discuss pneumatological experience of the pre-Christian life of some Corinthian Christians, which they unconsciously attempted to import into the Church (as evident in the pericope and Paul's teaching concerning Christian pneumatology and prophetism). I divide the pericope into six subtitles: exordium v. 26; exercising the gift of speaking in tongues in the church vv. 27-28; guidelines for prophets and prophecy in the church vv. 29-33a; restriction on women speaking in the church vv. 33b-36; a test for prophet's prophecies vv. 37-38; and concluding

---

1. Scott J. Hafemann, "Corinthians, Letters to the" in Gerald F. Hawthorne, Ralph P. Martin and Daniel G. Reid (Eds.) *Dictionary of Paul and His Letters* (Downers Grove, Illinois and Leicester, England: InterVarsity Press, 1993), 172.

remarks vv. 39–40. It asserts that, in the pericope, in view of the fact that many Christians can potentially have revelations and prophesy, prophetic ministry is a function not an office.

THE STRUCTURE OF 1 CORINTHIANS 14:26–40

There was a switch from exhortation/discussion about general religious conduct (in chapter 8 to the end of chapter 11) to spiritual matters (chapter 12–14). The preposition genitive περὶ (concerning",[2] "about",[3] in reference of) in 1 Corinthians 12:1 indicates a switch of attention or focus onto a new issue. 1 Corinthians 14:26–40 is the concluding remark of Paul's exposé concerning spiritual persons and their endowments in the Corinthian Church. Many scholars have structured 1 Corinthians 14:26–40 depending on the methodology used and the purpose for the study.

In the attempt to formulate Christian spirituality for the church, W. R. Willoughby structured 1 Corinthians 14:26–40 thus: "instruction to speakers" (14:26–33a); "instruction to women" (1 Cor.14:33b-37); and "instructions to the spiritually gifted" (14:36–40).[4] Willoughby's structure seems to support the notion that πνευματικῶν in 12:1 should be translated "spiritual persons" rather than "spiritual gifts".[5] Consequently, he did not take into account the other gifts of the Holy Spirit that Paul mentioned in the passage, especially the priority of prophecy over speaking in tongues in the Corinthian context. He likewise did not touch on the gloss interpolation of vv. 33b-36, which has been an issue of debate among New Testament scholars.

G. C. Morgan structured 14:26–40 as: "general principle" (14:26); "particular instruction" (14:27–33a); "parenthesis, women" (14:33b-35); and "final words" (14:36–40).[6] To a large extent, Morgan's structure agrees with that of Willoughby in translating πνευματικῶν as spiritual persons

---

2. Daniel B. Wallace, *Greek Grammar Beyond the Basics: An Exegetical Syntax of the New Testament* (Grand Rapids, Michigan: Zondervan, 1996), 379, 744.

3. John D. Kwamena Ekem & Seth Kissi, *Essentials of Biblical Greek Morphology with an Introductory Syntax* (Accra: SonLife Press, 2010), 59.

4. W. Robert Willoughby, *First Corinthians: Fostering Spirituality* (Camp Hill, Pennsylvania: Christian Publications, Inc., n.d.), 204–207.

5. Ekem, "Spiritual Gifts" or "Spiritual Persons"?, 58.

6. G. Campbell Morgan, *The Corinthian Letters of Paul: An Exposition of I and II Corinthians* (Old Tappan, New Jersey: Fleming H. Revell Company, 1946), 167.

Biblical, Traditional, and Theological Framework

and indicates that the instruction concerning women's participation in church service could be an interpolation. A. Robertson and A. Plummer structured (14:26–40) thus: (14:26–33) as instruction concerning the exercise of the gift of speaking in tongues and prophecy in the church, and (14:34–40) as instruction concerning women in public worship service and "final exhortation".[7] The structure propounded by Robertson and Plummer recognizes prophecy and tongue - speaking but does not show the preference of prophecy over speaking in tongues in the church. It does not seem to isolate 1 Corinthians 14:33b-37, the segment that is widely believed to be interpolated into the pericope.

In the pericope under discussion, there is paranomasia of key words featured repetitively and relatively. Critical analysis of these words will help frame an appropriate title and structure for the pericope. Λαλεω (speak) in its various forms appeared six times. Ἐν ἐκκλησίᾳ, ταῖς ἐκκλησίαις (In the church/the churches) and its cognate συνέρχησθε (assembly) appear five times. Σιγάτω (silent) in its various forms appeared three times. Προφητευω (prophesy), ἀποκάλυψις (revelation), and προφήτης (prophet) in their various forms appear eight times. Γλῶσσα (tongue) appeared three times in its various forms. This suggests that the pericope could be titled thus: Regulations concerning the exercise of the gifts of speaking in tongue and prophecy in church service to foster mutual growth. It could be structured as follows:

- Exordium (v.26)
- Exercising the Gift of Tongues in the Church (vv.27–28)
- Guidelines for Prophets and Prophecy in the Church (vv.29–33a)
- Restriction on Women Speaking in the Church (vv.33b-36)
- A Test for Prophets (vv.37–38)
- Concluding Remarks (vv.39–40)

---

7. Archibald Robertson and Alfred Plummer, *A Critical and Exegetical Commentary on the First Epistle of St Paul to the Corinthians* (Edinburgh: T&T Clark Ltd., 1999), 319–324.

Prophetism in Corpus Paulinum

Exordium (v.26)

In the opening statement of the pericope, Paul used ἀδελφοί, (brethren) to indicate the affectionate relationship that existed between him and the Corinthian Church. Ἀδελφοί, and ἀδελφη could be used to refer to biological siblings, however that is not the case in this context. According to W. Günther, ἀδελφοί, is the compound of *delphys,* which denotes the idea of being born from the same womb.[8] Stoic[9] philosophy,[10] which was dominant in Corinth, used ἀδελφοί, to express "monism" that existed among humans despite diversity in reasoning.[11] Hence Paul contended that, although there may exist diversities between him and the Corinthian Church, there was oneness and unity; in other words, there was the binding effect of ἀδελφοί, between him and the audience.

In the process of deifying Ptolemy II and his wife Arsinoe II, *theoi adelphoi* ("sibling gods") was used to describe their relationship,[12] since they were alive and living together. When Hegesippus of Palestine visited Corinth in the late first century, he testified of a feud in the Corinthian Church to the Church in Rome. The feud had to do with the charismatically gifted new generation who tried to overthrow the leadership of the Church and had started holding separate worship services beside the regular Church service.[13] Consequently, in the attempt to help resolve the impasse in the Corinthian Church, Clement of Rome used ἀδελφοί, (1 Clem.1:5; 2

---

8. W. Günther, "ἀδελφος" in Colin Brown (Ed.) *The New International Dictionary of New Testament Theology* (Grand Rapids, Michigan: Zondervan Publishing House, 1975), 255.

9. Stoicism was propounded by Zeno of Citium in Athens between (332–260 BCE). The name was derived from the Greek *stoa*—a painted porch in the market place where proponents of stoicism initially held public teachings. Stoicism was introduced in Rome in 161 CE by Panaetius and was given a louder voice by Seneca (ca. 4 BCE-65 CE) a contemporary of Paul. See Tate, *Handbook for Biblical Interpretation*, 55.

10. Philosophy is the love for wisdom and knowledge and the quest to seek them diligently. It also teaches strict ascetic living in search for wisdom and knowledge. Epicurean and Stoic philosophers were popular during Paul's day (Acts 17:18ff). See R. Allen Killen, "Philosophy" in Charles F. Pfeiffer, Howard F. Vos, John Rea (Eds.) *Wycliffe Bible Dictionary* (Peabody, Massachusetts: Hendrickson Publishers, Inc., 2008), 1336–1337.

11. Günther, "avdelfoj", 255.

12. David E. Aune, "Religions, Greco-Roman" in Gerald F. Hawthorne, Ralph P. Martin and Daniel G. Reid (Eds.) *Dictionary of Paul and His Letters* (Downers Grove, Illinois and Leicester: InterVarsity Press, 1993), 792.

13. Hans Lietzmann, *A History of the Early Church: The Beginning of the Christian Church* (Cleveland and New York: The World Publishing Company, 1953), 192–202.

Biblical, Traditional, and Theological Framework

Clem. 1:1) in the opening statements of his epistles to the Corinthians to signify that both the Roman and the Corinthian Christians believed in one Christ, therefore the need for harmony.

According to G. Kittel, Paul generally used ἀγαπητοὶ and ἀδελφοί, (1 Thess. 2:8–9; Phlm 16) interchangeably as a "guiding principle for the welfare of the brotherhood".[14] Paul's use of ἀδελφοί, was not for a biological relationship, but was used rhetorically to show his affectionate relationship as founder of the Corinthian Church in order to draw the attention of the recipients to pertinent issues. In other words, Paul used ἀδελφοί, to show the affection that existed among members of the brotherhood (Christ) to which he and the Corinthian Church belonged. The subjunctive compound συνέρχομαι, means "come together",[15] or "go with, gather together"[16] by ourselves. The subjunctive mood depicts a state of "volitional notion, . . . probability, . . . contingency",[17] and "doubtful assertion".[18] It may not have been about usual weekly meetings, but it is likely to be a gathering or amalgamation of house-churches in Corinth although it is not very certain.

However, J. W. Grundmann asserted that, in Pauline thought, συν is mostly used syntactically with datives to signify the idea of being together constantly with Christ.[19] Morgan postulates that, since some members of the Corinthian Church may come to the gathering with some gifts of the Spirit, συνέρχομαι is not gathering to preach to non-Christians in order to convert them to the faith. It is a gathering for fellowship among the Corinthian Christians themselves. Morgan's view suggests that all the Churches in Corinth come together in a fellowship periodically. This view could be supported by the use of the temporal particle ὅταν (whenever, any period). If this is so, Paul could have made reference to the organizers of the fellowship and tasked them for orderly conduct of the spiritually-gifted saints,

---

14. Gerhard Kittel, "ἀγαπαω, ἀγαπη,, ἀγαπητος ὅ φιλεω" in Gerhard Kittel (Ed.) *Theological Dictionary of the New Testament* Vol. I (Grand Rapids, Michigan: Wm. B. Eerdmans Publishing Company, 1964), 51.

15. Thomas A. Robinson, *Mastering New Testament Greek: Essential Tools for Students* (Peabody, Massachusetts: Hendrickson Publishers, Inc., 2007), 13.

16. Ekem & Kissi, *Essentials of Biblical Greek*, 165.

17. Wallace, *Greek Grammar Beyond the Basics*, 463.

18. Ekem & Kissi, *Essentials of Biblical Greek*, 135.

19. Jena Walter Grundmann, "σύν - μετά, "in Gerhard Kittel and Gerhard Friedrich (Eds.) *Theological Dictionary of the New Testament* Vol. VIII (Grand Rapids, Michigan: Wm. B. Eerdmans Publishing Company,1964), 781.

which Paul did not mention. Contrarily, C. Hodge argues that συνέρχομαι refers to any meeting of the Corinthian Church at separate venues where the gifts of the Spirit were expected to manifest.[20]

Συνέρχομαι occurred in 1 Corinthians 11:17, 18, 20, 33, 34 referring to coming together to worship. It is plausible that, in view of the fact that many members of the house churches in Corinth were not Jews,[21] Paul rhetorically used συνέρχομαι to refer to the gathering of individual members of the Corinthian Church at separate venues, so that both Jews and non-Jewish members of the Church would understand the scope of his instruction on the exercise of spiritual gifts. It is probable that Paul used συνέρχομαι in the exordium to refer to all meetings on any day because the use of ἐκκλησία in the exordium may have connoted a congregation with a deep Jewish background.

Scholars have divergent opinions concerning the use of ψαλμὸς (hymn or psalm). What is ψαλμὸς in a non-Jewish dominated Corinthian Church. Should ψαλμὸς be understood as the psalms in the Hebrew Bible or hymns in socio-religious culture of Corinth? According to H. G. Delling, "ψαλμὸς means 'plucking' the string of a bow ... or playing a string instrument".[22] During the time of Paul in Corinth, there was the worship of Isis and Serapis, Egyptian goddesses whose adherents use hymns as the major element for inspiration for spirit possession to prophesy.[23]

Archeologists have discovered a papyri on which a hymn had been composed by a Ptolemaic ruler who might have reigned from (221–205 BCE).[24] The hymn can be described as *epiclesis*. It praised and acknowledged the support and assistance of Hermes, "Sun god" and Zeus in making him a great King and then declared his love for Isis for future support. Delling further added that one of the means of receiving personal revelation

---

20. Charles Hodge, *A commentary on 1 & 2 Corinthians* (Edinburgh and Pennsylvania, The Banner of Truth Trust, 1994), 300.

21. Ekem, "Spiritual Gifts" or "Spiritual Persons"?, 63.

22. Halle Gerhard Delling, "ψαλμὸς" in Gerhard Kittel and Gerhard Friedrich (Eds.) *Theological Dictionary of the New Testament* Vol. VIII (Grand Rapids, Michigan: Wm. B. Eerdmans Publishing Company,1964), 491.

23. See Lietzmann, *A History of the Early Church*, 163–164. See also N. C. Croy, "Religion, Personal" in Craig A. Evans & Stanley E. Porter (Eds.) *Dictionary of New Testament Background* (Downer Grove, Illinois and Nottingham, England: InterVarsity Press, 2000), 929.

24. S. R. Llewelyn, "The King as 'Living Image' of Zeus" in S. R. Llewelyn (Ed.) *New Document Illustrating Early Christianity* Vol. 9 (Grand Rapids, Michigan and Cambridge: Wm. B. Eerdmans Publishing Company, 2002), 36.

Biblical, Traditional, and Theological Framework

from Isis was through the singing of hymns.[25] Some of the hymns were composed and documented while others were sung spontaneously without being documented.

J. Moffatt asserts that the transliteration of ψαλμὸς in 1 Corinthians as (psalms) is misleading because it directly points to the Old Testament Psalms. He elaborates that Paul meant ψαλμὸς to be understood as hymns that included praises and prayers to God.[26] On the basis of the English word supplied for ψαλμὸς as hymn in some Greek MSS,[27] C. K. Barrett and J. Murphy-O'Connor concluded that ψαλμὸς in this context refers to "fresh, perhaps spontaneous composition, not an Old Testament psalm".[28] Both Moffatt and Barrett's assertion took care of the fact that many of the Corinthian Christians might not have known the psalms in the Old Testament; neither did Paul set out time in his eighteen months ministry in Corinth to teach them the psalms.

In view of the significance of hymns in worship services in the Early Church (Col.3:16; Eph.5:18–20), and Paul's desire to win people for Christ without barriers, ψαλμὸς may not have been the psalms in the Old Testament. In order to make socio-religious meaning of ψαλμὸς, it may be understood as spontaneous or skillfully composed hymns, which may be parallel to the psalms in the Old Testament but not the same as the psalms in the Old Testament. In other words, ψαλμὸς could have referred to cultic[29] songs that led to inspiration and can be referred to as *epiclesis*. In the African Traditional Religious settings, ψαλμὸς could be referred to cult songs that usually lead to possession by a deity/spirit.

Διδαχή (teaching), expresses the idea of a pupil receiving instruction from a teacher. Hodge suggests that διδαχή refers to expounding doctrinal

---

25. Delling, "ψαλμὸς", 492.

26. James Moffatt, *The First Epistle of Paul to the Corinthians* (London: Hodder and Stoughton, 1938), 227.

27. MSS refers to a manuscript(s) of Church Fathers texts. In this case, it is probable to be a variant reading of Origen's manuscript.

28. See C. K. Barrett, *The First Epistle to the Corinthians* (London: Adam & Charles Black, 1971), 329. See also Jerome Murphy-O'Connor, "The First Epistle to the Corinthians" in Raymond E. Brown, Joseph A. Fitzmyer and Roland E, Murphy (Eds.) *The New Jerome Biblical Commentary* (London: Burns and Oates, 2007), 811.

29. Cultic acts are various religious rites that adherents of particular practice as means of worship. See J. Michael Matkin, *Early Christianity* (New York: Penguin Group, 2008), 196.

issues.³⁰ The kind of teaching Paul anticipated is 'sustained biblical reflection'³¹ as against some kind of spontaneous eloquence of an orator; in other words, forth telling. Since Paul referred to the Corinthian Christians as babes, it can be inferred that the teaching component of worship service was weak or not given much attention. In view of the competition to demonstrate one's spiritual gift, it is very likely that διδαχή here could have referred to spontaneous or charismatic exposition concerning spiritual gifts, rather than doctrinal teachings.

It was probably a *sensus plenior* interpretation directed towards discovering the intended meaning of a scripture passage, which was supposedly not well articulated by the author, rather than exegetical exposition intended to discover the intended meaning of a pericope by the author.³² This suggests that the Corinthian Church might have had some basic document for instruction, which is likely to be Pauline because there is evidence in 1 Corinthians 5:9, indicating that Paul wrote an earlier epistle to them prior to I Corinthians; meaning 1 Corinthian is actually 2 Corinthians. Accordingly, the earlier Pauline letter to the Corinthians would have been the basis for teaching in the Church.

Ἀποκάλυψις refers to "revelation, or to uncover". L. A. Oepke observes that manifestation/revelation by a deity to its adherents, which involved the removal of concealments was crucial for the survival of that religion/cult.³³ According to Garland, there were oracular cults and mystery deities such as "Apollo, Aphrodite/Venus, Asclepius, Athena Chalinitus, Demeter and Kore, Dionysus, Artemis of Ephesus, Hera Acraea, Hermes/Mercury, Jupiter Capitolinus, ... Egyptian mystery cults, Isis ... "³⁴ etc. that were highly celebrated in Corinth during the time of Paul.

Many of these oracular cults and mystery religions related to their subjects through revelation, communicating with them³⁵ about pressing issues or future happenings. These revelations could be received through

---

30. Hodge, *A commentary*, 300.

31. David E. Garland, *1 Corinthians* (Grand Rapids, Michigan: Baker Academic, 2003), 658.

32. William Sanford LaSor, "Prophecy, Inspiration, and Sensus Plenior" in *Tyndale Bulletin* 29 (1978), 49–60.

33. Leipzig Albrecht Oepke, "ἀποκάλυψις" in Gerhard Kittel (Ed.) *Theological Dictionary of the New Testament* Vol. III (Grand Rapids, Michigan: Wm. B. Eerdmans Publishing Company,1965), 564–565.

34. Garland, *1 Corinthians*, 9.

35. Croy, "Religion, Personal", 928–929.

Biblical, Traditional, and Theological Framework

dreams, trances and visions. Garland further expounds that ἀποκάλυψις in 14:26 refers to "divinely disclosed" issues either prior to or during worship service that may have been communicated[36] intelligibly to the Church through a prophet or any available Christian. G. D. Fee, Murphy-O'Connor and Hodge understood ἀποκάλυψις to be an aid to prophetic speech.[37] It implies that ἀποκάλυψις is prophecy yet to be proclaimed that makes it the undercurrents of prophecy.

Γλῶσσα could be used to refer to the human organ of speech (tongue)[38] and taste or ecstatic religious experience. In this case, it refers to ecstatic speech by people who are emotionally overcome by religious manifestations of the Spirit of God commonly termed "speaking in tongues". γλῶσσα, which is also referred to as glossolalia, is "an expression which in speech or manner is strange and obscure and needs explanation".[39] This emphasizes W. Mundle's assertion that the frenzied state that leads to speaking in tongues can be described thus "drive out of one's senses, . . . lose one's mind, be out of one's senses, . . . a change of location, madness".[40] It is significant to mention that speaking in tongues in the Corinthian Church was not "xenolalia (real 'foreign' languages)"[41] where some individuals in the audience may understand without interpretation, although we cannot rule out such a possibility.

It is very likely that many of the non-Jewish members of the Church knew the religious value of γλῶσσα prior to becoming a Christian. The famous oracular cult of antiquity - Pythia was located toward the "north coast of the Gulf of Corinth".[42] The prophetess in charge of the cult usually

---

36. Garland, *1 Corinthians*, 658.

37. Gordon D. Fee, *The First Epistle to the Corinthians* (Grand Rapids, Michigan: William B. Eerdmans Publishings Company, 1987), 690. Murphy-O'Connor, "The First Epistle to the Corinthians", 811. and Hodge, *A Commentary*, 300.

38. Verbrugge (Ed.), "γλῶσσα", 110.

39. Göttingen Johannes Belm, "glώssa" in Gerhard Kittel (Ed.) *Theological Dictionary of the New Testament* Vol. I (Grand Rapids, Michigan: Wm. B. Eerdmans Publishing Company, 1965), 720.

40. W. Mundle, "ἐκστασις" in Colin Brown (Ed.) *The New International Dictionary of New Testament Theology* (Grand Rapids, Michigan: Zondervan Publishing House,1975), 527.

41. Max Turner, *The Holy Spirit and Spiritual Gifts: Then and Now* (Cumbria, U. K.: Paternoster Press, 1999), 298.

42. Croy, "Religion, Personal", 926. Daniel Nii Aboagye Aryeh, "A Study of 'Prophetism' in the New Testament and its Implications for Ghanaian Christianity", B.Th. Long Essay *Trinity Theological Seminary*, Legon, (2013), 28.

spoke in tongues whilst the cult attendants interpreted it to the inquirers. γλῶσσα in the Corinthian Church does not bear resemblance with that of the cult, it was a new introduction in the Early Church.[43] It is true that the location of a cult did not necessarily mean that people living in that locality were adherents of the cult. Nonetheless, there is a high probability for the residents to subscribe or have knowledge of some of the practices in the cult. This does not suggest that speaking in tongues was a pagan importation. It was ingenuity by the Holy Spirit; the problem was that the Corinthian Christians sought to operate it like that of the cults in Corinth.

Moffatt reports that some adherents of sibyl oracles, which were known in Corinth, experienced the phenomenon of speaking in tongues. He adds that the ability to speak in tongues was a sign of belonging to a highly spiritual group, and that the Corinthian Christians may have used music, fasting and listening to tongues spoken by someone in order to arouse speaking in tongues.[44] It can be observed that speaking in tongues became inclusive and exclusive criteria for the Christian community in Corinth.[45] Speaking in tongues was given not to address humans or preach the gospel but for ministering praises and petition to God,[46] which one was impelled to utter.[47]

According to Belm, ἑρμηνεία basically means "to interpret," "to expound", "to explain" and that ἑρμηνεία of γλῶσσα in Pauline thought was not the "translation of ecstatic language" but rather conversion of unintelligible speech into intelligible[48] speech for the growth of the Christian community. As indicated above, there were many oracular cults in Corinth: Pythia, Sybil, and Cybele among others interpreted glossolalic messages to its inquirers. Therefore, the Corinthian Christians might have known or heard of ἑρμηνεία in their pre-Christian lives. Placing the gift of ἑρμηνεία of

---

43. C. Forbes, *Prophecy and Inspired Speech in Early Christianity and its Hellenistic Environment* (Peabody, Hendrickson, 1997) 73-74. Cited in Mark J. Cartledge, "The Nature and Function of New Testament Glossolalia" in *The Evangelical Quarterly*, Vol. 72, No. 2 (2000), 135-150.

44. Moffatt, *The First Epistle of Paul*, 209–211.

45. Gerd Theissen, *Psychological Aspects of Pauline Theology* (Edinburgh: T &T Clark, 1987), 300–303.

46. Morgan, *The Corinthian Letters of Paul*, 169.

47. Hodge, *A commentary*, 300.

48. Göttingen Johannes Belm, "ἑρμηνεία" in Gerhard Kittel (Ed.) *Theological Dictionary of the New Testament* Vol. II (Grand Rapids, Michigan: Wm. B. Eerdmans Publishing Company,1965), 665.

γλῶσσα as the last item in the list of gifts mentioned in 12:1–11 shows that the Corinthians highly valued this gift above others.[49] However, arranging gifts in some kind of sequential order does not necessary reflect hierarchy and importance.

Some scholars suggested that the gift of interpretation of tongues refers to tongues spoken in previous meeting(s) without spontaneous interpretation.[50] Others asserted that it is a spontaneous activity that flows after a tongue speaker ends his/her speech in tongues.[51] However, the distributive use of ἕκαστος (each one) indicates that the Spirit gives the interpretation to the one who has the gift of interpretation of tongues prior to the time of speaking in tongues. Alternatively put, since the Spirit had given tongues to be spoken by someone in the meeting, the Spirit had also given the interpretation of those particular tongues to someone coming to the meeting: many of the tongues to be spoken would be duly interpreted for the edification of the Church.

In the exordium, Paul mentioned five activities: ψαλμός, διδαχή, ἀποκάλυψις, γλῶσσα, and ἑρμηνεία, which the Church often experienced during worship service and had to be undertaken for the edification of the church. Surprisingly, Paul did not make mention of any leader in the Church who would coordinate these activities for edification. It is probable that the mention of a name may have suggested Paul's support for a particular group. However, it could be contended that not acknowledging the leaders of the Church also suggest Paul's disapproval of the leadership of the Church. I suggest that since the complaints were sent to Paul by some leaders of the Church such as Stephanas and leaders from the household of Chloe (16:15; 1:11), Paul might have dealt with them verbally, therefore there was no need to refer to them in the letter. It is also possible that the above mentioned names were not leaders in the Church, and since it was a charismatic community, Paul, being a theologian of the Spirit, expected that the Holy Spirit would coordinate all these activities.

Exercising the Gift of Speaking in Tongues in the Church (vv.27–28)

Paul gives regulations as to how to use the gift of speaking in tongues in public worship service for the benefit of the Church. The public speaking of

49. Barrett, *The First Epistle*, 286.
50. Hodge, *A Commentary*, 300.
51. Garland, *1 Corinthians*, 658.

tongues by the Church in Corinth points to Paul that they are infants in the things of God instead of being infants in doing evil.[52]

Verse 27

Paul limited the number of tongues speakers to a maximum of three persons who would speak one after the other and the spoken tongues should be interpreted as well. It suggests that there were many who spoke in tongues concurrently in the congregation without interpretation. Numbers played significant roles in many legal and religious settings in first century Corinth. The number of tongues speakers were limited to δύο ἢ τὸ πλεῖστον τρεῖς (two or at most three). Generally, δύο is a number of witnesses.[53] In the first century Roman legal system (which also governed Corinth), all cases to be heard by a magistrate or a jury went through three stages.[54] The first part consisted of formulation of charges in the presence of both plaintiff and defendant. The second stage was the formal laying of accusation before the court; and the third stage was the hearing and giving of judgment, which in many cases was final, and could only be appealed by academically and financially endowed persons.

Rhetorically, the "threefold execution of an act makes it definitive; threefold utterance of a word, expression or sentence, gives it full validity and power".[55] This does not refer to the doctrine of trinity, however, it was a philosophical and literary rule. Religious use of τρεῖς is dominant in first century oracular cults in Achaia and Corinth. Zeus, Poseidon and Hades who were considered as the "rulers of earth, sea and the underworld" respectively, usually formed a common triad[56] for protection and provision of good agricultural yield.

This proposes that Paul was using common philosophical and pre-Christian experiences of some Corinthian Christians to theologize to them. It is very likely that all the three tongues speakers' messages may agree on

---

52. Seth Kissi, *The Gifts and Spirituality: Understanding the Subject in the Context of First Corinthians, Addressing Some Popular Misconceptions* (Achimota, Ghana: African Christian Press, 2014), 80–81.

53. Verbrugge (Ed.), "δύο", 156.

54. A. A. Rupprecht, "Legal System, Roman" in Gerald F. Hawthorne, Ralph P. Martin and Daniel G. Reid (Eds.) *Dictionary of Paul and His Letters* (Downers Grove, Illinois and Leicester: InterVarsity Press, 1993), 546.

55. Delling, "τρεῖς", 216.

56. Delling, "τρεῖς", 216.

an issue the Spirit wants to communicate to the Church. Or it would agree with an earlier Pauline epistle that we currently do not have access to. In other words, the last two tongues speakers were likely to confirm the message of the first speaker. Fee argues that the statement 'two or at most three' is ambiguous because it is not clear if in every public worship there should be 'two or at most three' persons to speak in tongues.[57] Fee's argument suggests that there might have been different kinds of worship services in the Corinthian Church and that this gift should not manifest in some of the worship services. However, τὸ πλεῖστον (at the most) as a ceiling is an indication that, at any meeting of the Church[58] where the gift of the Spirit manifests, the rules must apply.

The insertion of ἀνὰ μέρος (apart, one after the other) points to the fact that two or more members attempted to speak in tongues at the same time[59] as it happened in non-Christian cults. It suggests that the tongues speaker is not in a frenzied or ecstatic state where he or she does not have control on what is happening to or through him or her. There should be one to interpret what is said in tongues. This is similar to what takes place in the cult led by the Pythia.

Verse 28

In the absence of an interpreter, the tongues speakers must be silent (σιγάτω) in the Church and speak to themselves and to God. Until someone speaks in tongues, one cannot know if there is an interpreter. It means that there could be a day where tongues could be spoken without an interpreter. In addition, the presence of a known interpreter does not necessarily guarantee a spontaneous interpretation of tongues spoken. However, since speaking in tongues and the interpretation are the singular work of the Spirit, it is believed that there will be spontaneous interpretation.

After the first speaker had finished speaking and there was no interpretation, subsequent individuals who intended to speak in tongues should keep silent,[60] σιγάτω (silent, say nothing, keep still). It implies that the

---

57. Gordon D. Fee, *God's Empowering Presence: The Holy Spirit in the Letters of Paul* (Grand Rapids, Michigan: Baker Academic, 1994), 250.

58. Garland, *1 Corinthians*, 658.

59. Robertson and Plummer, *A Critical and Exegetical Commentary*, 321.

60. David Prior, *The Message of 1 Corinthians: Life in the Local Church* (Leicester, England and Downers Groves, Illinois, 1985), 250.

speaker had control over the manifestation of the gift, and there could be an avenue where someone would speak in tongues in the Church without interpretation. However, what the Spirit wants to say to the Church should be intelligibly communicated in an orderly manner.[61] It shows that Paul does not see the gift of speaking in tongues as an overpowering ecstatic experience.[62] The gift of speaking in tongues is a spiritual gift subject to human control.

The regulation to keep silent concerning speaking in tongues would have to do with speaking in tongues in the Church (ἐν ἐκκλησίᾳ). Ἐκκλησία could mean called out assembly, assembly, meeting, and church.[63] In Greco-Roman settings, ἐκκλησία was used to denote a regular gathering by citizens to deliberate on issues concerning the city. The ἐκκλησία usually began with prayer and sacrifice to the city deity, after which any member had the right to speak concerning any issue relevant to the State.[64] Ἐκκλησία was later used to designate the gathering of "Jesus' movement" after the resurrection of Jesus.

Traditionally, there were two groups that one may belong to in the Greco-Roman world: *politeia* was the public gathering that discussed issues of public magnitude; and *oikonomia* was a household in which one was born[65] into and played an active role in. Paul's reference to the Church in the house of Gaius in Corinth (Rom.16:23); Chroe (1:11); Fortunatus, Stephanas, Achaicus (16:15-18) was an indication that Paul's use of ἐκκλησία was in respect of the latter option with modification on a limited number of people, who would speak in tongues and prophesy. This is reminiscent of imperial cults that were situated in households in Achaia.[66] One may think that Paul could have appealed to certain individuals in the Church for financial support to rent a social centre or a theatre for meetings that could accommodate a large number of members. However, Paul's adoption

---

61. Fee, *The First Epistle*, 692.

62. Richard B. Hays, *First Corinthians Interpretation: A Bible Commentary for Teaching and Preaching* (Louisville: John Knox Press, 1997), 242.

63. Verbrugge (Ed.), "ἐκκλησία", 170.

64. L. Coenen, "ἐκκλησία" in Colin Brown (Ed.) *The New International Dictionary of New Testament Theology* (Grand Rapids, Michigan: Zondervan Publishing House, 1975), 291.

65. Robert Banks, *Paul's Idea of Community: The Early House Churches in their Historical Setting* (Grand Rapids, Michigan: William B. Eerdmans Publishing Company, 1980), 15.

66. Garland, *1 Corinthians*, 12.

of *oikonomia* form of ἐκκλησία could serve as an alternative to household imperial cults, as a means of instilling Christian values in first century cosmopolitan Corinthian households. It had the potential of infringing on the privacy of the host family.

Some of the houses of the wealthy persons in Corinth were too big to hold meetings in. An example is the house of Gaius in Corinth (Rom.16:23); Chloe (1:11); Fortunatus, Stephanas, Achaicus (16:15–18). House-churches were a "small circle" of the Christian fellowship within the larger ἐκκλησία.[67] These house-churches, which were mainly located in urban areas in Corinth, were fundamentally composed of the host's family, slaves, business partners and other persons in the nearby community.[68] The slaves were likely to have served as attendants/ushers at worship services, which the Jews in the Church may not have been comfortable with due to their perception concerning non-Jewish slaves.

Neighboring individuals who were not on good terms with the host's family were not likely to come and worship; even if they should come, they may not have been comfortable. "The ἐκκλησία that gathered with the tentmakers Prisca, Aquila, and Paul in Corinth … might well have seemed to be neighbours, a club of the same sort".[69] It means that many of the members were likely to be working in the tent-making industry in Corinth. The overwhelming influence of the host of the house-churches, where the Church met may have meant that they tried to control worship services, which may have led to confusion in the Church.[70] These house-churches usually met at the hall or living room of the host that generally had the capacity to accommodate between 40 and 50 persons at a worship service.[71] The house-churches denote the idea of belonging to one's source of origin and the welfare of individual members was paramount; hence, every action and inaction ought to lead to edifying the Church.

---

67. P. T. O'Brien, "Church" in Gerald F. Hawthorne, Ralph P. Martin and Daniel G. Reid (Eds.) *Dictionary of Paul and His Letters* (Downers Grove, Illinois and Leicester: InterVarsity Press, 1993), 125.

68. Dennis C. Duling, *The New Testament: History, Literature and Social Context* 4th Ed. (Canada: Wadsworth, 2003), 150, 172, 175.

69. Wayne A. Meeks, *The First Urban Christians: The Social World of the Apostle Paul* (New Haven and London: Yale University Press, 1983), 32.

70. Garland, *1 Corinthians*, 2.

71. David W.J. Gill, "In Search of the Social Elite in the Corinthian Church" in Tyndale Bulletin 44.2 (1993) 323–337. And Dirk Jongkind, "Corinth in The First Century Ad: The Search For Another Class" in Tyndale Bulletin 52.1 (2001) 139–148.

Speaking in tongues to oneself and to God in the absence of an interpreter implies that the aspiring tongues speaker(s) may not have fully been participating in the worship service. Since the individual(s) had control over the manifestation of the gift, speaking in tongues to oneself and to God should not take place in the Church. The aspiring tongues speaker(s) must keep silent until he or she goes home to speak to him or herself and to God privately.[72] Although Paul pointed out in (14:18–19) that he could speak in tongues probably more than all Corinthian Church tongues speakers combined, there was, nevertheless, no evidence pointing to the fact that he was seen speaking in tongues publicly.[73] Instead, he would prefer to speak five intelligible words in the Church than many words in tongues (14:19). Speaking to one's self and to God shows that the speaker understands what he or she utters. It is significant to state that Paul did not condemn speaking in tongues; he, however, outlined rules for exercising tongues in public worship service.

Guidelines for Prophets and Prophecy in the Church (vv.29–33a)

Paul then gave some guidelines for prophets and prophecy in the Church.

Verse 29

In the Early Church, charismatically gifted persons were very active and given recognition in the Church.[74] Oracular cults were highly patronized in order to have insight into present happenings and foresight into the future. According to C. Brown, προφήτης (prophet) is the compound composed of the stem φή, (to say, proclaim) a religious issue/news and the prefix προ, which connotes the idea of "before, prior, fore, in advance." Therefore προφήτης is someone who tells before it happens.[75] However, B. K. Helmut argues that, originally, προ had the meaning of 'forth'. The idea of 'fore' was

---

72. Moffatt, *The First Epistle of Paul*, 209–228.

73. Aryeh, "Exegetical Analysis of 1 Corinthians 12:1–11", 211.

74. Williston Walker, *History of the Christian Church* (New York: Charles Scribner's Sons, 1922), 44.

75. C. Brown, "προφήτης" in Colin Brown (Ed.) *The New International Dictionary of New Testament Theology* Vol. 3 (Grand Rapids, Michigan: Zondervan Publishing House, 1975), 74–79.

Biblical, Traditional, and Theological Framework

very minimal and temporally until the 5th century BCE[76] when, for religious and oracular purposes, the meaning of 'fore' became intensive.

A famous oracle, the Pythia was, referred to as προφήτης and *promantis* (diviner). "This office belonged originally to one, two or three girls drawn from the local population" who later became elderly.[77] *Promantis* connotes the idea of revealing the future, which does not usually demand change of life style, while προφήτης connotes the idea of the gods using the voice of the Pythia to speak to its inquirers,[78] while demanding change of lifestyle. The Pythia spoke in glossolalic language while some officials at the shrine, also called προφήτης, interpret the message in an intelligible language to the inquirers.[79] The use of προφήτης by the Pythia was in a higher position than the use of προφήτης by cult attendants and interpreters. It implied that the Pythia took direct inspiration from the gods but προφήτης, who interpreted the language of the Pythia, did not.

Paul's instruction that at most three prophets may speak in public worship service can be likened to the three girls who sat on a triad at the Pythia. The difference is that the Pythia spoke in glossolalic language whilst the prophet in the Church spoke in an intelligible language to the Church or individuals. The prophets in the Church did not only interpret glossolalic language like as the prophets at the cult. In other words, Paul took some functions of the Pythia and her prophets to theologize concerning prophetic ministry in the Corinthian Church and added that others must judge what the prophets said in the Church. The basic meaning of διακρίνω is to measure an issue to find if it makes the required mark or qualifies.[80] It is not necessarily the determination of true and false prophecies. Prophets may want to defend their prophecies, which is likely to degenerate into confusion. Therefore διακρίνω should be understood as grading of prophecies in terms of importance and priority.[81] Unfortunately, Paul did not give criteria for the judgment of prophecies.

---

76. Bethel Krämer Helmut, "προφήτης" in Gerhard Kittel and Gerhard Friedrich (Eds.) *Theological Dictionary of the New Testament* Vol. VI (Grand Rapids, Michigan: Wm. B. Eerdmans Publishing Company,1964), 783–784.

77. C. Brown, "προφήτης", 75.

78. Helmut, "προφήτης", 787.

79. C. Brown, "προφήτης", 75.

80. Verbrugge (Ed.), "διακρίνω", 138.

81. Aryeh, "A Study of 'Prophetism' in the New Testament and its Implications for Ghanaian Christianity" , 41.

However, it does not suggest that three prophets implied three prophecies at a meeting.[82] Judgment of prophecies is likely to create some confusion and lengthy services in the Church. Judging of prophecy is done silently and personally to check one's inspiration during Church services,[83] so that it could not create confusion in the Church. Nonetheless, since Paul's objective was to instill orderliness in public worship service it was aimed at fostering togetherness.

Scholars are divided on who should exercise authority by judging prophecies in the church. Is it members of the Church or other prophets present in the service? One may ask how could people who are not prophets judge prophets? Barrett asserted that judgment of prophecies by members of the Church is much more plausible than other prophets present.[84] Robertson and Plummer argue that οἱ ἄλλοι (the others) should be interpreted as co-prophets who should judge prophecies of the prophets.[85] According to Fee, since all believers had the Spirit of God from whom prophecy proceeds,[86] they can judge prophecy. By this, Paul did not limit judgment of prophecy to prophets; all other Christians could judge prophesy. No individual prophet could take control and extra ordinarily influence in the Corinthian Church.[87] Therefore, prophetic ministry becomes a function in the Church not an office as was the case with the Pythia.

Verse 30

It is quiet unclear whether God, who is the author of peace and orderliness, would provoke someone to speak while the incumbent speaker had not finished speaking. Paul seemed to have made the point, that whilst someone is prophesying, a revelation could be given to ἄλλοι (someone who is not a prophet or someone who is not associated with giving prophecy) sitting and that attention should be given to the person with a new revelation. In other words, revelation or prophecy by prophets should not be rated above revelation/prophecy by other Christians. The issue is about prophecy from

---

82. Fee, *God's Empowering Presence*, 251.

83. Charles R. Erdman, *The First Epistle of Paul to the Corinthians: An Exposition* (Philadelphia, Pennsylvania: The Westminster Press, 1984), 149–150.

84. Barrett, *The First Epistle*, 328.

85. Robertson and Plummer, *A Critical and Exegetical Commentary*, 322.

86. Fee, *The First Epistle*, 694.

87. Hays, *First Corinthians Interpretation*, 242.

Biblical, Traditional, and Theological Framework

the same source as the Spirit who decides which vessel to use at any time. It is not a defense of ecclesiological designation. This again points to the fact that the role of the prophet is functional rather than an office. Revelation is not exclusive to one person or prophet.

Verse 31

Paul emphasized the assertion that all (πάντες) Christians could potentially prophesy. This again make the gift of prophecy available to all Christians: it is not the bonafied endowment of only prophets even though they might distinguish themselves concerning the giving of prophecies. Although Paul encourages the use of intelligible language in public worship services, he does not confide it in a person or group of persons. This verse also suggests that many members of the Corinthian Church were endowed with the gift of prophecy. The prophets are not to be "regarded as infallible and unanswerable"[88] to the local Church authorities.

Paul's statement "you can all prophesy" did not mean all members present must prophesy in a meeting but they all can prophesy in-turn of three persons in a meeting that must be aimed at learning and encouraging those present.[89] Μανθάνω refers to learning out of prophecies issued; probably learning personal life issues that draws one closer to God which is the goal of prophecy as against mere prediction of the future, likened to soothsaying. Encouragement here denotes that prophecy must not put the recipient in confusion or a state of despair.

Verse 32

Ὑποτάσσω connotes the idea of hierarchy: in other words, submitting to higher authority. The statement "the spirit of the prophet is subject to the prophet" means the spirit of the prophet is subject to "the prophetic Spirit", which is the source of prophecy and is higher in hierarchy than the prophet's spirit. He explains that the spirit of the prophet is subject to the prophet in the sense of timing and delivery of prophetic messages.[90] Since pagan cults were mostly polytheistic, many spirits could be manifesting at the

---

88. Garland, *1 Corinthians*, 662.
89. Hodge, *A commentary*, 302.
90. See Fee, *The First Epistle*, 696. See also Fee, *God's Empowering Presence*, 254.

same time through intermediary person(s). Christianity is monotheistic, therefore there could not be more than one manifestation of the Spirit of God at the same time in a gathering. Paul is here preventing pre-Christian experiences of some Corinthians from being part of Christian worship service, so that no prophet would claim to have been compelled by the Spirit to speak excessively.

Verse 33a

Γάρ (for) indicates the reason for the instruction of v.32 that orderliness portrays the character of God. If there is disorder in the Corinthian Church, it was not caused by God but by egocentric individuals.[91] Christian worship must express the orderly and peaceful character of God.

Restriction on Women in Public Worship Service (vv.33b-36)

Many scholars believe that vv.33b-36 was an interpolation into the text. Because Paul was dealing with speaking in tongues and prophecy in the Church and, suddenly, there was an immediate change of focus to prohibit women from speaking in the Church. If the assertion that these verses were interpolated into the pericope is correct, it was done at an early stage because it occurred after verse 40 in some manuscripts. He added that the phrase "the churches" and "the law" are not consistent with the content of the pericope; and that it was a gloss into the text by some Pauline students.[92] Many variant readings of manuscripts according to some Church Fathers' witnesses including P46, A, B, K, Ψ 0243 33 82 1739 has it as it is in *The Greek New Testament* (fourth revised edition)[93] with minor variations. In the entire Western tradition, D, F, G, a, b, d, f, g Ambrosiaster Sedulius-Scotus, it was found after verse 40.[94]

Taking out gender sensitive verses in 33b-36 does not really change the main focus of the pericope. He adds that there are three possible views concerning verses 33b-36: Either (1). It was an interpolation written and inserted into the pericope, which is why the English translation of the *New*

---

91. Barrett, *The First Epistle*, 328.
92. Hays, *First Corinthians Interpretation*, 245-247.
93. It was edited by Barbara Aland, Kurt Aland, Johannes Karavidopoulos, Carlos M. Martin and Bruce M. Metzger.
94. Fee, *The First Epistle*, 699. Garland, *1 Corinthians*, 675-677.

Biblical, Traditional, and Theological Framework

Revised Standard Version (NRSV) puts it in parenthesis to indicate its uncertainty; (2). It was a popular Corinthian formulation to bar women from being active in Church that Paul tried to refute because Paul usually quotes some Corinthian popular notions in order to respond to them accordingly (1:12; 2:15; 6:12; 10:23 . . .); or (3) It is an attempt to build strong husband and wife relationships in the Corinthian Church.[95] If Paul was dealing with popular Corinthian formulation and that he wanted to build strong marital relationships, he could have done it in (11:2–16) where he discussed head covering for women who would like to pray or prophesy in the Church. The first option is probable in that it is an early interpolation. Even if it is considered as original to Paul, it is probably an afterthought by him.[96]

Another argument is that Paul related to many women who were leaders in the Corinthian Church. For example, Chloe whose house was used as one of the house-churches in Corinth (1:11); and Phoebe who was a deacon in the Church at "Cenchreae (the eastern port at Corinth)".[97] It would have been highly ambiguous for Paul, who had related so well with these influential women, to turn around to silence them.

However, since they are contained in the majority of mss., it is imperative to make sense out of it despite the challenges. Women played significant roles in oracular cults in Corinth. The Pythia was under the leadership of women. Plato, as quoted by R. M. Grant, intimately said that a "'Corinthian girl' is bad for a man's health, Corinthian women make a lot of trouble".[98] The reason for silencing women, according to the author of this segment, is for the women to conform to the so-called law that has not been stated. The writer states that, if a woman has an issue, she should ask the husband at home. The question is: what of unmarried women? Or a husband who does not belong to the Church? Or a husband who is not learned in the scriptures?

A Test for Prophet (vv.37–38)

Paul then gave a criterion by which the Corinthians could determine which prophet to accept or reject.

95. Garland, *1 Corinthians*, 667–669.
96. Fee, *The First Epistle*, 701.
97. Duling, *The New Testament*, 251.
98. Robert M. Grant, *Paul in the Roman World: The Conflict at Corinth* (Louisville, London and Leiden: Westminster John Knox Press, 1989), 20, 125–126.

Verses 37–38

It is very difficult to name or specifically point out Paul's opponents in the Corinthian Church. Upon critical study of 1 Corinthians, it must have been "Gnosticism or over realized eschatology" that led to the misunderstanding of Paul's earlier letter (5:7) and social depositions.[99] Paul might have known that some elements in the Corinthian Church would like to reject his epistle because it does not favour their personal objectives. He was so definite to say that what he is writing to them is from the Lord. Therefore, he that claims to be a prophet and πνευματικός (spiritual person) from the Lord must acknowledge the source of the epistle as hailing from the same Lord. Paul used prophet and spiritual person interchangeably to emphasize the earlier view that the role of prophets is functional, not an office.[100] Whoever rejects this epistle must also be rejected. This further establishes Paul's apostolic authority over the Corinthian Church.

Concluding Remark (vv. 39–40)

In conclusion, Paul showed that he did not forbid speaking in tongues but that he encouraged prophecy over speaking in tongues in the Church. Even the exercise of prophecy in the Church ought to be conducted in order to exhibit the orderly character of God. Paul used ἀδελφοί,, in the opening statement of the pericope and repeated it in the concluding remark to indicate his strong affection for the Corinthian Church as the founder. We cannot be certain if Paul succeeded in solving the problem in Corinth at the time. However, a similar situation came up in the late first century as indicated above where the charismatically gifted youth wanted to take over the leadership role in the Church. This situation necessitated the first and second epistles of Clement of Rome to the Corinthians.

CONCLUSION

Paul's approach to the Corinthian problems was polemical. He considered the pre-Christian religio-cultural and social experiences of the Corinthian, which he employed to theologize to them. They did not assume that the

---

99. Charles H. Talbert, *Reading Corinthians: A New Commentary for Preachers* (London and New York: SPCK and Crossroad Publishing Company, 1987), xxii.

100. Fee, *The First Epistle*, 711.

Biblical, Traditional, and Theological Framework

gifts of speaking in tongues and prophecy were imported from the cults in Corinth, but that the gifts were given by the Spirit of God who is peaceful and orderly. Therefore, in exercising the gift, it must exhibit the peaceful and orderly character of the giver. Since Christianity believes in one God who is omnipresent, there could not be two manifestations of the same Spirit simultaneously in one worship service. The Spirit will manifest among Christians in-turns. The oracular cults were mostly polytheistic and so there could be many manifestations of different spirits at the same time. This pre-Christian experience of some of the members of the Church should not be imported into the Church for personal gains.

The gift of speaking in tongues is mainly for private communication with one's self and with God. It must be interpreted in public worship service so that those present will be edified. Where there is no interpreter, speaking in tongues must not be allowed. In the presence of an interpreter a maximum of three persons may speak in tongues in-turns. Prophecy must be encouraged in the Church with a ceiling of three persons to prophesy in-turns.

Every member of the church has the Spirit that gives revelations to Christians just like prophets. Revelation is not limited to only prophets, it is the Spirit that decides to whom to give revelation. Therefore a prophet plays a functional role as a vessel through whom the Spirit makes things known. He/she may be referred to as prophet or prophetess because he/she has developed the prophetic instinct that exists in all Christians. He or she is not the revealer but the Spirit of God. If the Spirit ceases to reveal to him or her, that will end his or her prophetic ministry.

Verse 33b-36 could better be described as a glossed interpolation at a very early period. It can be taken out of the pericope without affecting the main focus of the pericope. That is not to suggest that it should be taken out. Although it does not follow Paul's discussion on speaking in tongues and prophecy in the Church, many manuscripts by Early Church Fathers have it with minor variations. The text does not synchronize with Paul's teachings in 11:2–16 concerning women praying and prophesying in the Church; and Paul's collaboration with women such as Chloe and Phoebe who were leaders in the Church at Corinth.

Paul might have known that some prophets or spiritual persons may not accept his epistle simply because it may not favour them. He then used the epistle as a test case for true and false prophets. Paul knew that the epistle was the command of the Lord, not his personal suggestions. He that had the Spirit of the Lord would accept the epistle, but the one who did not have the Spirit of the Lord or have a personal interest may reject it. Paul finally encouraged the Corinthian Christians that they should desire intelligible gift—prophecy that edifies the Church rather than speaking in tongues. This does not suggest that Paul condemned the gift of speaking in tongues. It is significant to mention that Paul encouraged prophecy, not prophets. Therefore prophetic ministry is a function, not an office.

Chapter Eleven

Conclusions, Implications and Recommendations

CONCLUSION

CONTEMPORARY PROPHETS ARE GRADUALLY claiming to be the mouthpiece of God and that, if the Bible should be rewritten, their names and miracles would be added to the text. This claim is similar to that of the Montanists whose members claimed that their revelations were equal to scripture, and therefore must be added to it. Pentecostalism is the largest Christian denomination in Africa, Asia and Latin America and prophetism is a stream of Pentecostalism. If this phenomenon is not checked, it will escalate egocentricity in leaders in the Christian faith in Ghana. Some Pentecostals and Charismatics generally refer to "Pauline thought" in matters of faith as a primary authority, particularly, in pneumatology.

So far we have shown that the socio-religious and cultural context of Corinth and that of Ghana, share some commonalities: members in the Church in Corinth and prophets in Ghana have pre-Christian pneumatological experiences. In other words, they were familiar with oracular messages from the traditional religion before becoming a Christian. Persons with charismatic endowments seek for priority during public worship services. This phenomenon led to several prophets wanting to speak in every public worship service. Paul was compelled to limit the number of prophets to speak in each public worship service to a maximum of three persons

Conclusions, Implications and Recommendations

who would prophesy in-turns, while the congregations that have the Holy Spirit like the prophets, judge the prophecies of the prophets. Paul pointed out that all believers could prophesy, thereby making the prophetic gift not the preserve of prophets, although prophet have trained themselves to be spontaneous with prophecy.

Prophetism exists in some traditional religions in Ghana. The *Akan* and *Gã* words used to describe some religious functionaries indicate that the services of persons who claimed to have had some ability to mediate between the spiritual and the physical worlds for the benefit of inquirers were highly patronized before taking important decisions. These persons were held in high esteem since there were no sacred scriptures in primal religions to give guidance. Consulting them does not require the abandoning of one's religious affiliation or declaring one's allegiance to Jesus or any deity. In primal religions, the word of the prophet wields a lot of influence over inquirers and makes their ministry an office.

Paul's understanding and teaching concerning prophetic ministry is that of a function not an office. The individual manifests the prophetic grace by the will of the Holy Spirit. Meanwhile the scriptures are available to give guidance. Hence, the meaning of a prophet in Pauline thought is any individual Christian that the Holy Spirit deems fit to mediate a revelation/prophecy for the edification of the Church or the recipient without any benefit in kind or cash to the prophesier. In doing this, there are some individuals who have distinguished themselves for receiving prophecies for the Church or individuals who are referred to as prophets. However, they are prophets as long as the Holy Spirit communicates prophecies through them. They cease to be prophets when the Holy Spirit ceases to communicate to them.

There is a dichotomy between prophetism in Pauline literature and that of the Old Testament. The existence of a body of literature referred to as the *Nebi'im* (the prophets) points to the fact that prophetic ministry in the Old Testament is much more elaborate than that in the New Testament. In terms of content, the *Nebi'im* is a collection of the oracular messages from Yahweh to Israel, Judah, and other nations through the prophets. A study of the *Nebi'im* shows that the prophetic ministry was an established institution in ancient Israel. It is the oldest ministry with a well-organized history and a structured system on the conduct of prophets, a definition of what constitutes prophecy, and how to distinguish true from false prophets.

Biblical, Traditional, and Theological Framework

The training that some Old Testament prophets undergo in order to become a prophet resonates with the training of priests/priestesses, nevertheless, the content and duration vary. The unavailability of a canon suggests that the Old Testament prophetic ministry and that of traditional religion is an office. There were stipulations concerning how to determine false prophets from true prophets of Adonai. However, in 1 Corinthians. 14:26–40, the stipulation concerning prophecy was to evaluate it for priority and whether it conforms to his teachings concerning prophets and prophecy in the Church. This means that those who prophesy in the Church must first be genuine Christians. These clearly show that prophetism in the Old Testament and that of Pauline corpus are divergent.

The function of prophets and prophecy in traditional religion, Old Testament prophets, early Christianity, and Pauline corpus share some similarities:

(i) They have fore knowledge and fore-tell future events. For example, Samuel's fore knowledge about the lost asses of Saul's father (1Sam. 9:1–26); Jesus' had fore knowledge about the past life story of the Samaritan woman (John 4:16–19, 29); Agabus had fore knowledge concerning the arrest of Paul (Acts 21:11–14). Ɔkomfo Anokye had fore knowledge concerning the destiny of Osei Kofi; and Numbo Akrama often had fore knowledge concerning impending disaster.

(ii) They perform miracles and wonders. Examples include Moses in Egypt (Ex.7:14–11:1–10); the miracles of Jesus (Mark 6:14); the miracles of Ɔkomfo Anokye during the war between the Asantes and the Denkyira people; and the miracles of Paul and Barnabas. It is important to note that the forth telling component of prophecy which is the proclamation of the word of God is central to the New Testament prophet, and should be emulated by contemporary prophets in Ghana. It is obvious that contemporary understanding of "prophet" in Ghana has been largely influenced by traditional prophetism. It is due to the lack of good hermeneutical principles by some Pentecostal and Charismatic Ministers. Thereby picking scripture texts that seem to facially resonate with the African context without undertaking exegesis.

My thesis is that, prophet(s) who claim and place a high premium on prophetic ministry in Ghana that their ministry is guided by Pauline teachings concerning prophets and prophecy in the church is not correct. There is nowhere in Pauline corpus where Paul encouraged the payment of fees or

Conclusions, Implications and Recommendations

the mandatory purchase of any "anointing oils" or relics/substances as a prerequisite to receiving the service of a prophet. Although some contemporary prophets have impacted positively on some Ghanaians, it could be argued that contemporary Ghanaian prophetism is an amalgamation of Old Testament prophetism, prophetism by the AICs, and that of some Ghanaian traditional religions; an example being *Akan* and *Ga* tradition. They are very selective on Pauline thought. They partly limit Paul's statement: "Let two or three prophets speak, and let the others weigh what is said." (1 Corinthians 14:29), to "let the prophets speak", for undue advantage.

The gift of prophecy and prophets is still alive to this day. The Spirit of prophecy has not been withdrawn but in the exercise of these gifts caution must be taken: those who prophesy must not rate themselves above anybody in the church. All are equal before God. The prophet must not be the author of confusion in the church, but rather an ambassador of peace and unity. Spiritual gifts, especially prophecy, must be desired biblically under the tutelage of trained ministers of the gospel.

New Testament prophecy is not equal to scripture. Prophecy is situational and personal and is directed to an individual or a particular group of persons. The prophetic revelation must lead the recipient to Christ or foster a better relationship between the recipients and Christ. In other words, it must comfort, exhort and console the recipient. In view of what is happening in some 'prophetic churches/ministries' in Ghana today, it is important to note that prophecy must not be paid for. Anyone claiming revelation of new scripture must be watched carefully and his/her teachings discarded immediately.

In the New Testament, particularly Pauline epistles, the art of prophesying is not limited to few individuals. This is because the Holy Spirit dwells in the heart of every believer. Each believer can prophesy, although certain persons distinguished themselves and were called 'prophets'. Prophecy sometimes comes to confirm what the Holy Spirit has already revealed to the believer or what is in the heart of the believer. It is subject to judgment by other prophets and the word of God.

IMPLICATIONS

Deducing from the discussions in the chapters of this book, it implies that (i) prophet, prophecy and scripture should be clearly defined; (ii) the role

Biblical, Traditional, and Theological Framework

of traditional prophets and practices must be separated from that of Christianity; and (iii) the need for theological education.

Prophet, Prophecy and Scripture

There is a distinction between a prophet, prophecy and scripture. In the exegetical work, it is obvious that a prophet must recognize and give undivided attention to scripture, and it is a test to determine which prophet should be given attention to as the servant of God (1 Cor. 14:37–38). This agrees with the role of Old Testament prophets during the period of the monarchy in ancient Israel where prophets were covenant implementers. In other words, they kept reminding Israel concerning the covenant between them and Yahweh and its stipulations of curses and blessings. Since a prophet speaks for a particular deity (ies), the identity marker for a prophet who claims to speak for God in the name of Jesus must be scripture adherent and promote its content theologically.

Prophecy must not lead people from God through disorderly behaviors. In Pauline literature, he did not give advantage to prophecy over scripture, but he rather treated prophecy as a temporary gift, while scripture is permanent (1 Cor. 13). Therefore, prophecy is a gift that is limited by time and can be falsified by anyone, whilst scripture is permanent and can hardly be falsified but can be misinterpreted. The mad rush for Churches who emphasize prophetic activities could be attributed to challenging economic situations in Ghana. However, it is imperative that Christians be driven by the Holy Spirit and scripture rather than their economic situation even though it is also important. Due to the availability of scripture for the Christian faith, no individual prophet can claim to be the only mouth piece of God.

Christian Prophets and Traditional Prophets

There is a distinct dichotomy between a Christian prophet and a traditional prophet. The Christian prophet is subject to scripture and the rules of the local Church. Prophecies of a Christian prophet is subject to evaluation by the Church; it could be rejected or accepted. The prophecy of a Christian prophet is not sacrosanct but is subject to scriptural adherence; the Bible also serves as prophecies or a guide to solving existential needs.

Conclusions, Implications and Recommendations

In view of the lack of recognized scripture in some traditional religions including that of the *Akan* and *Ga* people of Ghana, prophets tend to assume significant positions and have become indispensable in the religious life of the community. It is important to note this so that Christian prophets will not assume the roles of traditional prophets in the name of contextualization. Since many members of the contemporary prophetic ministries still confess their affinity to TWMC such as Roman Catholic Church, Anglican Church, Presbyterian Church of Ghana, Methodist Church, Ghana, Evangelical Presbyterian Church, Ghana etc. there is the need for biblical and theological teachings on Christian prophetic ministry in the TWMC Churches. It also calls for critical consideration of the Ghanaian worldview of Christian worship.

Theological Education

Many contemporary prophets are not theologically trained. Therefore they interpret the Bible literally. Their hermeneutics lay emphasis on devotional and sermonic aspects of the text to the detriment of detail exegesis. These are popular interpretations that are directed towards inciting participants' or members' participation by shouting during preaching. It is clear that shouting does not necessarily indicate good and powerful exposition of the word of God. Contemporary prophets must submit themselves to theological education. Due to the weak methods/popular view of biblical interpretation by contemporary prophets and the general assertion among Ghanaians who believe in pneumatological manifestation in the church in prophecies, and that theological education does not support spirituality, many contemporary prophets have veered into traditional prophetism, which makes prophetic ministry an office rather than a function, as we have seen from the exegesis in chapter 10. There should be education concerning the dichotomy between traditional prophetism and Christian prophetism.

Financial demands by some contemporary prophets as a prerequisite for receiving the services of a prophet in order to pay for media expenses of the ministry is preventing many Christians from receiving the services of a prophet. Participants/members should be encouraged to give freely in support of media programs. The ministry of contemporary prophets is generally problem solving for Christians, and is not directed towards converting non-Christians to the Christian faith. This phenomenon compels them to condemn other churches so that they could appeal to their members. This does not foster the spirit of ecumenism and peaceful co-existence. Contemporary prophets must respect and recognize the good works of other churches.

Objects and substances given to participants/members for miracles generally resonate more with traditional prophetism than Christian prophetic ministry. This cannot be indigenization of Christianity but the appropriation of the traditional belief system into Christian worship. Christianity is not necessarily syncretistic; therefore contemporary prophets need to study Paul's teachings concerning prophetism in the church and implement it contextually. This points to the fact that there is the need to have a biblical and theological framework conducted in the New Testament, particularly in Pauline literature as a guide for the conduct and activities of contemporary prophets. It will also help members of the church to have a good understanding of biblical and theological understanding of prophetism.

RECOMMENDATIONS

This research is mainly based on Pauline stipulations concerning prophets and prophecies in the church and prophetism in *Akan* and *Ga* Traditional Religions, to access contemporary prophetic ministry in Ghana. In doing this, I drawn on prophetism in the Old Testament, the gospels, and early Christianity. There is the need to also undertake a research of other passages in Pauline corpus such as Romans 12:6–8; Ephesians 4:11–12; and 1 Thessalonians 5:21–22 that directly make reference to prophets and prophecy in the church, and prophetism in other Traditional Religions in Ghana.

Appendix: Images

A Portion of the Gbawe Palace

Appendix: Images

A Portion of the Gbawe Palace

Appendix: Images

Numbo Akrama, Gbawe wulɔmɔ standing in front of a shrine in his house in Gbawe.

Appendix: Images

Numbo Akrama, Gbawe wulɔmɔ standing at the entrance of his Gbatsu in Gbawe.

Appendix: Images

"Hope Miracle Water" of Prophet Dr. Eric Nana Kwasi Amponsah.

Appendix: Images

"Special Emergency Oil" of Prophet Dr. Eric Nana Kwasi Amponsah.

Appendix: Images

"Special Emergency Oil" of Prophet Dr. Eric Nana Kwasi Amponsah.

Appendix: Images

At the entrance of the building in which Ɔkɔmfo Anokye was born at Awukugua, in Akwapim

Appendix: Images

The shrine of Ɔkɔmfo Anokye at Awukugua, in Akwapim

Appendix: Images

Divination pot of Ɔkɔmfo Anokye at Awukugua, in Akwapim

Appendix: Images

Ɔkɔmfo Anokye's sword in the ground at Ɔkɔmfo Anokye teaching hospital at Kumasi, in the Ashanti Region.

References

PERIODICALS

A Communiqué Issued by the Ghana Catholic Bishops' Conference at their Annual Plenary
Assembly Held in Cape Coast from 10th to 15th July 2000.
A Communiqué Issued by the Ghana Catholic Bishops' Conference at their Annual Plenary
Assembly Held in Koforidua from 2nd to 10th July 1998.
A Communiqué Issued by the Ghana Catholic Bishops' Conference at their Annual Plenary
Assembly Held in Koforidua from 5nd to 9th July 1999.
A Communiqué Issued by the Ghana Catholic Bishops' Conference at their Annual Plenary
Assembly Held in Cape Coast from 10th to 15th July 2000.
"AMA Give Churches Deadline to Quit" *The Ghanaian Times* (21st January, 2015), 4.
"Assembly Warns Churches ... Install Soundproof or Face Closure" *The Ghanaian Times* (10th April, 2014), 1.
"Brain Drain Alarming" *Daily Graphic* (12th April, 2001), 1. 3.
"Bishops Decry Poverty" *Daily Graphic* (13th July, 2002), 1, 3.
"Bishop Obinim is Hot, Accused of Sending Someone to Perform Rituals at Rival's Camp" *Daily Graphic* (30th November, 2009),1.
"Churches, Business of Today" *The Mirror* (26th June, 1999), 2.
"Churches must Pay Tax on Sale of Anointing Oil" in *The Ghanaian Times,* (26th January, 2015), 1,4.
"Coup in Burundi" *Daily Graphic* (19th April, 2001), 1, 3.
"Deal with Nogokpo Shrine Now" *The Mirror* (26th June, 1999), 2.
"Economic Dialogue Next Month" *Daily Graphic* (6th April, 2001), 1,3.
"HIPC Shows Positive Signs" *Daily Graphic* (13th June, 2001), 1.
Ghana Aids Commission, Country Aids Response Progress Report - Ghana (January 2012 –December 2013), 29.
"Methodist Bishop Supports Tax on Anointing Oil" in The Ghanaian Times, (9th February, 2015), 15.
"Opambour Slaps T. B. Joshua" *The New P&P* (7th to 9th April, 2014), 3.

References

"Pentecost Disowns Edumfa...for Propagating 'False Doctrines" *The Ghanaian Times* (31st May, 2011), 1, 4.
"Rawlings Jabs Obinim, Kumchacha Calls Them False Prophets", *Daily Guide* (12th November, 2014), 1, 3.
"Use of Classrooms for Church Service" *Daily Graphic* (2nd December, 2014), 55.
"The Prophetic Ministry in Ghana: A Quandary" *Daily Guide* (13th November, 2014), 4.
"Three Fake Pastors Arrested" *Daily Guide* (13th November, 2014), 2.
"Probe Black Stars' Performance at World Cup – Prophet" *Daily Graphic*, 2 July 2014, 71.
"John Mahama will die this year unless... Rev. Owusu Bempah", 8 February 2013, on http://edition.myjoyonline.com/pages/news/201302/101142.php. Accessed on 27 August
2014.
Republic of Ghana, Local Government Act, 1993 (Act 462). Accra: Ghana Publishing Corporation. Assembly Press. 1993.
http/www.Ghanadistricts.com/gasouthmunicipalassembly

ARTICLES IN JOURNALS AND UNPUBLISHED THESIS

Agbeti, J. K. "The Need for Scholarship in the Training for the Christian Ministry" in *Trinity Journal of Church and Theology* Vol. 1 No.1 (June 1991), 25-34.
Akrong, Abraham A. "Salvation in African Christianity" in *Legon Journal of the HUMANITIES*, Volume 12 (1990-2001), 1-29.
Amevenku, Frederick Mawusi. "Mother-Tongue Biblical Interpretation and the Future of African Instituted Christianity in Ghana" in *Trinity Journal of Church and Theology* Vol. 18 No.1
(March 2014), 132-148.
Aryeh, Daniel Nii Aboagye. "A Study of 'Prophetism' in the New Testament and its Implications for Ghanaian Christianity", B.Th. Long Essay submitted to, Legon, 2013.
———. "Mission and Culture: An Expositional Analysis of Acts 1:8 and Mission in Some Ghanaian Market Places" a paper presented at *Valley View University*, School of Theology and Mission, 1st International Conference, (7th to 11th April, 2014).
———. "The Relevance of Mother-Tongue Biblical Hermeneutics in the Ghanaian Context" in *Journal of Applied Thought* (A Multidisciplinary Approach), Vol. 3, No 2 (May 2014), 282-301.
———. "Exegetical Analysis of 1 Cor. 12:1-11: Manifestations of the Gifts of the Holy Spirit in some Ghanaian Churches" in *Journal of Applied Thought* (A Multidisciplinary Approach) Vol. 3, No, 3 (November, 2014), 194-215.
———. "A Study of 'Prophetism' in the Gospels and Gᴁ South Municipal Area: A Way Forward for Prophetic Ministry in Ghana's Christianity" in *Journal of Applied Thought* (A Multidisciplinary Approach) Vol. 4, No, 1 (January, 2015), 196-221.
Asamoah-Gyadu, J. Kwabena "'On the "Mountain" of the Lord' Healing Pilgrimages in Ghanaian Christianity" in *Exchange Journal of Missiological and Ecumenical Research* Vol. 36 (2007), 65-86.
———. "Pentecostalism and the Missiological Significance of Religious Experience in Africa Today: The Case for Ghana 'Church of Pentecost' in *Trinity Journal of Church and Theology*, Vol. XII, No 1&2 (July/December 2002), 30-57.

References

Asante, Emmanuel. "The Relevance of Theological Education in the 21st Century" in *Trinity Journal of Church and Theology* Vol. XIII No.03 (July 2003), 77-82.

Atiemo, Abamfo O. "The Evangelical Christian Fellowship and the Charismatization of Ghanaian Christianity" in *Ghana Bulletin of Theology*, New Series, Vol. 2 (July 2007), 43-65.

Bayes, Jimmy D. "Five-Fold Ministry: A Social and Cultural Texture Analysis of Ephesians 4:11-16" in *Journal of Biblical Perspectives in Leadership* Vol. 3, No. 1 (Winter 2010), 113-122.

Brown, Colin. 'What was John The Baptist Doing?'. *Bulletin for Biblical Research* Vol. 7, (1997).

Bruce, F. F. "John the Forerunner," in *Faith and Thought* Vol. 94, No. 3. (Autumn, 1965).

Buama, Livingstone K. "Christian Witnessing in a Religious Plural Climate" in *Trinity Journal of Church and Theology* Vol. 1, No 1 (June 1991), 8-14.

Cartledge, Mark J. "The Nature and Function of New Testament Glossolalia" in *The Evangelical Quarterly* Vol. 72, No. 2 (2000), 135-150.

Dovlo, Elom "Religion and Politics of Fourth Republican Elections in Ghana (1992, 1996)" in *Ghana Bulletin of Theology*, New Series Vol. 1, No. 1 (July 2006), 3-19.

Ekem, John D. K. "Early Translators and Interpreters of the Judeo-Christian Scriptures on the Gold Coast (Ghana): Two Case Studies," in *Journal of African Christian Thought*, Vol. 13, No. 2 (December 2010), 34-37.

Farnell, F. David. "When Will the Gift of Prophecy Cease? In *Bibliotheca Sacra* Vol. 150 (April-June, 1993), 171-202.

Gill, David W.J. "In Search of the Social Elite in the Corinthian Church" in *Tyndale Bulletin* 44.2 (1993) 323-337.

Haliburton, G. M. "The Anglican Church in Ghana and Harris Movement in 1914" in *The Bulletin of the Society of African Church History* I (1964), 101-106

———. "The Calling of the Prophet" in *The Bulletin of the Society for African Church History*, Vol. 2, (1965), 84-96.

Jongkind, Dirk. "Corinth in The First Century Ad: The Search For Another Class" in *Tyndale Bulletin* Vol. 52, No. 1 (2001) 139-148.

LaSor, William Sanford. "Prophecy, Inspiration, and Sensus Plenior" in *Tyndale Bulletin* Vol. 29 (1978), 49-60.

Obeng, Pashington "Abibisom (Indigenous Religion) by Another Name: A Critical Look at Deliverance Ministry in Ghana" in *Trinity Journal of Church and Theology*, Vol. 18, No. 2 (September, 2014), 27-40.

Okyerefo, Michael Perry Kweku. "The role of Pentecostal Churches as an Influential Arm of Civil Society in Ghana" in *Ghana Social Science Journal* Vol. 11, No. 2 (2014), 77-101.

Omenyo, Cephas N. "The Spirit-Filled Goes to School": Theological Education in African Pentecostalism in Ogbomosho Journal of Theology Vol. XIII, No. 2 (2008), 41-55

Omenyo, N. Cephas & Atiemo O. Abamfo. 'Claiming Religious Space'.in *Ghana Bulletin of Theology*, New Series, Vol. 1, No.1 (July 2006).

Omulokoli, Watson A. O. "William Wade Harris: Premier African Evangelist" in *Africa Journal of Evangelical Theology* Vol. 21, No. 1 (2002), 3-24.

Quarshie, Benhardt Y. 'Doing Biblical Studies in the African Context-the Challenge of Mother-Tongue Scriptures,' in *Journal of African Christian Thought*, Vol. 5, No. 1 (June 2002), 4-14.

References

———. 'The Bible in African Christianity: Kwame Bediako and the Reshaping of an African Heritage,' in *Journal of African Christian Thought*, Vol. 14, No. 2 (December 2011), 3-16.

Rowe, Arthur J. "1 Corinthians 12 - 14: the Use of a Text for Christian Worship" in *Evangelical Quarterly* Vol. 77, No. 2 (2005), 119-128.

Yayi, Jonathan Aremu. "Language Barrier: A Serious Handicap for Theologizing and Mission Input in West Africa: A Case Study of French in Nigeria" in *Ogbomosho Journal of Theology* Vol. XV, No. 2 (2010), 179-186.

2010 Population & Housing Census: Summary Report of Final Result. Accra: Ghana Statistical Service, May, 2012), 6.

Unpublished 2010 Head count Population Census of Ga South Municipal Assembly. Source: GSMA.

Unpublished census of Churches in the Ga South Municipal Assembly, source: GSMA

ARTICLES ON WEBSITES

Ekem, John D. "Spiritual Gifts" or "Spiritual Persons"? 1 Corinthians 12:1A Revisited on www.axbe40.pipex.com/archive/381/381 sample-ekem.pdf. Accessed 2/8/2014.

Boyer, James L. "The Office of the Prophet in the New Testament" in *Grace Journal* on http://www.biblicalstudies.org.uk/pdf/grace-journal/01-1_13.pdf. Accessed 18/72014.

Odamtten, Harry Nii Koney. "They Bleed but they Don't Die: Towards a Theoretical Canon On
Ga-Adangbe Gender Studies" in *The Journal of Pan African Studies*, vol.5, no.2, (April 2012), 110-127.

Odotei, Irene K.. "The History of Gã people: Introduction" on http://www.justiceghana.com/index.php/en/2012-01-24-13-47-17/6642-the-history-of-ga people-introduction. Accessed 3/7/2015.

Ghana's HIV Prevalence for 2013 Declines on
http://www.ghanaweb.com/GhanaHomePage/health/artikel.php?ID=314325 Accessed 22/03/2015.

Shank, David A. "Wadé Harris, William c. 1860 to 1929 Harrist Church (Église Harriste) Liberia/Ghana/Côte d'Ivoire" in G. H. Anderson et al (eds.). 1994. On http://www.dacb.org/stories/liberia/legacy_harris.html. Accessed 6/6/2014.

The Spectator , "The Story of Tema" on http://www.ghanaculture.gov.gh/index1.php?linkid=65&archiveid=2230&page=1&adate=14/12/2013. Accessed 3/7/2014.

Walls, Andres F. "Sam(p)son Oppong c. 1884-1965 Methodist Ghana" in *Dictionary of African
Christian Biography.* On http://www.dacb.org/stories/ghana/opon_sampson2.html 6/6/2014.

Watson-Quartey, Mustapha. "Origin of the Gã Speaking People of Accra" on http://www.kpakpatseweroyalfamily. Wordpress.com/2011/06/18/origin-of-the- Gã-people-in-Ghana. Accessed 3/7/2015.

Zarwan, John. "William Wade Harris: The Genesis of an African Religious Movement" in *Mission: An International Review,* 431-450, http://www. mis.sagepub.com. Accessed 21/5/2014.

http://ghananewsagency.org/human-interest/illiteracy-rate-among-women-still-high-in-ghana fao-54631 Accessed 22/03/2015.

References

http://www.ghanaweb.com/GhanaHomePage/religion/artikel.php?ID=276602. Accessed 28/03/2015.

http://gadangme.weebly.com/kings-of-the-ga-state.html. Accessed 5/4/2014.

BOOKS

Adutwum, Ofosu. *The Faithful and the Power of God: The Testimony of the Book of Daniel.* Accra, Ghana: Buck Press, 2013.

Agbeti, J. Kofi. *West African Church History, Christian Missions and Church Foundations: 1482-1919.* Leiden, The Netherlands: E. J. Brill, 1986.

Ago, E., Anang E. Adzei and Bekoe, Adjei. *Teshi Administrative and Cultural Practices.* Tema, Ghana: Ronna Publishers, 2004.

Alford, Henry. *Alford's Greek Testament: An Exegetical and Critical Commentary*, Vol.1. Michigan: Baker Book House, 1980.

Annorbah-Sarpei, James. "The Rise of Prophetism — A Socio-Political Explanation" in *The Rise of Independent Churches in Ghana.* Accra: Asempa Publication, 1990.

Anto, Isaac. *The Office of the Prophet.* Accra: Nobles Multimedia, 2011.

———. *Deeper Insight into the Prophetic.* Accra: Nobles Multimedia, 2014.

Arhin, Samuel Acquaah. "HIV/AIDS, the Church and Pastoral Care: African Perspectives" in J. Kwabena Asamoah-Gyadu (Ed.) *Christianity, Mission and Ecumenism in Ghana, Essays in honour of Robert K. Aboagye-Mensah* (Accra: Asempa Publishers, 2009.

———. "Spirit and Spirits African Religious Traditions" in Veli-Matti Kärkkäinen, Kirsteen Kim, and Amos Yong (Eds.), *Interdisciplinary and Religio-Cultural Discourses on a Spirit-Filled World: Loosing the Spirits.* New York: Palgrave Macmillan, 2013.

———.*African Charismatics: Current Developments within Independent Indigenous Pentecostalism in Ghana.* Leiden, The Netherland: African Christian Press under License from Koninklijke Brill NV, 2005.

———. *Contemporary Pentecostal Christianity: Interpretations from an African Context.* Oxford, U. K.: Regnum Books International, 2013.

———."'The Promise is for you and your Children': Pentecostal Spirituality, Mission and Discipleship in Africa" in Wonsuk Ma and Kenneth R. Ross (Eds.) *Mission Spirituality and Authentic Discipleship.* Oxford: Regnum Books International, 2013.

———. "Theological Education and Religious Pluralism in Ghana" in J. Kwabena Asamoah-Gyadu (Ed.) *Christianity, Mission and Ecumenism in Ghana, Essays in honour of Robert K. Aboagye-Mensah.* Accra: Asempa Publishers, 2009), 158-159.

Asante, Emmanuel K. *The Prophetic and Apocalyptic Phenomena in Israel: A Theological Introduction.* Accra: Son Life Press, 2011.

Asiedu, Henry Ampaw "Gaddiel R. Acquaah and the Hermeneutics of Vernacular Hymns" in Kwabena Asamoah-Gyadu (Ed.) *Christianity, Mission and Ecumenism in Ghana, Essays in honour of Robert K. Aboagye-Mensah.* Accra: Asempa Publishers, 2009.

Atiemo, Abamfo O. *The Rise of the Charismatic Movement in the Mainline Churches in Ghana.* Accra: Asempa Publishers, 1993.

Aune, David E. *Prophecy In Early Christianity and the Ancient Mediterranean World.* Michigan: William B. Publishing Company, 1983.

———. "Religions, Greco-Roman" in Gerald F. Hawthorne, Ralph P. Martin and Daniel G. Reid (Eds.) *Dictionary of Paul and His Letters.* Downers Grove, Illinois and Leicester: InterVarsity Press, 1993.

References

Ayerh, Lawrence K. *Constitutional Amendment in Heaven: Why the Lord Jesus Christ, the Anointed One, did not Use Oil*. Accra: Forever Grateful Ministries International Publishing, n.d.

Banks, Robert. *Paul's Idea of Community: The Early House Churches in their Historical Setting*. Grand Rapids, Michigan: William B. Eerdmans Publishing Company, 1980.

Baëta, Christian G. *Prophetism in Ghana: A Study of Some 'Spiritual' Churches*. Achimota, Ghana: Africa Christian Press, 2004.

Barclay, William. *And He Had Compassion*. Valley Forge, PA: Judson Press, 1975

———.The New Daily Study Bible, The Gospel of John, Vol.2. Bangalore: Theological Publication in India, 2009.

Barnett, Paul. *Paul Missionary of Jesus*. Grand Rapids, Michigan: Wm. B. Eerdmans Publishing Co., 2008.

Barnett, Paul W. "Tentmaking" in Gerald F. Hawthorne, Ralph P. Martin and Daniel G. Reid (Eds.) *Dictionary of Paul and His Letters*. Downers Grove, Illinois and Leicester: InterVarsity Press, 1993.

Barrett, C. K. *The First Epistle to the Corinthians*. London: Adam & Charles Black, 1971.

———. *A Commentary on the Epistle to the Romans*. London: Adam & Charles Black, 1957.

Bartels, F. L. *The Roots of Ghana Methodism*. Cambridge: The Cambridge University Press in Association with Methodist Book Depot Ltd Ghana, 1965.

Bediako, Kwame. *Christianity in Africa: The Renewal of a Non-Western Religion*. Edinburgh: Edinburgh University Press and New York: Orbis Books, 1995.

Belm, Göttingen Johannes. "γλῶσσα" in Gerhard Kittel (Ed.) *Theological Dictionary of the New Testament* Vol. I. Grand Rapids, Michigan: Wm. B. Eerdmans Publishing Company, 1965.

———. "ἑρμηνεία" in Gerhard Kittel (Ed.) *Theological Dictionary of the New Testament* Vol. II. Grand Rapids, Michigan: Wm. B. Eerdmans Publishing Company, 1965), 665.

Bernhard Bierlich, *The Problem of Money: Africa Agency and Western Medicine in Northern Ghana*. New York and Oxford: Berghahn Books, 2007.

Blomberg, Claig L. with Markley, Jennifer Foutz. *A Handbook of New Testament Exegesis*. Grand Rapids, Michigan: Baker Academic, 2010.

Boadi, Lawrence Kwadwo. *Linguistic Barriers to Communication in the Modern World*. Accra: Ghana Academy of Arts and Sciences, February 1994.

Bornkamm, Gunther. *Paul*. London, Sydney, Auckland and Toronto: Hodder and Stoughton, 1980.

Brown, Colin. *That You May Believe: Miracles and Faith Then and Now*. Grand Rapids, Michigan and Devon, UK: William B. Eerdmans Publishing Company and The Paternoster Press, 1985.

———. "προφήτης" in Colin Brown (Ed.) *The New International Dictionary of New Testament Theology* Vol. 3. Grand Rapids, Michigan: Zondervan Publishing House, 1975.

———. "σοφία" in Colin Brown (Ed.), *The New International Dictionary of New Testament Theology* Vol. 3. Grand Rapids, Michigan: Zondervan, 1978.

Bruce, F. F. "Paul in Acts and Letters" in Gerald F. Hawthorne, Ralph P. Martin and Daniel G. Reid (Eds.) *Dictionary of Paul and His Letters*. Downers Grove, Illinois and Leicester: InterVarsity Press, 1993.

References

———. *Paul: Apostle of the Heart Set Free*. Grand Rapids, Michigan: William. B. Eerdmans Publishing Company, 1990.

———. *New Testament History*. New York: Doubleday & Company, Inc., 1972.

Buckmaster, Henrietta. *Paul: A Man who Changed the World*. New York, Toronto and London: McGraw-Hill Book Company, 1965.

Budd, P. J. "Γαβριήλ" in Colin Brown (Ed.) *The New International Dictionary of New Testament Theology*. Grand Rapids, Michigan: Zondervan Publishing House, 1975.

Commey, Richard Oswald. *Ministry Gifts: Apostles, Prophets, Evangelists, Pastors and Teachers*. Summerville. SC: Holy Fire Publishing, 2008.

———.*Prophecy and Prophets*. Summerville. SC: Holy Fire Publishing, 2007.

Carson, D. A. "pseudonymity and pseudepigraphy" in Craig A. Evans & Stanley E. Porter (Eds.),*Dictionary of New Testament Background*. Downers Grove, Illinois: InterVarsity Press, 2000.

———. *The Cross and the Christian Ministry: Leadership lessons from 1 Corinthians*. Grand Rapids, Michigan: Baker Academic, 1993.

Carter, Warren. *Seven Events that Shaped the New Testament*. Grand Rapids, Michigan: Baker Academic, 2013.

Coenen, L. "Ε,κκλησία" in Colin Brown (Ed.) *The New International Dictionary of New Testament Theology*. Grand Rapids, Michigan: Zondervan Publishing House, 1975.

Chilton, B. D. "Rabbis" in Craig A. Evans & Stanley E. Porter (Eds.), *Dictionary of New Testament Background*. Downers Grove, Illinois: InterVarsity Press, 2000.

Chisholm Jr, Robert B. *Handbook of the Prophets*. Grand Rapids, Michigan: Baker Academic, 2002.

Clarke, Peter B. *West Africa and Christianity*. London: Edward Arnold Publishers Ltd, 1986.

Coleman, William L. *Today's Handbook of Bible Times & Customs: Cultural, Social & Political Background on the Land & People of the Bible. Based on all the Recent Archaeological Discoveries*. Minneapolis, Minnesota: Bethany House Publishers, 1984.

C.M., Vawter Bruce. "Introduction to Prophetic Literature" in *The New Jerome Biblical Commentary*. Bangalore: Theological Publications in India, 1992.

Conteh, Prince S. *Essays in African Religion and Christianity*. n. c. :n. p., 2012.

Coppes, Leonard J. 'Nabi' in R. Laird Harris, Gleason L. Archer Jr., Bruce K. Waltke Eds, *Theological Wordbook Of The Old Testament*, Vol.2. Chicago: Moody Press, 1980.

Croy, N. C. "Religion, Personal" in Craig A. Evans & Stanley E. Porter (Eds.) *Dictionary of New Testament Background*. Downer Grove, Illinois and Nottingham, England: InterVarsity Press, 2000.

Cousland, J. R. C. 'Prophets and Prophecy' in Craig A. Evans & Stanley E. Porter Eds, *Dictionary of New Testament Background*. Illinois: Inter Varsity Press, 2000.

Dakubu, M.E. Kropp (Ed.), *Gã - English Dictionary with English - Gã Index* 2nd Ed. Accra, Ghana: Black Mask Ltd, 2009.

Debrunner, Hans W. *A History of Christianity in Ghana*. Accra: Waterville Publishing House, 1967.

References

Delling, Halle Gerhard. "ψαλμὸς" in Gerhard Kittel and Gerhard Friedrick (Eds.) *Theological Dictionary of the New Testament* Vol. VIII. Grand Rapids, Michigan: Wm. B. Eerdmans Publishing Company, 1964.

Duling, Dennis C. *The New Testament: History, Literature and Social Context* 4th Ed.. Canada: Wadsworth, 2003.

Dunn, J. D. G. *Jesus and the Spirit*. Philadelphia: Westminster, 1975.

Dunnett, Walter M. "Paul" in Charles F. Pfeiffer, Howard F. Vos, John Rea (Eds.) *Wycliffe Bible Dictionary*. Peabody, Massachusetts: Hendrickson Publishers, Inc., 2008.

Dyer, Anne E. "Angels and Pentecostals: An Empirical Investigation into Grassroots Opinions on Angels among Assemblies of God, UK Members" in Veli-Matti Kärkkäinen, Kirsteen Kim, and Amos Yong (Eds.) *Interdisciplinary and Religio-Cultural Discourses on a Spirit-filled World: Loosing the Spirits*. New York; Palgrave Macmillan, 2013.

Eicken, E. von and Lindner, H. "αvpostε,llw" in Colin Brown (Ed.) *The New International Dictionary of New Testament Theology* Vol.1. Grand Rapids, Michigan: Zondervan Publishing House, 1975.

Ekem, John D. Kwamena & Kissi, Seth. *Essentials of Biblical Greek Morphology with an Introductory Syntax*. Accra: SonLife Press, 2010.

Ekem, D. K. John. *Priesthood in Context: A Study of Priesthood in Some Christian and Primal Communities of Ghana and its Relevance for Mother-Tongue Biblical Interpretation*. Accra: Son Life Press, 2008.

———. "Wesleyan Methodist and Bible Translation in the Gold Coast" in J. Kwabena Asamoah-Gyadu (Ed.) *Christianity, Mission and Ecumenism in Ghana, Essays in Honour of Robert K. Aboagye-Mensah*. Accra: Asempa Publishers, 2009.

———. *Early Scriptures of the Gold Coast (Ghana): The Historical, Linguistic, and Theological Settings of the Gã, Twi, Mfantse, and Ewe Bibles*. Rome and Manchester: Edizioni di Storia e Letteratura and St Jerome Publishing, 2011.

Elwell, Walter A. and Yarbrough, Robert W. *Encountering the New Testament: A Historical and Theological Survey*. Grand Rapids, Michigan: Baker Academic, 2005.

Erdman, Charles R. *The First Epistle of Paul to the Corinthians: An Exposition*. Philadelphia, Pennsylvania: The Westminster Press, 1984.

Essamuah, Casely B. "Heart Music as Identity Marker: Ebibindwom and Ghanaian Methodism" in J. Kwabena Asamoah-Gyadu (Ed.) *Christianity, Mission and Ecumenism in Ghana, Essays in honour of Robert K. Aboagye-Mensah*. Accra: Asempa Publishers, 2009.

Evans, C. A. "Sons of God Texts (4Q246)" in Craig A. Evans & Stanley E. Porter (Eds.), *Dictionary of New Testament Background*. Downers Grove, Illinois: InterVarsity Press, 2000.

Fee, Gordon D. *The First Epistle to the Corinthians*. Grand Rapids, Michigan: William B. Eerdmans Publishings Company, 1987.

———. *God's Empowering Presence: The Holy Spirit in the Letters of Paul*. Grand Rapids, Michigan: Baker Academic, 1994.

Field, Margaret J. *Social Organization of the Gã people*. London: The Crown Agents for the Colonies, 1940.

Fitzmyer, Joseph A. "Paul" in Raymond E. Brown, Joseph A. Fitzmyer and Roland E, Murphy (Eds.) *The New Jerome Biblical Commentary*. London: Burns and Oates, 2007.

References

Forbes, C. *Prophecy and Inspired speech in Early Christianity and its Hellenistic Environment.* Peabody, Hendrickson, 1997.

Freeman, Hobart E. *An Introduction to the Old Testament Prophets.* Chicago: Moody Press, 1972.

Gaiser, Frederick J. *Healing in the Bible: Theological Insight for Christian Ministry.* Grand Rapids, Michigan: Baker Academic, 2010.

Garland, David E. *1 Corinthians.* Grand Rapids, Michigan: Baker Academic, 2003.

Gerhardsson, B. 'The Mighty Acts of Jesus', in Raymond E. Brown, Joseph A. Fitzmyer, Roland E. Murphy (Eds), *The Jerome Biblical Commentary.* London: Burns & Oates, 2007.

Gifford, Paul. *Ghana's New Christianity: Pentecostalism in a Global African Economy.* Bloomington & Indianapolis: Indiana University Press, 2004.

Goetchius, Eugene Van Ness. *The Language of the New Testament.* New York: Charles Scribner's Sons, 1965.

Granberg-Michaelson, Wesley. *From Times Square to Timbuktu: The Post-Christian West Meets the Non-Western Church.* Grand Rapids, Michigan / Cambridge, U.K.: William B. Eerdmans Publishing Company, 2013.

Grant, Robert M. *Paul in the Roman World: The Conflict at Corinth.* Louisville, London and Leiden: Westminster John Knox Press, 1989.

Grudem, Wayne. *Systematic Theology: An Introduction to Biblical Doctrine.* Nottingham, England: Inter-Varsity Press, 1994.

Günther, W. "ἀδελφος" in Colin Brown (Ed.) The New International Dictionary of New Testament Theology. Grand Rapids, Michigan: Zondervan Publishing House, 1975.

Grundmann, Jena Walter. "σύν-μετά" in Gerhard Kittel and Gerhard Friedrick (Eds.) *Theological Dictionary of the New Testament* Vol. VIII. Grand Rapids, Michigan: Wm. B. Eerdmans Publishing Company,1964.

Guthrie, Donald. *New Testament Introduction.* Leicester, England: Inter-Varsity Press, 1970.

Hayes, John H. *An Introduction to Old Testament Studies.* Nashville: Abingdon Press, 1991.

Hill, David. *New Testament Prophecy.* London: Marshall, Morgan & Scott, 1979.

Porter, H. "Shekel" in James Orr Ed., *The International Standard Bible Encyclopedia*, Volume IV. Grand Rapids: Michigan, WM.B. Eerdmans Publishing Co., 1949.

Hafemann, Scott J. "Corinthians, Letters to the" in Gerald F. Hawthorne, Ralph P. Martin and Daniel G. Reid (Eds.) *Dictionary of Paul and His Letters.* Downers Grove, Illinois and Leicester, England: InterVarsity Press, 1993.

Helmut, Bethel Krämer. "προφήτης" in Gerhard Kittel and Gerhard Friedrick (Eds.) *Theological Dictionary of the New Testament* Vol. VI. Grand Rapids, Michigan: Wm. B. Eerdmans Publishing Company,1964.

Hesselgrave, David J. *Today's Choices for Tomorrow's Mission: An Evangelical Perspective on Trends and Issues in Missions.* Grand Rapids, Michigan: Zondervan Publishing House, 1988.

Hodge, Charles. *A commentary on 1 & 2 Corinthians.* Edinburgh and Pennsylvania, The Banner of Truth Trust, 1994.

———.*Commentary on the Epistle to the Romans.* Grand Rapids, Michigan: Wm. B. Eerdmans Publishing Company, 1993.

Hagin, Kenneth E. *The Holy Spirit and His Gifts.* Tulsa, Ok: Faith Library Publications, 2007.

References

Haliburton, G. M. *The Prophet Harris: A Study of an African Prophet and his Mass Movement in the Ivory Coast and the Gold Coast, 1913-1915*. London: Longman, 1971.

Hamon, Bill. *Prophets and the Prophetic Movement: God's Prophetic Move Today*. Shippensburg, PA: Destiny Image, 1990.

Hill, David. *New Testament Prophecy*. London: Marshall, Morgan & Scott, 1979.

Howell, Allison M. "Beyond Translating Western Commentaries: Bible Commentary Writing in African Languages" in Gillian Mary Bediako, Benhardt Y. Quarshie and J. Kwabena Asamoah-Gyadu (Eds.) *Seeing New Facets of the Diamond: Christianity as a Universal Faith, Essays in Honour of Kwame Bediako*. Oxford: Regnum Africa, 2014.

Jenkins, Philip. *The Next Christendom: The Coming of Global Christianity*. New York: Oxford University Press, 2007.

Jewett, Robert. *Dating Paul's Life*. London: SCM Press, Ltd, 1979.

Josephus, Flavius. *The New Complete Works of Josephus*. Michigan: Kregel Publications, 1999.

Karris, Robert J., 'The Gospel According to Luke" in Raymond E. Brown, Joseph A. Fitzmyer, Roland E. Murphy Eds. *The Jerome Biblical Commentary*. London: Burns & Oates, 2007.

Kee, Howard Clark. *Miracle in the Early Christian World: A Study in Sociohistorical Method*. New Haven and London: Yale University Press, 1983.

Keil, C. F. and Delitzsch, F. Keil & Delitzsch. *Commentary on the Old Testament* Vol. 1, the Pentateuch. Peabody, Massachusetts: Hendrickson Publishers, 1989.

Kilson, Marion. *African Urban Kinsmen: The Gã of Central Accra*. London: C. Hurst & Company, 1974.

Kissi, Seth. *The Gifts and Spirituality: Understanding the Subject in the Context of First Corinthians, Addressing Some Popular Misconceptions*. Achimota, Ghana: African Christian Press, 2014.

Kittel, Gerhard. "ἀγαπάω, ἀγάπή, ἀγαπητος – φιλεω" in Gerhard Kittel (Ed.) *Theological Dictionary of the New Testament* Vol. I. Grand Rapids, Michigan: Wm. B. Eerdmans Publishing Company, 1964.

Killen, R. Allen. "Philosophy" in Charles F. Pfeiffer, Howard F. Vos, John Rea (Eds.) *Wycliffe Bible Dictionary*. Peabody, Massachusetts: Hendrickson Publishers, Inc., 2008.

Klein, William W.; Blomberg Craig L. and Hubbard, Robert L. Jr., *Introduction to Biblical Interpretation*. Nashville, Dallas, Mexico City and Rio de Janeiro: Thomas Nelson, 2004.

Kummel, Werner Georg. *Introduction to the New Testament*. Nashville: Abingdon Press, 1975.

Ladd, George Eldon. *A Theology of the New Testament* Rev. Ed.. Grand Rapids, Michigan: William B. Eerdmans Publishing Company, 2001.

Lambert, J.C. 'Spirit' in James Orr Ed., *The International Standard Bible Encyclopedia*, Volume V. Grand Rapids: Michigan, WM.B. Eerdmans Publishing Co., 1949.

Lang, Bernhard. *Monotheism and the Prophetic Minority: An Essay in Biblical History and Sociology*. Sheffield: The Almond Press, 1983.

Laryea, Philip Tetteh. *Yesu Hɔmɔwɔ nuŋtsɔ*. Akropong-Akuapem, Ghana: Regnum Africa, 2011.

Lawrence, Paul. *The Lion Atlas of Bible History*. Oxford, England: Lion Hudson plc., 2006.

References

Yonge, C. D. translated, The Works of Philo: Complete and Unabridged, New Updated Version. n.c.: Hendrickson Publishers, 2013.

Lietzmann, Hans. *A History of the Early Church: The Beginning of the Christian Church.* Cleveland and New York: The World Publishing Company, 1953.

Llewelyn, S. R. "The King as 'Living Image' of Zeus" in S. R. Llewelyn (Ed.) New Document Illustrating Early Christianity Vol. 9. Grand Rapids, Michigan and Cambridge: Wm. B. Eerdmans Publishing Company, 2002.

Larbi, Emmanuel Kingsley. *Pentecostalism: The Eddies of Ghanaian Christianity.* Accra: SAPC, 2001

Matkin, J. Michael. *Early Christianity.* New York: Penguin Group, 2008.

Mallone, George. *Those Controversial Gifts: Prophecy, Dreams, Visions, Tongues, Interpretation, Healing.* Illinois: InterVarsity Press, 1983.

Matthews, H. Victor and Benjamin, C. Don. *Old Testament Parallels, Law and Stories From The Ancient Near East,* Third Edition. New Jersey: Paulist Press, 2006.

Mbiti, S. John. *Introduction to African Religion,* Second Edition. Oxford: Heinemann Educational Publishers, 1991.

Meyer, Jena Rudolf. "The End of Prophecy" in Gerhard Kittel, Gerhard Friedrich, (Eds), *Theological Dictionary of the New Testament* Vol.vi (Michigan: WM.B. Eerdmans Publishing Company, 1968

Michel, Halle Otto. "καλυπτω" in Kittel and Friedrich Eds, *Theological Dictionary of the New Testament* Vol.iii. Michigan: WM.B.Eedmans Publishing Company, 1965.

Motyer, Stephen. "Apocalyptic and Revelation" in Walter A. Elwell Ed, *Baker Theological Dictionary of the Bible.* Michigan: Baker Books, 1996.

Murphy, Carolyn & Jim. *Prophets and Prophecy in Today's Church.* California: Hundredfold Press, 1994.

Marshall, I. Howard. *A Concise New Testament Theology.* Downers Grove, Illinois and Leicester, England: InterVarsity Press, 2008.

Maxwell, David. *African Gifts of the Spirit: Pentecostalism & the Rise of a Zimbabwean Transnational Religious Movement.* Oxford, Ohio and Harare: James Currey, Ohio University Press and Weaver Press, 2006.

Mbiti, John S. *Introduction to African Religion* 2nd Rev. Ed.. Oxford: Heinemann Educational Publishers, 1991.

Meeks, Wayne A. *The first Urban Christians: The Social World of the Apostle Paul.* New Haven and London: Yale University Press, 1983.

Meier, Samuel A. *Themes and Transformations in Old Testament Prophecy.* Downers Grove, Illinois: IVP Academic, 2009.

Menzies William W. and Menzies, Robert P. *Spirit and Power: The Foundation of Pentecostal Experience.* Grand Rapids, Michigan: Zondervan Publishing House, 2000.

Meyer, Jena Rudolf "Prophecy and Prophets in the Judaism of the Hellenistic-Roman Period" in Gerhard Kittel and Gerhard Friedrich (Eds), *Theological Dictionary of the New Testament* Vol.vi. Michigan: WM.B. Eerdmans Publishing Company, 1968.

Michaels, J. R. "Paul in Early Church Tradition" in Gerald F. Hawthorne, Ralph P. Martin and Vos, Howard F. "Tarsus" in Charles F. Pfeiffer, Howard F. Vos, John Rea (Eds.) *Wycliffe Bible Dictionary.* Peabody, Massachusetts: Hendrickson Publishers, Inc., 2008.

Moffatt, James. *The First Epistle of Paul to the Corinthians.* London: Hodder and Stoughton, 1938.

References

Morgan, G. Campbell. *The Corinthian Letters of Paul: An Exposition of I and II Corinthians.* Old Tappan, New Jersey: Fleming H. Revell Company, 1946.

Mundle, W. "ἐκστασις" in Colin Brown (Ed.) *The New International Dictionary of New Testament Theology.* Grand Rapids, Michigan: Zondervan Publishing House, 1975.

Murphy-O'Connor, Jerome. "The First Epistle to the Corinthians" in Raymond E. Brown, Joseph A. Fitzmyer and Roland E, Murphy (Eds.) *The New Jerome Biblical Commentary.* London: Burns and Oates, 2007.

Mwaura, Philomena Njeri. "Spirituality and Healing in African Indigenous Culture and Contemporary Society" in Gillian Mary Bediako, Benhardt Y. Quarshie and J. Kwabena Asamoah-Gyadu (Eds.) *Seeing New Facets of the Diamond: Christianity as a Universal Faith, Essays in Honour of Kwame Bediako.* Oxford: Regnum Africa, 2014.

Nii Abbey, H. *Homoho in Ghana.* Accra, Ghana: Studio Brian Communications, 2010.

Obeng, Pashington. *Asante Catholism: Religion and Cultural Reproduction Among the Akan of Ghana.* Leiden and New York: E. J. Brill, 1996.

O'Brien, P. T. "Church" in Gerald F. Hawthorne, Ralph P. Martin and Daniel G. Reid (Eds.) *Dictionary of Paul and His Letters.* Downers Grove, Illinois and Leicester: InterVarsity Press, 1993.

Oepke, Leipzig Albrecht. "ἀποκάλυψις" in Gerhard Kittel (Ed.) *Theological Dictionary of the New Testament* Vol. III. Grand Rapids, Michigan: Wm. B. Eerdmans Publishing Company, 1965.

Omenyo, Cephas N. *Pentecost Outside Pentecostalism: A Study of the Development of Charismatic Renewal in the Mainline Churches in Ghana.* The Netherlands: Boekencentrum Publishing House, 2002.

Onyinah, Opoku. "Faith, Healing and Mission: Perspectives from the Bible" in J. Kwabena Asamoah-Gyadu (Ed.) *Christianity, Mission and Ecumenism in Ghana, Essays in honour of Robert K. Aboagye-Mensah.* Accra: Asempa Publishers, 2009.

Orelli, C. Von. "Prophecy, Prophets" in James Orr Ed., *The International Standard Bible Encyclopedia*, Volume IV. Grand Rapids: Michigan, WM.B. Eerdmans Publishing Co., 1949.

Opoku, Kofi Asare. "A Brief History of Independent Church Movement in Ghana Since 1862" in *The Rise of Independent Churches in Ghana.* Accra: Asempa Publication, 1990.

Prior, David. *The Message of 1 Corinthians: Life in the Local Church.* Leicester, England and Downers Groves, Illinois, 1985.

Quayesi-Amakye, Joseph. *Prophetism in Ghana Today: A Study on Trends in Ghanaian Pentecostal Prophetism.* n.c.: n. p., 2013.

Quarcoopome, T. N. O. *West African Traditional Religion.* Ibadan: African University Press, 1987.

Bernard Ramm, *Protestant Biblical Interpretation* 3rd Rev. Ed. Grand Rapids, Michigan: Baker Book House, 1993.

Reasoner, M. "Citizenship, Roman and Heavenly" in Gerald F. Hawthorne, Ralph P. Martin and Vos, Howard F. (Eds.) *Wycliffe Bible Dictionary.* Peabody, Massachusetts: Hendrickson Publishers, Inc., 2008.

Robeck, C. M. Jr., "Knowledge, Gift of Knowledge" in Gerald F. Hawthorne, Ralph P. Martin and Daniel G. Reid (Eds.), *Dictionary of Paul and His Letters.* Downers Grove, Illinois and Leicester, England: Intervarsity Press, 1993.

Robertson, Archibald and Plummer, Alfred. *A Critical and Exegetical Commentary on the First Epistle of St Paul to the Corinthians.* Edinburgh: T&T Clark Ltd., 1999.

References

Robbins, Vernon K. *Beginnings and Developments in Socio-Rhetorical Interpretation.* Atlanta, GA: Emory University, 2004.

Robinson, Thomas. A. *Mastering New Testament Greek: Essential Tools for Students.* Peabody, Massachusetts: Hendrickson Publishers, Inc., 2007.

Reid, Daniel G. (Eds.) *Dictionary of Paul and His Letters.* Downers Grove, Illinois and Leicester: InterVarsity Press, 1993.

Ruff, John. *Paul's First Letter to Corinth.* London: SCM Press Ltd, 1977.

Rupprecht, A. A. "Legal System, Roman" in Gerald F. Hawthorne, Ralph P. Martin and Daniel G. Reid (Eds.) *Dictionary of Paul and His Letters.* Downers Grove, Illinois and Leicester: InterVarsity Press, 1993.

Sanneh, Lamin. *Translating the Message: The Missionary Impact on Culture.* Maryknoll, New York: Orbis Books, 2009.

Schmitz, E. D. "Γινώσκω" in Colin Brown (Ed.), *The New International Dictionary of New Testament Theology* Vol. 2. Grand Rapids, Michigan: Zondervan, 1978.

Sintim-Koree, Stephen. *The God Who Answers by Thunder: An Account of Christian Persecution in Nzemaland During the Ban on Drumming 1993-1996.* Accra, Ghana: SonLife Press, 2013.

Soards, Marion L. *The Apostle Paul: An Introduction to his Writings and Teaching.* New York/Mahwah: Paulist Press, 1987.

Stegner, W. R. "Diaspora" in Gerald F. Hawthorne, Ralph P. Martin and Daniel G. Reid (Eds.) *Dictionary of Paul and His Letters.* Downers Grove, Illinois and Leicester: InterVarsity Press, 1993.

Stott, John R. W. *The Message of Romans.* Nottingham, England: Inter-Varsity Press, 2012.

Stowers, Stanley K. *Letter Writing in Greco-Roman Antiquity.* Philadelphia: The Westminster Press, 1989.

Talbert, Charles H. *Reading Corinthians: A New Commentary for Preachers.* London and New York: SPCK and Crossroad Publishing Company, 1987.

Tate, W. Randolph. *Handbook for Biblical Interpretation: An Essential Guide to Methods, Terms, and Concepts* 2nd Edi. Grand Rapids, Michigan: Baker Academic, 2012.

———. *Biblical Interpretation: An Integrated Approach* 3rd Ed. Massachusetts: Hendrickson Publishing, Inc., 2008.

Tenney, Merrill C. *New Testament Times.* Grand Rapids, Michigan: William. B. Eerdmans Publishing Company, 1965.

Tetteh, Lawrence. *Benefit of the anointing.* London: LT Media Ministries, 2002.

Theissen, Gerd. *Psychological Aspects of Pauline Theology.* Edinburgh: T &T Clark, 1987.

Thiessen, Henry Clarence. *Introduction to the New Testament.* Grand Rapids, Michigan: Wm. B. Eerdmans Publishing Company, 1964.

Thomson, J. E. H. "Background of Apocalyptic" in James Orr Ed., *The International Standard Bible Encyclopedia*, Volume V. Grand Rapids: Michigan, WM.B. Eerdmans Publishing Co., 1949.

Turner, Max. *The Holy Spirit and Spiritual Gifts Then and Now.* London: Paternoster Press, 1999.

Verbrugge Verlyn D. (Ed.), "καλύπτω" in *New International Dictionary of New Testament Theology* Abri. Edi.. Grand Rapids, Michigan: Zondervan Corporation, 2000.

Vincent, R. Marvin. *Vincent's Word Studies in the New Testament* Vol.1. Massachusetts: Hendrickson Publishers Inc, 2009.

References

Viviano, Benedict T. "The Gospel According to Matthew" in Raymond E. Brown, Joseph A. Fitzmyer, Roland E. Murphy (Eds), *The Jerome Biblical Commentary*. London: Burns & Oates, 2007.

V. Iain Provan, Long, Philips and Longman, Tremper III. *A Biblical History of Israel*. Louisville, London: Westminster John Knox Press, 2003.

Wagner, C. Peter. *Your Spiritual Gifts Can Help Your Church Grow*. California: Regal Books, 2005.

Walker, Williston. *History of the Christian Church*. New York: Charles Scribner's Sons, 1922.

Wallace, Daniel B. *Greek Grammar Beyond the Basics: An Exegetical Syntax of the New Testament*. Grand Rapids, Michigan: Zondervan, 1996.

Watson, D. E. "Education: Jewish and Greco-Roman" in Craig A. Evans & Stanley E. Porter (Eds.) *Dictionary of New Testament Background*. Downers Grove, Illinois and Nottingham, England: InterVarsity Press, 2000.

Wellington, H. Nii Adziri. *Stones Tell Stories at Osu: Memories of a Host Community of the Danish Trans-Atlantic Slave Trade*. Accra, Ghana: Sub-Saharan Publishers, 2011.

William Whiston (trans), *The New Complete Works of Josephus*. Grand Rapids, Michigan: Kregel Publications, 1999.

Williamson, P. R. "Circumcision" in T. Desmond Alexander & David W. Baker (Eds.), *Dictionary of the Old Testament Pentateuch*. Downer Grove, Illinois/Leicester, England: InterVarsity Press, 2003.

Willoughby, W. Robert. *First Corinthians: Fostering Spirituality*. Camp Hill, Pennsylvania: Christian Publications, Inc., n.d.

Yankah, Kwesi. *Education, Literacy and Governance: A Linguistic Inquiry into Ghana's Burgeoning Democracy*. Accra: Ghana Academy of Arts and Sciences, March 2006.

Index of Authors

Abbey, H. Nii, 13, 13n5
Aboagye-Mensah, Robert K., 56n59
Acquaah, Gaddiel Robert, 62
Addo, Stephen Ayisi, 49
Adubofour, S., 39
Afriyie, Kwame Dwoben Poku, 4n10, 5n13, 6n14, 6n15, 6n17, 7n18, 7n19, 8, 8n23, 8n24, 10n27
Agbeti, J. K., 69, 69n98
Ago, E., 16, 16n20
Ahinful, Kwamena, 40
Akrama, Numbo, 20, 20n34, 21
Akrong, Abraham, 79, 79n8
Aland, Barbara, 133n93
Aland, Kurt, 133n93
Alford, Henry, 93n34
Amevenku, Frederick Mawusi, 37n9, 38, 38n13, 69n97
Ammah, E. A., 13
Amponsah, Eric Nana Kwas, 60, 60n74, 60n76, 61, 63, 64, 65, 68, 69
Anang, E. Adzei, 16, 16n20
Anderson, G. H., 26n5
Annorbah-Sarpei, James, xxin26, 33, 33n42, 33n43, 33n44, 37, 37n8
Anquandah, James, 36n5, 37n7
Anto, Isaac, xix, xixn17, xviiin10, 46n9, 53, 53n43, 59, 59n70, 60, 60n71, 60n75, 67, 67n92
Archer, Gleason L., Jr., 90n29
Arhin, Samuel Acquaah, 49n22
Arthur, Wonderful Adjei, xvi–xvii, xvin6–xviin6, xviin7

Aryeh, Daniel Nii Aboagye, xviin9, xxivn33, 36n4, 38n16, 40n22, 42n29, 43n31, 46n10, 47n12, 53n45, 54n50, 57n65, 122n42, 129n73, 130n81
Asamoah-Gyadu, J. Kwabena, xvi, xvin2, xviiin15, xxin26, 20, 20n32, 25n2, 25n3, 26n4, 32–33, 33n39, 36, 36n3, 36n6–37n6, 37, 37n10, 38n12, 40, 40n21, 47, 47n11, 47n14, 49n20, 49n22, 50n26, 50n27, 50n28, 50n29, 51n33, 52n35, 52n38, 54n47, 54n49, 55, 55n52, 55n53, 56n59, 56n61, 57n62, 57n63, 58n69, 62, 62n80, 62n81, 62n82, 66, 66n91, 68n95, 69n97, 70, 70n101
Asamoah-Gyadu, Paul J. K., xviii
Asante, Emmanuel K., 1n1, 69n99, 82n1, 84n8, 92n31, 94, 94n41, 94n42
Asiedu, Henry Ampaw, 62, 62n81
Atiemo, Abamfo O., 37n11, 39, 39n18, 43n32, 52n36
Aune, David E., xvi, xvin4, xx, xxn21, 77n5, 84, 84n9, 85, 85n10, 85n11, 86n14, 86n15, 90, 90n26, 92, 92n32, 93, 93n35, 98n2, 98n3, 100n9, 102, 102n17, 102n18, 103n19, 103n20, 117n12
Ayerh, Lawrence K., 67, 67n94
Baëta, Christian G., xxin26, 25n2, 35, 35n1, 37, 38n14, 38n15, 43n30, 60n73
Banks, Robert, 127n65

Index of Authors

Barclay, William, 93n34, 99n6, 99n7
Barrett, C. K., 120, 120n28, 124n49, 131, 131n84, 133n91
Bartels, F. L., xvn1, 25n2, 26n7
Bayes, Jimmy D., xixn18
Bediako, Gillian Mary, 50n26, 56n61
Bediako, Kwame, 26n4
Bekoe, Adjei, 16, 16n20
Belm, Göttingen Johannes, 122n39, 123, 123n48
Benjamin, C. Don, 83n5, 84n7, 90n27
Berger, Klaus, 103
Blenkinsopp, Joseph, 95, 95n48, 95n49
Boyer, James L., xxi, xxin25
Brown, Colin, 99, 99n8, 117n8, 127n64, 129, 129n75, 130n77, 130n79
Brown, Raymond E., 46n10, 93n36, 101n13, 101n14, 120n28
Bruce, F. F., 98, 98n5
Budd, P. J., 62, 63n84

Cartledge, Mark J., 123n43
Clarke, Peter B., 26n9, 27, 27n11
Coenen, L., 127n64
Commey, Richard Oswald, xviii–xix, xviiin11, xixn16, 41n27, 41n28, 53n40, 53n41, 53n44
Coppes, Leonard J., 90n29
Cousland, J. R. C., xxii–xxiii, xxiiin29
Croy, N. C., 119n23, 121n35, 122n42

Dakubu, M. E. Kropp, 12, 12n1–13n1
Debrunner, 30n23, 30n29, 33, 33n40, 33n41
Delitzsch, F., 21, 21n40, 91, 91n30, 93n34
Delling, Halle Gerhard, 119, 119n22, 120n25, 125n55, 125n56
Dovlo, Elom, 45n2, 45n3
Duling, Dennis C., 128n68, 134n97
Dyer, Anne E., 62, 62n83, 63, 63n85

Ekem, John D. Kwamena, 2n2, 2n5, 2n6, 56, 56n59, 57n65, 82n2, 115n3, 115n5, 118n16, 118n18, 119n21
Erdman, Charles R., 131n83
Essamuah, Casely B., 62n80
Evans, Craig A., xxiiin29, 119n23

Farnell, F. David, xx–xxi, xxin23
Fee, Gordon D., 122, 122n37, 126, 126n57, 127n61, 131, 131n82, 131n86, 132n90, 133n94, 134n96, 135n100
Field, Margaret J., 13–14, 13n6, 14n8, 14n9, 14n11, 15n12, 15n13, 15n15, 15n16, 16, 16n17, 16n19, 17, 17n21, 17n23, 18, 18n27
Fitzmyer, Joseph A., 46n10, 93n36, 101n13, 101n14, 120n28
Forbes, C., 123n43
Friedrich, Gerhard, 92n33, 94n39, 102, 118n19, 119n22, 130n76
Frimpong, Gordon, 4n11, 6n16, 7n18, 7n20, 8, 8n25

Gaiser, Frederick J., 50, 50n24, 50n25
Garland, David E., 121, 121n31, 121n34, 122, 122n36, 124n51, 126n58, 127n66, 128n70, 132n88, 133n94, 134n95
Gifford, Paul, xxii, xxiin28, 40, 40n23, 40n24, 58n67
Gill, David W. J., 128n71
Granberg-Michaelson, Wesley, 54n48
Grant, Robert M., 134, 134n98
Grundmann, Jena Walter, 118, 118n19
Günther, W., 117, 117n8, 117n11

Hackett, R. I. J., 55
Hafemann, Scott J., 114, 114n1
Hagin, Kenneth E., 41n27, 53n40
Haliburton, G. M., 28, 28n14, 30n24, 30n26, 31, 31n33
Hamon, Bill, 40–41, 41n25, 67, 67n93
Harris, R. Laird, 90n29
Hasler, V., 103
Hastings, A., 37
Hawthorne, Gerald F., 114n1, 117n12, 125n54, 128n67
Hays, Richard B., 127n62, 131n87, 133n92
Helmut, Bethel Krämer, 129, 130n76, 130n78
Hesselgrave, David J., 65, 65n88
Heward-Mills, Dag, 51, 51n32

Index of Authors

Hill, David, xvin5, xixn20, xix–xx, xxiii, xxiiin31, xxiiin32, 100, 100n10, 101, 101n12, 102, 102n15, 102n16, 103n21, 103n22
Hodge, Charles, 118, 119n20, 120, 121n30, 122, 122n37, 123n47, 124n50, 132n89
Howell, Allison M., 56, 56n61

Jenkins, Philip, 55n55
Jongkind, Dirk, 128n71
Josephus, Flavius, 98, 98n4

Karavidopoulos, Johannes, 133n93
Kärkkäinen, Veli-Matti, 20n32, 52n35, 62n83
Keil, C. F., 21, 21n40, 91, 91n30, 93n34
Killen, R. Allen, 117n10
Kilson, Marion, 17n25
Kim, Kirsteen, 20n32, 52n35, 62n83
Kissi, Seth, xxi, xxin24, 115n3, 118n16, 118n18, 125n52
Kittel, Gerhard, 92n33, 94n39, 118, 118n14, 118n19, 119n22, 121n33, 122n39, 123n48, 130n76
Kudadjie, J. N. K., 69
Kwadwo, Osei, 3n7, 3n8, 3n9, 4n11, 7n20, 8n21, 8n22
Kyeremanteng, K. Nkansa, 2n4

Lambert, J. C., 87n18
Larbi, Emmanuel Kingsley, 29n20, 30, 30n22, 30n24, 30n27, 31n31, 31n34, 31n35, 32n36, 32n38, 38n17–39n17, 79n7
Larbi, Nana, 5n12, 7n18, 7n20
Laryea, Philip Tetteh, 21, 21n38, 22n41
LaSor, William Sanford, 121n32
Lietzmann, Hans, 117n13, 119n23
Lindblom, J., 89, 89n24, 95, 95n45, 95n46, 95n47
Llewelyn, S. R., 119n24

Ma, Wonsuk, xviiin15
Mantse, Gbawe Kpoboo, 19
Martin, Carlos M., 133n93

Martin, Ralph P., 114n1, 117n12, 125n54, 128n67
Martinson, E. D., 30
Matkin, J. Michael, 120n29
Matthews, H. Victor, 83n5, 84n7, 90n27
Maxwell, David, xviiin14
Mbiti, John S., 14, 14n10, 20n33, 48, 48n18, 78n6, 79n9
McCutchan, R. G., 62
Meeks, Wayne A., 128n69
Meier, Samuel A., 82, 83n3, 85n12, 85n13, 88n21, 89, 89n23, 89n25, 90, 90n28
Menzies, Robert P., 52, 52n39, 53n46
Menzies, William W., 52, 52n39, 53n46
Metzger, Bruce M., 133n93
Meyer, Jena Rudolf, 92
Michel, Halle Otto, 94n39
Moffatt, James, 120, 120n26, 123, 123n44, 129n72
Moltman, J., 50
Morgan, G. Campbell, 115, 115n6, 118, 123n46
Motyer, Stephen, 94n40
Mundle, W., 122, 122n40
Murphy, Jim & Carolyn, 83n4
Murphy, Roland E., 46n10, 93n36, 101n13, 101n14, 120n28
Murphy-O'Connor, Jerome, 120, 120n28, 122, 122n37
Mwaura, Philomena Njeri, 37, 50, 50n26, 51n30

Obeng, Pashington, 55n56
O'Brien, P. T., 128n67
Odamtten, Harry Nii Koney, 21n37
Odotei, Irene K., 13, 13n3, 13n4
Oepke, Leipzig Albrecht, 121, 121n33
Okanfani, Nii Abbey, 19, 19n31
Okyerefo, Michael Perry Kweku, 41n26, 55, 55n54
Omenyo, Cephas N., xvi–xvii, xvin6–xviin6, xviin7, xxin26, 25n1, 26n4, 28n13, 29, 29n16, 29n21, 30n25, 30n28, 31n31, 31n32, 31n33, 31n35, 32n36, 37n11, 43n32, 54n47

Index of Authors

Omulokoli, Watson A. O., 27n12–28n12, 29n15, 29n17, 29n19
Onyinah, Opoku, 50, 50n29
Opoku, Kofi Asare, 9n26, 26–27, 26n9, 27n10
Orelli, C. Von, 84n6, 86n16, 88n20, 88n22
Orr, James, 86n16, 87n18, 93n37

Pfeiffer, Charles F., 117n10
Plummer, Alfred, 116, 116n7, 126n59, 131, 131n85
Pobee, J. S., 69
Poku, Kofi Asare, xxin26
Porter, Stanley E., xxiiin29, 119n23
Prior, David, 126n60

Quarcoopome, T. N. O., 48, 48n16
Quarshie, Benhardt Y., 50n26, 55, 56n57, 56n61, 57n65
Quartey, Solomon Nii Atutu, 18n28, 19
Quayesi-Amakye, Joseph, xvii, xviin8, xixn19, 35, 35n2, 36n4, 39, 39n19, 39n20, 46n5, 47n13, 53, 53n42, 54n47, 60n72, 70, 70n100, 70n102

Rea, John, 117n10
Reid, Daniel G., 114n1, 117n12, 125n54, 128n67
Reindorf, Carl Christian, 17, 56
Robertson, Archibald, 116, 116n7, 126n59, 131, 131n85
Robinson, Thomas A., 118n15
Ross, Kenneth R., xviiin15
Rowe, Arthur J., xx, xxn22
Ruff, John, xxiin27
Rupprecht, A. A., 125n54

Sanneh, Lamin, xvi, xvin3, 56, 56n58, 56n60

Shank, David A., 26n5, 26n8, 29n18
Sintim-Koree, Stephen, 19n29
Southon, A. E., xv
Sumrall, Lester, 53n44

Talbert, Charles H., 135n99
Tate, W. Randolph, 117n9
Tetteh, Lawrence, 51, 51n31
Theissen, Gerd, 123n45
Thomson, J. E. H., 93n37
Turner, Max, 80, 80n10, 80n11, 87n17, 88, 88n19, 122n41

Verbrugge, Verlyn D., xxiiin30, 93n38, 94n43, 95n44, 97n1, 122n38, 125n53, 127n63, 130n80
Vincent, Marvin R., 101n11
Viviano, Benedict T., 46n10, 93n36, 101n13, 101n14
Vos, Howard F., 117n10

Wagner, C. Peter, 52, 52n37
Walker, Williston, xviiin13, 129n74
Wallace, Daniel B., 115n2, 118n17
Walls, Andres F., 31n30, 31n31, 32n37
Waltke, Bruce K., 90n29
Warrington, Keith, 52n34
Watson-Quartey, Mustapha, 13, 13n2, 15n14, 17n22, 17n24, 17n26
Wellington, H. Nii Adziri, 16n18
Willoughby, W. Robert, 115, 115n4

Yankah, Kwesi, 2, 2n3, 58n66
Yayi, Jonathan Aremu, 57n64
Yong, Amos, 20n32, 52n35, 62n83

Zarwan, John, 26n6

Index of Subjects

Abiathar, 21
Abraham, 83–84, 91
Abram, renaming of, 61
Accra, called Gã, 14
Accra Gã people, origin of, 17–18
Acquaah, Gaddiel Robert, 62
Acts (book of)
  on the Holy Spirit, xvi
  individuals called prophets in, 106
  other people who prophesied in, 108
Addo, Stephen Ayisi, 49
Adonai, 11
Adu, Grace, 39
Adumfa Prayer Camp, 39
Afoakye dwarfs, 19
African Christian prophet, Harris' reference to himself, 28
African Traditional Religion (ATR), 5, 79
African/Ghanaian cosmology, 2
Africanism, as a form of prophetism, 24
Agabus, 106, 107–8, 140
Agape Prayer Camp, 39–40
agba, cleaning away of harmful influences, 16
King Ahab, group of Baal prophets, 86
AICs (African Initiated/Instituted/Indigenous/Independent Churches)
  characteristics of, 38
  declining in membership in the 1970s, 37
  expressing the Christian faith, 79
  founders of, 35
  not selling prophylactics, 42
  numerical decline of, 69
  prophetic ministries of, 24
  prophetism first experienced during the period of, xvii
  prophets taking authority mainly from the Old Testament, xix
  provoked acceptance of charismatic inclinations in TWMCs, 68
  referred to as *sunsum sorè* (spiritual churches), 36
  singing local choruses as spontaneous with Spirit possession, 62
  use of mother-tongue, 55–56
AIDS, 48–49
Akan language, 2, 57
Akan people, 1, 2
Akan tradition, xxiv
Akan traditional prophetism, 10
Akan Traditional Religion, xvii, 1–11, 82
Akrama, Numbo, 140, 147, 148
Akwamu kingdom, 15
Akwapim *Twi*, 2
Aladura Churches, in Nigeria, 36
Amoako, Elisha Salifu, 41
Amos, 85, 86
Amponsah, Eric Nana Kwasi, 41
  advocating training for prophets, 69
  background and education of, 59
  counselling troubled persons, 68
  gifted in the area of music, 61–62
  image of "Hope Miracle Water," 149
  images of "Special Emergency Oil," 150, 151
  prophecy about, 59
  prophetic ministry of, 44
Amponsah, Janet, 59

Index of Subjects

Amponsah, Joseph, 59
Ana, called a prophetess, 93
Ananias, 106
angelic encounters, of the forerunner prophets, 32
angels, coming from the "immediate presence" of God, 62–63
Anglican Church, benefited from the ministry of Swatson, 30
Anim, Kwame Siaw, 9
animal parts, 5, 6
Anna, as prophet, 111
"Ano, Kye," meaning Anor see the wonders of your son, 4
anointing, 40, 51
King Ansah Sasraku, 6
Antioch Church, teachers and prophets in, 107
antiretroviral drugs, scarcity of, 49
anti-witchcraft cult, 33
Anto, Isaac, 41, 59, 60
apocalyptic phenomena, rise of, 93–94
apostle, as an ecclesiological title, 52
apostolic succession, leadership by, 113
Appiah, Joseph William, 60
asafo (church, assembly, gathering), 36
Asante (*Akan*) people, 3
Asante Catholicism, 55
Asante *Twi*, 2
Asantes, war with the Denkyira people, 8
Asaph, seer of King David, 86
ATR (African Traditional Religion), 5, 79
authority
    over the prophecies of the prophets, 110
    submitting to higher, 132
Ayiwasu (Ayi has arrived), 17

Balaam, prophecies from Yahweh, 92
bamboo, use of in Harris' day, 27
baptism, form of John's, 99
Barnabas
    miracles of, 140
    as a prophet, 106
bath qol, usage of, 92–93
Benjamin, naming of, 61
Bezalel, 87–88

Bible
    acceptance of, 54
    translated into thirteen Ghanaian languages, 56
bill boards, advertising contemporary prophets, 54
Bishop O'Rorke, commissioned and licensed Swatson, 30
Bleku spirits, 14
blessings, from giving something precious to God, 65
King Boa Amponsem, 6
Bokete Lawei, first chief of Nungua Gã, 15
Bonigas, Daniel, 42
brain drain, from Ghana, 46
brethren, Paul's use of, 117, 118
Bronsam, Nana Kwaku, 47

call experiences
    of Jeremiah, xx
    of Old Testament prophets, 82–83
    of Paul, xx
Catholic Church, encouraging the use of native languages, 55
cessation, of prophecy, 92–93, 112–13
charisma
    exhibited by women, 38
    giving rise to contemporary prophetic ministry, 51–54
    of prophets, xvi, 43
charismata, 52
Charismatic denomination, 80
charismatic endowments, 138
charismatic leaders, claims concerning the prophetic ministry, 79
Charismatic Ministers, lack of good hermeneutical principles, 140
Charismatic Ministries (CMs), xvii, 41, 52, 57, 61
charismatic prayer groups, 52
charismatically endowed persons, 70
charismatically gifted new generation, tried to overthrow the leadership of the Church in Corinth, 117
charismatically gifted persons, in the Early Church, 129

Index of Subjects

Charismatics, giving attention to "experience over theology," 53
Chloe, 134, 136
"Christ Church Mission," of Swatson, 30
Christian alternative, to *Tigare* shines, 37
Christian faith, not limited to the language of the founder, 55
Christian prophet(s). *See also* prophet(s)
  combining both forth-telling and fore-telling, xxiv
  compared to traditional prophets, 142–43
  Hill defining, xxiii
  office of established in Ephesians 4:11–12, xix
  subject to scripture and the rules of the local Church, 142
Christian prophetism in Ghana, assessing in the light of 1 Corinthians 14:26–40, xxi
Christian spirituality, formulating for the church, 115
Christianity
  emergence of prophetism in Ghana's, xxiv–xxv, 24–34
  future of prophetism in Ghana's, 65–66
  as monotheistic, 133
  prophetism in early, xxv, 105–13
Christians
  having the Bible as a guide, 23
  rendered the ministry of *Gbaloi* unpopular, 19
Church, institutionalization of, 113
Church denominations
  Ghana blessed with many, 79
  having a prophetic position, xviii
  leaders commenting on electoral matters, 45
Church of Christ (Spiritual Movement), 38
Church of Jesus Christ, role of "prophets and prophecy" in today's, 79–81
Church of Pentecost (CoP), xix, 39, 59, 80
churches
  changing the name of, 61
  new, advertising services and programs in the media, 64

civil wars, created fear among Ghanaians, 46
clans, of the Asante people, 3
Classical Pentecostals (CPs), led by Apostle Peter Newman Enim, 38
Clement of Rome, 117–18, 135
Cleopas, 102
clergy vestment, of Harris, 27
CMs (Charismatic Ministries), xvii, 41, 52, 57, 61
communication, between the material and the immaterial worlds, 22
"computer man," Amponsah referred to as, 63
conditional prophecies, 78
confusion, God not the author of, 110
Constitutional Amendment in Heaven: Why the Lord Jesus Christ, the Anointed One, did not Use Oil (Ayerh), 67
consultation fees, prophets collecting from clients, 80
contemporary Ghanaian prophetism, 141
contemporary prophetic ministry
  claiming to have powers to heal all illnesses, 49
  described, xvii–xviii
  Eric Nana Kwasi Amponsah's Hope Generation Ministry International as a case of, 58–66
  external factors giving rise to, 45–51
  as the fifth phase of neo-prophetism, 70
  in the Gã Municipal Area, xxv, 72–81
  impact of, 68, 71
  internal factors giving rise to, 51–58
  issues of, xxv
  leaders of became the alternative for the services of traditional shrines, 48
  many members confessing affinity to TWMC, 143
  perception of, 66–70
  reminding TWMCs to sustain the charismatic activities, 68
contemporary prophetism. *See* neo-prophetism

Index of Subjects

contemporary prophets. *See also* prophet(s)
   as agents of *ebisa* in Ghanaian Christianity, xvii
   Bible versions preferred by, 57
   claiming the authority from the New Testament, xviii
   claiming to be the mouth piece of God and mediators of spiritual issues, 67
   complaining of being misinterpreted, 58–59
   on formal theological education not supporting spiritual formation, 69
   Ghanaians following without scrutiny, 66
   giving considerable attention to music, 61–62
   gradually claiming to be the mouthpiece of God, 138
   holding worship services in places not requiring any elegant ecclesiological features, 54–55
   initially members of TWMCs or Classical Pentecostal Churches (CPCs), 59
   lacking literacy in the use of English language, 58
   making themselves indispensable in the lives and minds of seekers or members, 66
   making time to meet their members, 68
   motivated by money and snatching other men's wives, 65–66
   moving out to establish their own Churches, 70–71
   needing formal theological education, 71
   needing to study Paul's teachings concerning prophetism, 144
   nick names depicting endowment(s), 63
   not following the concepts of mother-tongue biblical hermeneutics, 57
   not theologically trained, 143
   possessing at least two revelational gifts in addition to the gift of prophecy and sometimes healing, 53
   prophecy diagnosing illnesses, 50
   relying on the translated versions to preach in the *Akan* language, 57
   resisting "wise counselling" from other Pastors, 70
   seeking to take the church to the public sphere, 55
   sought to restore a "lost concern of the Early Church," 51–52
   use of the English language for worship service as the promotion of clericalism, 58
   use of the media, 54–55
   using the *Akan* mother-tongue for worship service, 58
   veering into traditional prophetism making prophetic ministry an office, 143
"contortionist hermeneutics of Scripture," 54
CoP (Church of Pentecost), xix, 39, 59, 80
CoP prayer camp, sanctioned, 71
co-prophets, judging prophecies of the prophets, 131
Corinth, cults in, 23
Corinthian Christians
   gathering for fellowship among, 118
   not knowing the psalms in the Old Testament, 120
   pre-Christian life of some, 114
   speaking in tongues like that of the cults in Corinth, 123
Corinthian Church
   gathering at separate venues, 119
   interest of being called a prophet in, 109
   Paul's strong affection for, 135
Corinthian women, making a lot of trouble, 134
1 Corinthians 12:1, switching attention or focus onto a new issue, 115
1 Corinthians 12:14, on prophetism in the church, xxii

Index of Subjects

1 Corinthians 14:26–40
  structure of, 115–35
  subtitles of, 114–15
1 Corinthians 14:33b-37, 116
Cornelius, 106
Corpus Paulinum, prophetism in, 114–37
cosmic dualism, of apocalyptic literature, 94
counsellee, indicating the kind of counselling, 64
counselling, forms of in HGMI, 63
counselling days, for Amponsah, 68
counselling sessions, "emergency oil," "miracle water" sold during, 68
court prophets, in the Old Testament, 86
cross
  breaking of Oppong's by the District Commissioner, 31
  held by Harris, 27–28
Cross of Miracle Evangelistic Ministry, 42
cult, temple, and classical/literary prophets, in the Old Testament, 85
cultic acts, described, 120n29
cultic songs, leading to inspiration referred to as *epiclesis*, 120

dancing, in worship services, 38
Daniel, 91, 100
Daniel (book of), standing out as fully apocalyptic, 94
David
  effect of anointing on, 51
  seers and prophets of, 86
  used Abiathar's *Urim* and *Thummim*, 21
"Day of Atonement," 22
Day of Pentecost, 105, 113
deities, of the Tema, 14
Denkyira Kingdom, 3
disciples
  in Ephesus said to have spoken in tongues and prophesied, 108
  referred to Jesus as a prophet, 102
  in Tyre prophesied concerning the arrest of Paul, 108
"ditto-ditto" (detail, detail), xvii
Divination, defined, 98
divination pot, of Okomfo Anokye, 154

"divine council," call event as, 82–83
Divine Healers Church, 38
divine healing
  emphasized in Phase 2, 38
  where faith and healing are inseparable, 50
"divinely disclosed" issues, prior to or during worship service, 122
divinities, punishing those disobeying norms, 48
dufa, found in *Okomfo Anokye*'s hand at birth, 4
Dzranowoyei (market priestesses), women elected as, 15

early Christian prophetism, in Ghana, 24–34
early Christianity, "prophets" in, 105–8
Early Church, prophets and prophecy in, xvi
Ebenezer Miracle Worship Centre, 42
Ebibindwom (vernacular choruses), 62
ebisa (to inquire or ask), xvii
economic factors, giving rise to contemporary prophetic ministry, 46–47
ecstatic speech, 122
ecumenism, 144
Elijah
  messenger formula indicating the voice of God to, 90
  mighty works of in relation to raising the dead, 101
  not having a grave, 10
  prophecy by, 42
  training of, 86
Elisha
  fore knowledge of what the King of Aram was planning, 100
  mighty works of in relation to raising the dead, 101
  prophecy by, 42
  telling the secret plans of the King of the Arameans to the King of Israel, 7
  training of, 86
Elizabeth, 98
Elkanah, 65

Index of Subjects

"emergency" counselling, 63–64
"emergency" fees, 64
"emergency oil," 64
"emic" viewpoint, versus an "etic" viewpoint, 32–33
English language, skills and proficiency in, 58
Enim, Peter Newman, 38
epiclesis, 119, 120
Esa-nti-foo . . ., having both political and economic values, 3
Eschatology, Old Testament prophecy and, 94–95
Ethiopian Eunuch, Philip ministering to, 106
Evangelical Presbyterian Church, autonomy of, 24–25
evil angels, fact of, 63
exordium (v.26), 117–24
Ezekiel, 85, 100

failed prophecy, punishment for, 10
faith
    expressing in other languages, 55
    necessary for prophecy, 111
    of the patient, 50–51
"faith healing," as an anti-medicine doctrine, 50
Faithway International Chapel, songs at, 62
false claims, of prophetic ministry and prophecy, 76
false prophecy, of *Okomfo Anokye*, 6
false prophets, 89, 90–92
family planning, limiting the number of children, 48
famine, prophesied, 106–7
fees
    charged for *sunsum akwankyere* as a hardship on the poor, 78
    paid by survey respondents for spiritual direction, 74–75
financial accountability, lack of in Phase 6, 42
financial demands, by some contemporary prophets as a prerequisite for receiving services, 143

fore knowledge, having, 140
forerunners of the prophetic ministry, 33, 34
foretelling prophecy, in the Old Testament, 88
formulas, that occurred in prophetic speeches in the Old Testament, 89–90
forth telling
    anticipated by Paul, 121
    central to the New Testament prophet, 140
    as declaring the message of God as revealed to the prophet, xxiii
    as preaching the gospel, xxiii
    of prophecy in the New Testament, 100
Fosuhene, Rev., 31
founder/leader, as sole signatory to the account of the church/ministry, 80–81
founding prophet, everything revolving around, 69
freelance prophets, in the Old Testament, 86
frenzied state, leading to speaking in tongues, 122
Frimpong, Ayi, became the first Asere chief, 17
Frimpong, Kwame Agyei. *See Okomfo Anokye*
fufu (boiled pounded cassava eaten with soup), 5
fulfillment, for authentication of the ministry of the intermediary, 10
future events, fore-telling, 140

Gã, ethnic and contract meanings of the word, 12–13
Gã Boni party, 15, 17
Gã language, 13
Gã *Mashie* on the hill, as Greater Accra, 17
Gã Mashie party, 17
Gã Obutu party, 17
Gã people, concise history of, 12–18
Gã South Municipal Area (GSMA), 18, 72–73

Index of Subjects

Gã State, leaders of came to inquire of the deities or spirits through the *Gbalo*, 19
Gã Traditional Prophetism, xxiv, 12–23
Gã Wo party, 17
Gad, as King David's seer, 86
Gaius, house of in Corinth, 128
Gamaliel I, xix
Gana (dangerous black big soldier ants), term Gã derived from, 13
Gãs. *See* Gã people
Gbalo (prophet or foreteller). *See also* prophet(s)
    ability to communicate both vertically and horizontally, 22
    communicating with deities promptly, 20
    in Gã language referring to a prothet, 18
    Lomotshokona as, 18
    over reliance on, 22
    speaking of happenings as a foretelling enterprise, 19
Gbaloi, 17–18, 19
Gbatsu (shrines/sacred places)
    defined, 21
    image of Numbo Akrama's, 148
    playing two major functions, 21–22
    role of in Gã primal religions, 20–21
    sizes and shapes of, 21n36
"Gbawe," meaning of, 18
Gbawe *Gbatsu*, housing myriads of spirits, 22
Gbawe Palace, images of, 145, 146
Gbawe Traditional Area, 12, 18–22
Gbawe wulomo, 147, 148
Gentile nations, form of prophecy, 88–89
Ghana, heavily indebted to its development partners, 46
Ghana AIDS Commission, 49
Ghana Catholic Bishops' Conference, communiqué on voting in 2000, 45
Ghana Health Service, 49
Ghanaian world-view, considering in religious life, 25

Ghanaians, perception of contemporary prophetic ministries, 66–70
Ghana's New Christianity (Gifford), 40
gift of prophecy, many members of the Corinthian Church endowed with, 132
gift of speaking in tongues. *See* speaking in tongues
gifts, given for the perfecting of the saints, 112
glossed interpolation, at a very early period, 136
glossolalia, described, 122
Gnosticism, in the Corinthian Church, 135
God
    allowed false prophets to rise in order to try the faith of the Israelites, 91
    anointed many priests, kings, judges, and other individuals to accomplish specific tasks in the Old Testament, 87
    compelling the prophets to prophesy, 88
    serving in a non-Western manner, 27
    speaking to provide solutions for needs, xv
    used Moses to deliver the Israelite from slavery in Egypt, 8
God's Public Relations Officer, Ayerh as, 67
"God's town-crier," prophet of the Bible as, xvi
"Golden Age of Business," in Ghana, 46
gospels
    activities of prophets and prophecy limited in, 103
    presentation of Jesus as a prophet, 100–102
    prophetism in, xxv, 97–104
gourd, Harris's use of as a bowl for baptism, 28
grassroots prophets, 39
Great Fire Pentecostal Ministry, 42
Greco-Roman religions, prophetism in, 97–98

Index of Subjects

Greco-Roman world, groups one may belong to, 127
Gua (a blacksmith god), 14

Habakkuk, 85
Hades, 125
Haggai, 85
Hannah and Elkanah, gave Samuel to the Lord, 65
Harris, William Wadè
   arrested and his cross and gourd were broken, 29
   conversions by, 28–29
   directed converts to join the established churches, 29
   dress of as a prophet, 26–27
   early background of, 26
   as an influential prophet, 26–29
   ministry in phase 1, 35–36
   ministry "transcended denominational barriers," 29
   resemblance to traditional priests from Liberia, 27
   special powers of, 28
   visited by the biblical angel Gabriel in a vision, 26
healing
   drawing the individual close to Jesus, 50
   encouraging masses of people to seek refuge, 49
   as a means of communicating with God and the community, 50
   prophecy helping in diagnosis, 66
health factors, giving rise to contemporary prophetic ministry, 48–51
heavenly voice, subjected to interpretation, 93
Heavily Indebted and Poor Country (HIPC) initiative, 46
Hegesippus of Palestine, 117
Heman, seer of King David, 86
hermeneutics, not followed in AICs, 38
Herod Antipas, 100, 101
King Hezekiah, 85
HGMI. See Hope Generation Ministry International (HGMI)

Historic Mission Churches, 24, 80
The History of the Gold Coast and Asante (Reindorf), initially written in Gã, 56
HIV/AIDS, 48–49
Holy Spirit
   in Acts, 105
   as the counsel of all believers, 70
   dwelling in the heart of every believer, 141
   experienced by Swatson, 30
   in the heart of believers, 111
   interpretation and categorization of the gifts of, 41
   living in each believer, 106
   poured out, 113
   as the Spirit of prophecy, xvi
   using any Christian to prophesy, 22
homowo, festival of the Gã people, 22n41
hooting at hunger, 22n41
hope, giving to the hopeless, 61
Hope Generation Ministry International (HGMI), 44
   "emergency" counselling in, 63–65
   located near the Oblogo Health Centre, 59
   revealed to Prophet Dr. Amponsah in a vision, 61
"Hope Miracle Water," images of, 149
Hosea, 86
house-churches, 128
household imperial cults, 128
houses, of wealthy persons in Corinth, 128
Human Immunodeficient Virus/Acquired Immune Deficiency Syndrome (HIV/AIDS), 48–49
human society, health as a major concern, 48
hunters
   meeting spirit beings in the forests, 19
   misfortune of, 5–6
hunting, as a prophetic art to "see" and "discern," 18
hymns, 119, 120

identity marker, 142
imperial cults, 127

Index of Subjects

indigenous charismatic Ghanaians, began Phase 5, 40
indigenous church movements, under local charismatic figures, 36–37
indigenous mother tongue, 38
inflation, high level of, 46
institutionalized prophets, expected gifts of the Spirit, 53
instruction, receiving from a teacher, 120–21
intermediaries, in African Traditional priesthood and prophetism having taboos, 9
International God's Way Church, 42
interpolation, into the text as the original vv.33b-36, 133
interpretation, of speaking in tongues, 124, 136
interpretations and reinterpretations, of prophetic writings, 89
Isaiah, 85
Isis, worship of, 119
Israelites, requested that Adonai not speak to them directly, 91
Ivorians, perception of Harris' regalia and manner of service, 27

Jacob, renaming of, 61
Jeduthun, 86
Jeremiah, xx, 85, 91
Jeremias, 107
Jeshua ben Jozadak, 85
Jesus Christ
    ability as a prophet to reveal secrets, 101
    ability to predict His death and resurrection, 99–100
    accused before the Supreme Council of being a false prophet, 101
    anointing of, 101
    asked the disciples "who do people say that I am?" 101
    biblical stories of, 59
    feeding of the five thousand persons by, 5
    forgiving sin, 102
    as human and divine, 102
    identified as the Messiah by John the Baptist, 98–99
    identified as the "promised prophet" by Moses, 102
    messianic concept of, 88
    ministry of synonymous with the ministry of the Old Testament prophets, 101
    miracles of, 140
    not presenting Himself as a prophet like those of the Old Testament, 103
    prophecy concerning the birth of, 78
    as a prophet, 99–102
    prophetic features in the ministry of, 102–3
    prophetic speeches of, 103
    regarding John the Baptist as more than a prophet, 98
    revealed the past life story of the Samaritan woman at the well, 78, 81, 140
    statement on welcoming a prophet, 93
    unique authority claimed by, 103
Jewish theology, associating prophecy with the presence of the Spirit of God, 113
Jewish wisdom tradition, 94
Jews, perception concerning non-Jewish slaves, 128
Jezebel, 86
Joel, 85, 105
John the Baptist
    ascetic life of, 108
    biblical stories of, 59
    as "more than a prophet," 103
    prophecy concerning the birth of, 78
    as a prophet, xxi, 93, 98–99
    sent his disciples to Jesus, 99
Jordan River, use of for baptism as significant, 99
Judas, as a prophet, 107
judgment of prophecies, by members of the Church, 131

king, request for as not the will of Yahweh, 84

Index of Subjects

King of Aram, 100
klote lagoon, worship of, 16
Kpeshi dialect, 14
Kpeshie lagoon, spirit of, 18
Kpledzo festival, 14, 15
Kufuor, John Adjekum, 45
Kundum dance and festival, origin of, 19
Kushi, Ayi, 17
Kushi, Ayite, 17
Kwa language group, 13
Kwame Nkrumah University of Science and Technology (KNUST), 39
Kwei, Okai, 17
Kyenekye, died at Adansi, 10

Labadi Gã people, origin of, 15
language, importance of, 57
last events, study of, 94
Law, freelance prophets interpreting, 86
Lawson, Gilbert Ablorh, 38
lay persons, prophesying during the quiet moment, 40
Levitical high priesthood, as a prophetic type, 21
life situations, of the forerunner prophets, 32
literacy levels, in Ghana, 58
literary/classical prophets, 85
Loei, dangerous evading brown ants, 17
Loeiabii (progenies of *Loei*), 17
Lomotshokona, caught the spirit of the *Kpeshie* lagoon, 18

magic wound, found in *Okomfo Anokye*'s hand at birth, 4
magicians, using the name of Jesus for money, 66
Mama Grace, 39–40, 80
Manasseh, Atsu, 60
manifestation/revelation, by a deity to its adherents, 121
Mansa, Bukyia, 8
"Mari letters," messenger formula in, 90
Martinson, E. D., on the work of Swatson, 30
McKeown, James, 38

meanings, Ghanaians reading into miracles, 68
Mecaiah, participating in a divine council, 83
media
    prophets as good clients for networks, 71
    support of programs, 143
    use of by contemporary prophetic ministry, 54–55
    used in Phase 6, 42
members. *See* seekers/members
Mensah, John, 38
mentorship, under senior prophets, 69
"messenger formula," in the writings of prophets in the Old Testament, 90
Messiah, with prophetic activities, 103
messianic expectation, of apocalyptic literature, 94
Methodist Church, Oppong's trouble with, 32
Micah, 86
Mills, John Evans Atta, 45
ministers, taking up certain titles, 67
Ministries
    financial challenges for new, 61
    given for the perfecting of the saints, 112
    as offerers of spiritual panacea, 46
    preaching the word of God, 67
ministry, conferred by ordination, 113
"miracle water," buying, 63
miracles
    in other Christian denominations, 80
    performing, 140
Mireku, Kofi, 59
"misfortunes," rooted in the other, 70
missional reasons, for naming or renaming in some CMs, 61
missionaries, deportation of during the First World War, 33
missions, costs of, 65
mistakes, God's people making, 110
monarchy period, in the Old Testament, 84–86
money

Index of Subjects

demanded from seekers or members, 42
realized out of "emergency" counselling, 64–65
"monism," existing among humans, 117
Montanism, xviii, 112, 112n22
Montanists, xx, 138
Morgan, G. C., 115–16
Moses
    experience with the burning bush, 82
    miracles in Egypt, 140
    not having a grave, 10
    Okomfo Anokye as the biblical, 5
    promising another prophet, like himself, 91
    as a prophet, 84
mother Churches, reasons for contemporary prophets leaving, 60
MSS, referring to manuscript(s) of Church Fathers texts, 120n27
Musama Disco Christo Church (MDCC), 60
music, 61, 62
mystery deities, celebrated in Corinth, 121

Na Afiyei (a grandmother deity), 14
"Nabi," Old Testament designation of, xxi
Nackabah, John, 29
Nahum, 85
naming and renaming, reflecting ministry objectives, 61
Nathan, 86
National Democratic Congress (NDC), 45
National Economic Dialogue, in 2001 in Accra, 46
Nebi'im (the prophets), 139
"necromancy and technical witchcraft," practiced by Gentile nations, 88–89
"negative Eschatology," 95
neo-prophetism. *See also* contemporary prophetism
    emerged in Ghana after the AICs, xvii
    phases of in Ghana's Christianity, 35–43
New Patriotic Party (NPP), 45
New Religious Movements (NRMs), 32
New Testament
    available in twenty-six Ghanaian languages, 56
    prophecy, 109, 112, 141
    references to Old Testament prophets, xxi
Nii Ayi Kushi, Gã State established by, 13
nkrang, corrupted by the Portuguese to *Akra*, 17
Nmashi, Nuumo Okang, 16
"nomistic rationalism," 92
non-rational aspect of religion, over-emphasis on, 69
non-Western Christianity, demand for, 25
normal counselling, in HGMI, 63
Nsiah, Bernard Opoku, 41
King Ntim Gyakari, of the Denkyira Kingdom, 8
Nungua Gã people, 15–16
Nzema language, Anglican Prayer book and Hymns translated into, 30

Obinim, Daniel, 42
objects, given to participants/members for miracles, 144
Obutu, referring to huts made out of palm branches, 14
offerings, decreasing, 64
office, in the Church, xviii
official or institutionalized prophets, trained and accepted by the Church, 39
Oholiab, 87–88
oikonomia, 127, 128
oils, water, stones, and sand, selling of not seen in the Bible, 78
Okley, Nii Afotey, 16
Oko, *wulomo* of the deity *La-kpa*, 15
okom, meaning prophesying, 2
okomfo, 2
Okomfo Anokye
    birth narrative of, 4
    building of his birth, image of the entrance of, 152
    changing the color of cows, 7
    charmed a golden stool to Osei Kofi Tutu I, 7

Index of Subjects

Okomfo Anokye *(continued)*
  closing days of, 8–10
  delivering the Asantes from the hands of the Denkyira people, 8
  divination pot, image of, 154
  early life of, 4–5
  education of, 5
  failed prophecy later fulfilled, 6
  fore knowledge concerning the destiny of Osei Kofi, 140
  gifted by the deities/spirits from birth, 4, 10
  history of, 4–11
  impact of the work of on *Akan* traditional prophetism, 10
  imprisoned a second time, 6
  led the Asantes in war, 8
  miracles of, 140
  not supposed to eat tilapia, 9
  performed thirty wonders in Asante, 8
  projected himself above all except the King, 11
  prophecies of, 6, 10
  returning with anti-death medicine, 9
  showing that traditional prophets are fallible, 11
  shrine of, image, 153
  study of the exploits of, 1–11
  sword in the ground at Okomfo Anokye teaching hospital, 155
  tested by the Asante, 7
  wonders with rivers, 8
  works of, 5–8
Okomfo Anokye teaching hospital, construction of, 10
Old Testament
  classifications of prophets in, 83–86
  evidence concerning giving to prophets, 80
  false prophets, 90–92
  freelance prophets, 86
  monarchy period, 84–86
  no mention of the gifts of utterance of wisdom, knowledge, and discernment of spirits, 42
  pre-monarchical period, 83–84
  prophecy in, 88–89
  prophetic speeches in, 89–90
  prophetism in, xxv, 82–96
  prophets, categories of, 84
  prophets, Spirit of God and, 87–88
  training of prophets, 86–87
  use of by Christians today, xvi
"'On the "Mountain" of the Lord' Healing Pilgrimages in Ghanaian Christianity" (Asamoah-Gyadu), 55
"one man church(es)," 80
"*Onyame wo ho daa*" ("God lives perpetually"), 61
opponents, of Paul in the Corinthian Church, 135
Oppong, Sampson
  baptized into the Christian faith by Rev. Fosuhene and introduced to the Methodist Church, 31
  lost his preaching abilities, 32
  ministry characterized by wonders and mass conversions, 31–32
  ministry in Phase 1, 35–36
  traditional priest without any Christian background, 31
oracles, 89, 91
oracular cults
  in Corinth, 121, 123
  giving insight, 129
  mostly polytheistic, 136
oracular messages
  from a deity, xv
  Nebi'im as a collection of, 139
  receiving from a god, 97
oral theology, expressed in music, 62
orderliness
  in the Church, xxi
  portraying the character of God, 133
King Osei Kofi Tutu I, 3, 7
Osu Gã people, origin of, 16
the "other," the evil person causing problems, 70
over realized eschatology, in the Corinthian Church, 135
Owusu-Bempah, Isaac, 41

pagan cults, as mostly polytheistic, 132–33

Index of Subjects

paranomasia, 116
parent Church, phenomenon of leaving, 60
participants/members. *See* seekers/members
pastors, taking up certain titles, 67
patients, prayed for by the laying on of hands, 51
Paul
    admonition for orderliness in Christian worship, xxi
    Ananias comforted, 106
    as an apostle whose functions included prophetic ministry, xx
    apostolic authority over the Corinthian Church, 135
    as a Christian prophet, xix
    collaboration with women such as Chloe and Phoebe, 136
    defining activities of prophets in the Church, 109
    earlier epistle prior to 1 Corinthians, 121
    encouraged prophecy rather than speaking in tongues, 137
    giving a criterion by which Corinthians could determine which prophet to accept or reject, 134–35
    indebted to Old Testament prophetism, xx
    knowledge of Hellenistic prophecy, xix
    limiting the number of prophets speaking in each worship service, 138–39
    miracles of, 140
    not condemning speaking in tongues, 129
    not despising prophecy, 108
    not encouraging the payment of fees or mandatory purchase of any "anointing oils" or relics/substances, 140–41
    not forbidding speaking in tongues, 135
    not giving clues on the gifts of utterance of wisdom and utterance of knowledge, 54
    not giving criteria for the judgment of prophecies, 130
    not limiting judgment of prophecy to prophets, 131
    not seeing the gift of speaking in tongues as an overpowering ecstatic experience, 127
    on Old Testament prophets, xix
    permitting women to prophecy in the Church, 111
    polemical approach to the Corinthian problems, 135
    on predictive prophecy as revelation leading to repentance, 111
    preventing pre-Christian experiences of some Corinthians from being part of Christian worship, 133
    as a prophet, 107
    on prophetic ministry as a function not an office, 139
    on purpose for ministries, 67
    referring to himself as "aspostle," 109
    related to many women who were leaders in the Corinthian Church, 134
    revelations concerning the voyage to Rome, 106
    speaking in tongues himself but not publicly, 129
    teachings regarding prophetism foundational for prophetic ministry, xviii
    unique teaching on prophetism, xx
    urged the Corinthian Church to desire prophecy, 110
    used prophet and spiritual person interchangeably, 135
    used the epistle as a test case for true and false prophets, 136–37
    using common philosophical and pre-Christian experiences of Corinthian Christians, 125

Index of Subjects

Pauline communities, prophets and prophecy as a common phenomenon in, xvi
Pauline corpus, xxv, 144
Pauline instruction, concerning prophetism not part of the forerunners' guiding principles in ministry, 34
Pauline literature, 108–11
"Pauline thought," referring to in matters of faith, 138
Pentecost prayer camp, at Ablekuma-Agape, 80
Pentecostal Churches, demonized the AICs as ritualistic and occultic, 37
Pentecostalism
    believing in the manifestation of the gift of prophecy and prophets today, 80
    encouraging experience with the Holy Spirit, 52
    lack of good hermeneutical principles by, 140
    as the largest Christian denomination in Africa, Asia and Latin America, 138
    pioneers of in Ghana, 25
    spirituality relying heavily on oral theology, 62
Pentecostals
    categorizing the gifts of the Spirit into three parts, 52
    giving attention to "experience over theology," 53
    making room for participatory worship in vernacular language, 57
    pointing to Pauline thought as the primary source of authority, xviii
    preferring spirituality over scholarship, 69
"perennial phenomenon," prophetism as, 43
perpetuity, need for paramount in the minds of many founding prophets, 65
personal prophecies, 40, 47
"persons of the Spirit," 88
Peter, 106
Pharisees, not acknowledging Jesus as a prophet, 101
Phases, of prophetism, 35–42
"pheet" – to speak, xxiii
"phee"-"to say" or "to speak," xxii
Philip
    as a prophet, 105–6
    unmarried daughters of, 108
philosophy, 117n10
Phoebe, 134, 136
Plange, Bart, 31
Plato, on a "Corinthian girl," 134
Plummer, A., 116
pneumatic Christianity, 38
politeia, as public gathering, 127
political factors, giving rise to contemporary prophetic ministry, 45–46
popular interpretations, of scripture by contemporary prophets, 143
Poseidon, 125
"positive Eschatology," 95
post-exilic prophecy, taking the form of "nomistic rationalism," 92
poverty, weakening individual family responsibilities, 48
power(s)
    of forerunners of the prophetic ministry, 34
    Harris' demonstration of, 28
power gifts
    as categorized by CMs, 41
    of the Spirit, 52
prayer camps, 39, 40
prayer centres, with leaders promising a diagnosis of misfortunes, 47
pre-Christian pneumatological experiences, in Corinth and in Ghana, 138
pre-exilic prophecy, reinterpreting to include the future, 95
Pre-monarchical period, in the Old Testament, 83–84
The Presbyterian Church of Ghana, autonomy of, 24–25

Index of Subjects

priesthood, in *Akan* Traditional Religion, 2
priests/priestesses, training of, 140
primal religions
    having no sacred scriptures to give guidance, 139
    prophetism in, 20, 22
    prophets in, 19
private sector, as the engine of growth, 46
pro "pro" – before, xxii
pro "pro" – on behalf of, xxiii
promantis, revealing the future, 130
prophecy
    amounting to new revelations, 112
    available to all Christians, 132
    cessation of, 92–93, 112–13
    of a Christian prophet as not sacrosanct, 142
    crucial to the growth of the Corinthian Church, 110–11
    differentiating between true and false, 110
    encouraged over speaking in tongues, 135
    encouraging in the Church, 136
    establishing the cause of one's condition, 47, 66
    experienced in other Christian denominations, 80
    false prophets and, 90–92
    fulfillment of for survey respondents, 74
    gift of, 53, 142
    given according to the proportion of faith, 111
    grading of, 109
    in the Greco-Roman world, 97–98
    in Israel seen as the influence of the Holy Spirit on the prophets, 93
    judgment of, 130, 131
    made up of forth-telling and fore-telling, xxiii
    meant to edify, exhort and comfort, 112
    must not be paid for, 141
    not all from God, 91
    not leading people from God through disorderly behaviors, 142
    not putting the recipient in confusion or a state of despair, 132
    in the Old Testament, 88–89
    as partial knowledge, 112
    postponed fulfillment of, 6
    received from prophets not coming to pass, 77
    receiving through the laying on of hands, 108
    some not fully fulfilled, 95
    strengthening the relationship that God always desires to have with His creation, 88
    survey respondents receiving, 74
    taking a different form due to the *sitz im leben* of the people, 92
    as a temporary gift, 142
prophecy (*Akan: nkonhye*), 2
"prophecy (Greek: "propseetees")
    in the context of 1 Corinthians 14:26–40, xxii
    dominated by frenzied experience, xix
    meaning speaking on behalf of/for God or gods, xxiii
    not limited to early Christian usage, xxiii
prophecy and prophets, gift of still alive to this day, 141
prophesies, leading to total salvation, 81
"prophet"
    bearers of the title compared to "pastor," "reverend minister," 71
    as an ecclesiological designation attracting people to Pentecostal and Charismatic Churches, xvii
    selling water in a bottle to cure barrenness, 77
prophet(s). *See also* Christian prophet(s); contemporary prophets; *Gbalo* (prophet or foreteller)
    accepting or rejecting, 134–35
    African Traditional Religious practices and manticism compared to New Testament, 78
    as the announcer of God's message, xx

Index of Subjects

prophet(s)(*continued*)
   in the book of Acts, 105–8
   call experience of Old Testament, 82
   charisma of attracted both Christians and non-Christians to their meetings, 52
   classes of, 95–96
   classification of in the OT, 83–86
   continuity of in the New Testament, xxi
   in the CoP, 39
   as covenant implementers, 142
   creating confusion and hatred among family members, 80
   defined, xxiii–xxiv, 52, 67
   determining false from true, 139, 140
   expected to possess and demonstrate at least two revelational gifts and the gift of prophecy by CMs, 41
   functional role rather than an office, 132
   functioning in the courts of the kings, 86
   Jesus as, 99–102
   leading clients to worship other gods, 77
   as long as the Holy Spirit communicates prophecies through them, 139
   missionary minded in their role, 108
   as the mouth piece of God, xviii
   must not be the author of confusion in the church, 141
   in the New Testament described, xxiii
   non-literary in the Old Testament, xv–xvi
   participating in the divine council, 83
   in Pauline thought, 139
   performance of miracles authenticating ministry, 71
   ranked next to the Apostle, 110
   recognizing and giving undivided attention to scripture, 142
   referred to as "persons of the Spirit," 88
   revelation or prophecy by, not rating above revelation/prophecy by other Christians, 131
   revelations of leading to salvation, 78
   roles in the establishment and growth of the Church, 107
   as someone telling before it happens, 129–30
   as someone who received information from a higher authority, 90
   speaking for different deities or God/gods, 1–2
   traditional understanding of the functions of, 66
   training of Old Testament, 86–87
   unfulfilled prophesies expected to be fulfilled, 6
   visiting company of in Acts, 110
prophet and apostle, as ecclesiological titles, 52
prophet of God, not measured by the number of miracles, 91
"prophetic," meaning of the word, 40
prophetic activities, attributed to challenging economic situations in Ghana, 142
"prophetic acts," by some contemporary prophets criticized as ritualistic and occultic, 71
prophetic churches/ministries
   claims made concerning, 79
   dominant in Gã South Municipal Area, 77
   in the Gã South Municipal Assembly, 73
   not belonging to ecumenical bodies, 80
   offerings given by members of, 78
   referred to as "one man church(es)," 80
"prophetic direction," receiving from a study of scripture, 113
prophetic gift
   described, xix
   misinterpretation of, xviii
   as an office in the Church, xviii
prophetic ministry

Index of Subjects

aimed at replicating and perpetuating prophetism, xvi
becoming a function in the Church and not an office, 131
compared to other ministries, 67
contemporary in Ghana, 44–71
contemporary nature and structure in the New Testament, xxii
contemporary resonating with the Ghanaian phenomenon of religion, xvi
established institution in ancient Israel, 139
factors giving rise to contemporary, 45–58
as a function, not an office, 115, 137
of *Gbalo*, as indispensable, 20
geared towards giving hope and restoration, 61
ministry of pioneers of in Ghana's Christianity, 32–34
pioneers of, 25
recognized as offices in Pauline literature, 110
respondents' views on belief in, 73
as the single most popular and most chastised, 58
prophetic narrative, in the Hebrew Bible finding writing less important, 89
prophetic office, xix
prophetic phenomenon, in Ghana, 79
prophetic power, as the "last stop" for life challenges, xvii
prophetic revelation
    glorifying and leading people to Christ, 111
    leading the recipient to Christ, 141
"prophetic rhetoric," in the speech of Jesus, 102–3
prophetic speeches
    of Jesus, 103
    in the Old Testament, 89–90
"the prophetic Spirit," spirit of the prophet subject to, 132
prophetic writings, editing and enlargement of, 89
prophetism
    in *Akan* Traditional Religion, 1–11
    attracting patronage to a deity and a religious intermediary in many Traditional Religions, 12
    in the CoP demystified Ghana's prophetism, 40
    in Corpus Paulinum, 114–37
    defined, 35
    in early Christianity, 105–13
    emergence of in Ghana's Christianity, 36
    found among all races, xv
    in Gã Traditional Religion, 12–23
    in Gbawe Traditional Area, 12, 18–22
    in Ghana's Christianity as a "perennial phenomenon," 43
    in the gospels, 97–104
    in Israelite's religion, 95–96
    not new to Ghana's Christianity, 34
    in the Old Testament, 82–96
    in the Old Testament divergent with the Pauline corpus, 140
    in Pauline literature versus that of the Old Testament, 139
    as a "perennial phenomena," 35
    phases in Ghana's Christianity, 35
    referring to a system or means of receiving oracular information, xix
    as a stream of Pentecostalism, 138
    in traditional religions, 20, 22, 139
prophets and prophecy
    function of having similarities, 140
    in Ghana today, 79–81
    guidelines for in the Church, 129–33
    overview of survey respondents concerning, 76
prophylactics, 37, 42
prosperity gospel, 54
Ptolemy II and his wife Arsinoe II, process of deifying, 117
public worship service, instilling orderliness in, 131
Pythia oracular cult, 122–23
    under the leadership of women, 134
    messages required interpretation, 97
    oracular cult of, 23
    took direct inspiration from the gods, 130

Index of Subjects

Quarcoopome, T. N. O., 48
Qumran community, leaders of as "Teachers of Righteousness," 98

Rawlings, Jerry John, 45
red oil or bottled water, survey respondents payments for, 74–75
reinterpretation, need for resulted in Eschatology, 95
religion, as a matter of both words and music, 62
religious and social factors, giving rise to contemporary prophetic ministry, 47–48
religious broadcast space, filled by prophetic churches/ministries, 81
"religious functionaries," 20
religious intermediaries, diagnosing and prescribing solutions, xv
religious mediators, in the Ghanaian society, 41
religious syncretism, prophets called to speak against, 85
religious washings, in Jewish culture, 99
repentance, required for baptism, 99
restoration, prophesied by Jeremiah not fully materializing, 95
revelation
    not constituting prophecy, 78
    not exclusive to one person or prophet, 132
    not limited to only prophets, 136
    not necessarily constituting prophecy, 81
    of oracular cults and mystery religions, 121–22
revelational gifts, 41, 52
ritual objects, selling, 41
Robertson, A., 116
Roman incubation oracles, 77
Roman legal system, stages of, 125
"rulers of earth, sea and underworld," formed a common triad, 125
rural areas, activities of the pioneers of prophetism concentrated in, 37

sacred places, of the Tema, 14
sacred scriptures
    absence of in many traditional religions, 22
    lack of in African/Ghanaian Traditional Religions, 20
sacrificial animals, used by religious intermediaries for omens, 89
salvation, leading to total wellbeing in this present life, 79
Samaritan woman, called Jesus a prophet, 102
Samson, 4, 78
Samuel, 65
    birth narrative of, 4
    first prophet to have the "school of the prophets," 86
    fore knowledge about the lost asses of Saul's father, 140
    as a king maker and priest, 100
    meeting with Saul, 100
    prophecy by, 42
    as prophet, priest and king maker, 84
Sarai, renaming of, 61
Sarpong, Gabriel Akwasi, 42
Satan, emphasizing the work of, 43
King Saul, visited a diviner, 92
"school of the prophets," 86
scripture
    available to give guidance, 139
    contortionist hermeneutics of, 54
    as permanent, 142
Scripture Union (SU), 39
seekers/members
    continuing to identify themselves as Catholic, Anglican, Presbyterian, Methodist, 68
    encouraging to give freely in support of media programs, 143
    "falling under the anointing," 39
    judging the prophecies of the prophets, 139
    making time for, 68
    many not satisfied with engagement with some contemporary prophets, 47
    of ministries versus seekers or inquirers, 67–68

Index of Subjects

not always supporting churches
financially, 64
not usually satisfied with the outcome
of encountering a prophet, 43
told that misfortunes were caused by
close relatives, 47
"self-proclaimed men of God," exploitative
whims of, 47
Sempe people, origin of, 17
Seneca, 117n9
sensus plenior interpretation, 121
Serapis, worship of, 119
shamanistic prophets, composed of
Samuel, Elijah, and Elisha, 84–85
shouting, during preaching, 143
shrines, re-emergence of competing with
the church for members and
adherents, 47
sibyl oracles, adherents of experienced of
speaking in tongues, 123
sickness, causes of, 50
Silas, 107
similarities, of prophets and prophecy, 140
social and religious reformers, freelance
prophets as, 86
social factors, giving rise to contemporary
prophetic ministry, 47–48
social reformers, Old Testament prophets
as, 96
socio-religious and cultural context, of
Corinth and that of Ghana sharing
some commonalities, 138
son of God, "knowing the mind of God,"
100
songs, singing leading to Spirit possession,
62
"sons of the prophets," first school of, 87
soothsayers/diviners, Christian prophets
appearing as, xxiv
sorè, derived from the word for worship or
adoration, 36
sowing seed, 64n87
speaking in tongues, 122
exercising the gift of, 124–29
as inclusive and exclusive criteria
for the Christian community in
Corinth, 123
mainly for private communication
with one's self and with God, 136
to oneself and to God not taking place
in the Church, 129
Paul not forbidding, 135
during a quiet moment seen as a
prelude to prophecy, 40
receiving through the laying on of
hands, 108
regulations as to how to use, 124–25
as a spiritual gift subject to human
control, 127
as stimulus for the manifestation of
prophecy, 108
"Special Emergency Oil," 64, 150, 151
Spirit
giving the interpretation to one who
has the gift of interpretation of
tongues, 124
influence of, 87
manifestation of as synonymous with
prophecy, 88
spirit beings, complementary role to the
welfare of humans, 2
Spirit of God
manifesting among Christians in-
turns, 136
played the role of an intermediary
between God and humans, 88
as the power of God on the prophets,
87
as a seal of ownership of the prophets,
88
Spirit of prophecy
members of the church encouraged to
be receptive of, 40
restored at the inauguration of
Christianity, xvi
spirit of the prophet, subject to the
prophet, 132
"Spirit of Yahweh"
as an indispensable topic in Old
Testament studies, 87
no evidence of withdrawal of, 92
using the prophets as intermediaries
between God and humans, 88

Index of Subjects

Spirit possession, leading to the release of angels, 62
spirits
  discerning of, 41, 63
  manifesting in game form, 18
  testing every, 110
spiritual causality, physical happenings/situations, xv
spiritual direction (*sunsum akwankyere*)
  issue of gaining popularity in Gã South Municipal Area, 78
  making a person dream of lotto numbers, 77
  needing in order to have prophecy fulfilled, 78
  paying a fee before being given, 78
  received by survey respondents, 74
  with and without fee for survey respondents, 75
"spiritual directions," giving, 41
spiritual endowments, of the forerunners of the prophetic ministry, 34
spiritual giftedness, 52
spirituality, over-emphasis on, 69
spiritually-gifted saints, orderly conduct of, 118
Stoic philosophy, 117
stoicism, propounded by Zeno of Citium, 117n9
substances, given to participants/members for miracles, 144
sunsum, as God's or the Devil's, 78
sunsum asafo, translated as spiritual Church, 36
sunsum sorè (spiritual churches), 36
supernatural, revelatory/visionary of, 94
supernatural creatures, 82
supernatural events, not necessarily authenticating the work of the prophet to others, 83
survey research, analysis of findings, 77–78
"sustained biblical reflection," anticipated by Paul, 121
Swatson, John
  background of, 29–30
  met Prophet William Wadè Harris and became his disciple, 30
  ministry in phase I, 35–36
  referred to himself as "Bishop," 30
  supported Phase 1, 36
  translated Anglican Prayer book and Hymns into the Nzema language, 30
sword, pushing into the ground at Kumasi in 1697, 8
sword in the ground, at Okomfo Anokye teaching hospital, 155
symbolic messages, interpreting from the gods, 98

Tani, Grace, joined the evangelistic team of Harris, 38
Tanne, Grace, converted by Harris, 29
"Teachers of Righteousness," 98
Tema Gã people, origin of, 14–15
tent-making industry, in Corinth, 128
tertiary institutions, revival of Christian fellowships in, 39
Teshie Gã people, origin of, 16–17
theological education
  lack of formal by many contemporary prophets, 69–70
  limiting mistakes and building control over challenges, 32
  need for, 143–44
theology, influenced by socio-cultural issues, xv
1 Thessalonians, earliest epistle of Paul advocating prophecy, xvi
threefold execution, of an act making it definitive, 125
Thummim, as a "medium" given by Yahweh for the high priest to access divine direction for Israel, 21
"Thus sayeth the Lord," not necessary to prefix "prophecy," 113
Tigare shines, activities and popularity of curtailed, 37
"Tigare" traditional cult, 33
tilapia bone, lodged in *Okomfo Anokye*'s throat, 9

Index of Subjects

Timothy, cautioned not to ignore a word of prophecy, 112
tongues speakers, 125, 126
traditional belief system, appropriation into Christian worship, 144
traditional prophetism, combination with Old Testament prophetism, 34
traditional prophets, compared to Christian prophets, 142–43
Traditional Western Mission Churches. *See* TWMCs (Traditional Western Mission Churches)
trainee prophets, called "the sons of the prophets," 84–85
training, of Old Testament prophets, 140
translations, colonial influence on, 56
Trebi, Nii, 16
Trinity College (now Trinity Theological Seminary), 69
Tutu, Osei Kofi, 6, 10
Twi language, 2
TWMCs (Traditional Western Mission Churches)
  charismatic activities and, 68
  charismatic prayer groups in, 52
  need for biblical and theological teachings on Christian prophetic ministry in, 143
  revival in, 26
  use of mother-tongue by, 58

unclean persons, touching of, 102
unintelligible speech, conversion into intelligible speech, 123
Urim, as a "medium" given by Yahweh for the high priest to access divine direction for Israel, 21
utterance of knowledge, gift of, 41, 53
utterance of wisdom, gift of, 41, 53

venereal diseases, considered as immoral, 49
vernacular Bible, outdistanced and outlasted the forces of ephemeral colonial rule, 56
vernacular language, use of giving rise to contemporary prophetic ministry, 55–58
vestments, of the forerunner prophets, 32
vision, of Oppong while serving a jail term, 31
vocal or inspirational gifts
  as categorized by CMs, 41
  of the Spirit, 52–53
voice of God, ministers hearing, xv

"*wasu*," Dangme word meaning "you have arrived," 16
Waterworth, W. G., 31
wellbeing, quest for, 79
Wesleyan Methodist Missionary Society, attempts to translate the Bible into Ghanaian languages by, 56
Western Christianity, inability to integrate Charismatic experiences in Africa, 36
Western missionary societies, handing over leadership roles to Ghanaians in the early twentieth century, 24
"when the perfect comes," interpreting, 112
white stone, of Oppong, 31, 32
Willoughby, W. R., 115
witches/wizards, accused by prophets, 80
women
  identified with property, 111
  not recorded working miracles, 111
  played significant roles in oracular cults in Corinth, 134
  prohibiting from speaking in the Church, 133
  restriction on in public worship service, 133–34
wonders
  performed by *Okomfo Anokye*, 5
  performing, 140
worship
  as described by Harris, 27
  in the midst of the activities of the Spirit, 37

Index of Subjects

worship services
    challenge in obtaining a permanent place for, 61
    characterized by prophecy in Phase 3, 39
    liberal approach drawing people to, 55
wrist bands and chains
    bought for protection by survey respondents, 75
    traced to amulets worn in African Traditional Religion, 78
wulomei, *agba* differentiated from, 16
wulomei (high priests)
    roles in the socio-political and religious life of the Asere clan, 17–18
    words of, 15
wulomo, 20–21, 22

"xenolalia (real 'foreign' languages)," 122

Yahweh
    changed/varied His mode of communication with the prophets, 92
    communication with Moses, 84
    dichotomizing the voice of from the prophet, 90
    expected repentance from Israel, 91
    fed the Israelites with manna and quails in the wilderness, 102
    speaking through the occurrence of natural phenomena, 93
    spiritual encounters with, 82
    spoke to Samuel concerning Saul, 100
yam farmers, *Kpeshi* dialect *Gã* speaking people of Tema as, 14
Yankah, Kwesi, 2
Yiadom, Ebenezer Opambour, 42
Your Spiritual Gifts Can Help Your Church Grow (Wagner), 52

Zachariah (father of John the Baptist), 98
Zechariah (prophet), 85, 93
Zeno of Citium, 117n9
Zephaniah, 85
Zerubbabel, 85
Zeus, 125
Zionist Churches, in South Africa, 36

Index of Scripture

OLD TESTAMENT

Genesis

2:8–10	88
8:1	87
15	91
17	61
20:7	83
32:22–32	61
35:16–26	61

Exodus

3	82
7:14_11:1–10	140?
12:40	91
16	5
19	91
28:3	87
28:30	21
31:1–11	88

Leviticus

15	99
16	22
19:26	89
31:20	89

Numbers

11:25–29	88
11:29	111
11:31	87
12:6	84
19	99
22:7	80
22–24	92
27:21	21

Deuteronomy

13:1–5	77, 90
18:10	89
18:15	102
18:15–18	91
18:22	77, 91

Joshua

3	99
4	99
5	99

Judges

13	4
13–16	78
14:19–20	88
15:14	87
15:14–16	88

Index of Scripture

1 Samuel

1	4
2:18–20	84
2:21	65
3:1, 19–20	84
8	100
8:1–18	84
9	100
9:1–26	140
9:7, 8	80
10:1–11	88
10:10	87
10:12	84, 87
19:18	87
20:1	87
23:1–14	21
28:3–25	92
31:1–13	92

2 Samuel

1:18	89
7:4–17	86
12:1–17	86
24:11	86

1 Kings

1:8, 10, 23–37	86
6:8–23	100
10:35	85
11:41	89
14:19, 29	89
17:14–16	90
17:14A	90
17:14B	90
17:15	90
17:16	90
18:19	86
22:19	82
22:19–28	83

2 Kings

2:1–12	87
2:3, 7, 15	85
2:12	84, 87
3:13	86
4:1, 38	85
5:22	85, 87
6:1	85
6:8–23	7
6:21	84, 87
9:1	85
13:14	87
23:2–3, 21, 24	89

1 Chronicles

21:9	86
25:5	86

2 Chronicles

29:25	86
35:15	86

Ezra

1:1	91
5:1–2	85

Job

1:6	82
2:1	82
12:10	87
15:30	87
37:4–5	93

Psalms

18:14	93
20	85
21	85
50	85
60	85
61	64
68:38	93
72	85
75	85
94:9	92

Index of Scripture

Isaiah

1:15–16	99
2:2	95
6:1–12	94
6:2	82
9	95
16:13–14A	95
24–27	94?
30:30	93
36–39	85
48:16	88
49:1	xx

Jeremiah

1:4–5	xx
1:4–19	4, 82
1:7–8	xxiii
23:20	95
25:11	91
26:2	85
27:16–22	85
28:1, 5	85
29:10–14	91
31:34	88

Ezekiel

11:19	87
13	83
30	94
37:1	87
37–39	94?
38:16	95

Daniel, 9:1–2

	91

Joel

2:28	88
2:28–29	105

Amos

1:1, 6	90
7:10–13	85
7:14	85

Habakkuk, 1:2–4

	83

Zechariah

3:1–10	94
7:12	88
9–14	94?
13:2–6	92

APOCRYPHA,

1 Maccabees, 4:46

	92

NEW TESTAMENT

Matthew

3:12	99
5–7	100
7:39	101
10:41	93
11:2–6	98
11:11	98
13:57	100
14:13–22	5
16:13–20	101
16:18	36
18:17	36
21:11	101
26:68	101

Mark

6:14	140
6:30–44	5
8:31_9:1	99
14:65	101
16:17–18	106

Luke

1:5–25, 57–66	98
1:5–38	59, 78
2:36	111
4:18FF	100
7:15	101
9:10–17	5
13:33	100
22:64	101
24:19	102

John

3:23	99
4:1–42	78, 81
4:16–19, 29	140
6:14	102
7:40	102
7:52	102
12:28–29	93
16:4–15	100

Acts

	XVI, 36, 43, 106, 113
2:17	39
5:3	106
7:6	91
10	108
10:9–21	106
11:27–30	106, 110
13:1	107
13:1–3	54, 107
13:15–16, 42	110
13:27	XIX
14:21–28	106
15:32	107, 110
17:10–15	110
17:18FF	117N10
19:6	108
21:1–16	54
21:4	108
21:9	108
21:10FF	107
21:11–14	140
21:27–36FF	107
27:21–24	106

Romans

1:2	XIX
1:11	127, 128
12:6	111
12:6–8	144
16:15–18	127, 128
16:23	127, 128

1 Corinthians

1:11	124, 134
1:12	134
2:15	134
3:16	106, 111
5:7	135
5:9	121
6:12	134
8–11	115
10:23	134
11:2–16	134, 136
11:5	111
11:17, 18, 20, 33, 34	119
11:23	XX
12:1	115
12:1–11	41
12:8–11	52
12–14	XVIII, XX, XXII, 115
12:28	110
12:29	109
13	142
13:8	112
14	XVI, 109
14:1	110
14:3	112
14:18–19	129
14:19	129

14:20–33A	116
14:23–25	53
14:24–25	111
14:26	114, 115, 116, 117–24, 122
14:26–33	116
14:26–33A	115
14:26–40	XX, XXI, XXII, XXV, 34, 114, 115–35, 116, 140
14:27	110
14:27–28	114, 116, 124–25
14:27–33A	115
14:27–38	114
14:28	126–29
14:29	129–31, 140
14:29–31	XX
14:29–33A	114, 129–33
14:29A	109
14:29B	109
14:30	131–32
14:31	39, 132
14:32	132–33
14:33	110
14:33A	133
14:33B-35	115
14:33B-36	114, 115, 116, 133–34
14:33B-37	115, 116
14:34–40	116
14:36–40	115
14:37–38	XIX, 116, 134–35, 142
14:39–40	115, 116, 135
16:15	124
33B–36	136

Ephesians

2:20	112
4:11	110, 112
4:11–12	XIX, 144
4:12–13	67
5:18	106
5:18–20	120

Colossians, 3:16

	120

1 Thessalonians

2:8–9	118
5:19–22	XVI
5:21	108
5:21–22	144

1 Timothy, 4:14

	112

Philemon, 16

	118

1 John, 4:1

	110

Revelation

	36

EARLY CHRISTIAN WRITINGS

1 Clement, 1:5

	117

2 Clement, 1:1

	117–18

www.ingramcontent.com/pod-product-compliance
Lightning Source LLC
Chambersburg PA
CBHW070314230426
43663CB00011B/2128